Law and Risk

Legal Dimensions Series

This series stems from an annual legal and sociolegal research initiative sponsored by the Canadian Association of Law Teachers, the Canadian Law and Society Association, the Council of Canadian Law Deans, and the Law Commission of Canada. Volumes in this series examine various issues of law reform from a multidisciplinary perspective. The series seeks to advance our knowledge about law and society through the analysis of fundamental aspects of law.

The essays in this volume were selected by representatives from each partner association: Pierre Noreau (Canadian Law and Society Association), France Houle and Philip Girard (Canadian Association of Law Teachers), Serge Rousselle (Council of Canadian Law Deans), and Lorraine Pelot and Nathalie Des Rosiers (Law Commission of Canada).

1 *Personal Relationships of Dependence and Interdependence in Law*
2 *New Perspectives on the Public-Private Divide*
3 *What Is a Crime? Defining Criminal Conduct in Contemporary Society*
4 *Law and Risk*

Edited by the Law Commission of Canada

Law and Risk

UBCPress · Vancouver · Toronto

© UBC Press 2005

All rights reserved. No part of this publication may be reproduced, stored in a retrieval system, or transmitted, in any form or by any means, without prior written permission of the publisher, or, in Canada, in the case of photocopying or other reprographic copying, a licence from Access Copyright (Canadian Copyright Licensing Agency), www.accesscopyright.ca.

15 14 13 12 11 10 09 08 07 06 05   5 4 3 2 1

Printed in Canada on acid-free paper

Library and Archives Canada Cataloguing in Publication

Law and risk / edited by the Law Commission of Canada.

(Legal dimensions series, ISSN 1701-2317)
Includes bibliographical references and index.
ISBN 0-7748-1191-9

1. Law – Canada. 2. Risk assessment – Canada. 3. Risk management – Canada. 4. Risk communication – Canada. I. Law Commission of Canada. II. Series.

K487. R48L39 2005   349.71   C2005-902174-8

Canadä

UBC Press gratefully acknowledges the financial support for our publishing program of the Government of Canada through the Book Publishing Industry Development Program (BPIDP), and of the Canada Council for the Arts, and the British Columbia Arts Council.

UBC Press
The University of British Columbia
2029 West Mall
Vancouver, BC V6T 1Z2
604-822-5959 / Fax: 604-822-6083
www.ubcpress.ca

Contents

Preface

Contracts manage risks of non-performance. Regulations manage perceived risks to the health and safety of citizens. Sentencing principles aim to manage the risks of recidivism or violence. Law is often about managing risk.

In Chapter 1, William Leiss and Steve E. Hrudey suggest that the "bond between law and risk becomes tighter over time." Indeed, risk assessment has become part of decision making in many areas of law. This collection of essays examines, through a multidisciplinary approach, the connections between law and risk.

The study of risk assessment and risk management provokes a great deal of debate and these essays are no less controversial. Three of the essays (Chapters 2, 3, and 6) cover the hotly debated issues of the use of the precautionary principle, the role and regulation of research ethics boards, and determination of the likelihood of re-offence. The two other chapters (Chapters 4 and 5) use a number of examples, including social assistance, child pornography, marijuana possession, and Megan's Law to examine the legal system's use of facts and risk knowledges. The study of evidentiary principles and constitutionality examines the uncertainty involved in "objective" judicial determinations, while the other demonstrates the dynamic interaction that exists between the science of risk and legal networks.

The interplay between law and risk covers many domains and involves many actors: judges, policy makers, police officers, and even citizens who are often asked to judge or participate in the calculation of risk. This book illustrates the complex links that exist between law and risk and how law reform in this area could address a number of different issues: control over information, access to knowledge by experts and non-experts, power imbalances in the ability to bear risks and participate in their evaluation, and the need for transparency and legitimacy in decision making.

The law is often called upon to provide some certainty, whether this involves allocating responsibility for a risk or determining the extent of reparations where the full extent of the damages is unknown. *A priori* risk management through laws or regulations provides greater certainty and objectivity. However, once engaged in legal interpretation or determination of risk *a posteriori*, interested parties become subject to many of the same uncertainties and subjectivities that arise in the scientific arena. Sometimes these uncertainties are obscured by language rooted in the premise of objective decision making.

In a legal arena, which is very dependent on a high degree of certainty and premised on objectivity, a number of challenges arise. Rules and traditions that have long determined the flow of information face challenges due to an increasing complexity of facts and a plethora of expertise. One might say that regulation and adjudication, which are the preventive and remedial aspects of law, are becoming riskier endeavours as decision makers rely on experts armed with conflicting information. Along with the uncertainty comes a greater degree of subjectivity in choosing between options. Greater demands for accountability through the revelation of underlying facts, values, assumptions, and subjective aspects of decision making may require reforms to practices governing the sources and flow of information.

The law reform questions are numerous: Are the concepts used in law to manage risks still relevant? Do they raise new issues of institutional competence or new challenges to our democratic values? Are our legal concepts and institutional mechanisms adaptable to new scientific and social realities? A consideration of law and risk requires us to attempt to reconcile scientific knowledge and democratic principles, individual behaviour and collective fears, and concepts of efficiency and equality. It is one of the core elements of law reform in our society.

This collection is the result of a partnership between the Council of Canadian Law Deans, the Canadian Association of Law Teachers, the Canadian Law and Society Association, and the Law Commission of Canada. Through the Legal Dimensions initiative, we seek to stimulate critical thinking on emerging law and society issues. The Law Commission of Canada wants to thank its partners, the authors of the essays, the guest commentators William Leiss and Steve E. Hrudey, and the participants of the Legal Dimensions workshop that was held in Halifax in June 2003. The Law Commission of Canada hopes that this collection of essays will further discussions on the many facets of law and risk.

Law and Risk

1

On Proof and Probability: Introduction to "Law and Risk"

William Leiss and Steve E. Hrudey

Law and the Management of Risk

The public policy disciplines of law, on the one hand, and risk management, on the other, come together in their reliance on two key modes of reasoning: proof and probability. Attribution of blame under our system of justice requires proof of culpability, either on balance of probabilities or beyond reasonable doubt. And the management of health and environmental risks – where risk is the probability of encountering adverse consequences under specified conditions – is governed by a requirement for evidence of possible harm that by definition can be represented only as a range of probabilities. Both disciplines have no choice but to live with uncertainties, even though, in both, the consequences of erroneous decisions can be (and sometimes are) catastrophic. Precaution is the balm that both seek to apply in order to forestall the worst forms of error, but the practitioners in both domains know full well that some mistakes will happen no matter how large a dollop of precaution has been applied.

As modern society matures, the bond between law and risk becomes tighter over time.[1] In the penal system, for example, formal risk-based instruments of assessment are devised in order to assist judges in evaluating the "likelihood of re-offence." In social-policy jurisprudence, in cases such as possession of child pornography or the marketing of a hazardous substance (tobacco), judges must assess whether certain probabilities of harm (serving as a proxy for an inherently unprovable cause-effect nexus) are sufficient grounds for restrictions on the freedom of expression that are "reasonable" in terms of the *Canadian Charter of Rights and Freedoms*.[2]

At the same time, risk management practitioners are challenged to answer hard questions about the "burden of proof" where possible harms may occur, because some uncertainties cannot be resolved until long after actual harms occur. In occupational risk, for example, the traditional approach involved "waiting for the body count" – the scientific calculus of association between cause and effect, uncovered through painstaking epidemiological analysis of mortality and morbidity records. Only after the findings were confirmed and reconfirmed did workers' compensation regimes begin paying out benefits to victims or surviving families. Typically, the first generation of victims and their families, who provided the data for the analyses, were never compensated. Where environmental risk is concerned, North America came perilously close to losing some of its raptor populations for good, due to DDT exposure, because it was difficult to assemble and defend the evidence for the cause-and-effect relation. To compound these intrinsic problems, disputes over the assessment and management of these types of risks can (at least in the United States) end up in court, under the purview of criminal law, where scientific studies confront the legal demand for proof "beyond a reasonable doubt."

During the last forty years, we have witnessed in advanced economies a profound elaboration of the risk management approach with respect to health and environmental risks. As explained briefly in the next section, this approach has two main characteristics: first, it seeks to use a rigorous and consistent "language"; second, it strives for a sequential, step-wise form of decision making in which each step builds upon and moves forward from the preceding one. The term "risk society," which was taken from the title of a 1986 book of that name by the German sociologist Ulrich Beck, has entered academic discourse (Leiss 1993). More recently, the "language of risk" increasingly has entered public and popular discourse and there is every reason to believe that this trend will strengthen. The essays collected in this volume illustrate well how the interplay between law and risk is affecting some very important areas of jurisprudence. This project of the Law Commission of Canada is, therefore, both timely and welcome.

Language of Risk

There is clearly an imperative to explain what meaning we assign to risk for the purposes of managing risk. In our view, the most useful and comprehensive notion of risk can be built upon the concepts first outlined by S. Kaplan and B.J. Garrick (1981) in the inaugural issue of the journal for the Society for Risk Analysis, the primary scientific organization for risk studies. They proposed that risk is a multidimensional entity comprising the answers to three questions:

- What can go wrong?
- How likely is it?
- What are the consequences?

The answers to these questions, which effectively amount to an assessment of risk, combined with a need to specify a time frame and with consideration of some essential human issues that have been well described by O. Renn (1992), can lead to a functional notion of the kind of risk that we attempt to assess and to manage. The imperative of adopting a common working definition of risk was later stressed again by Kaplan (1997) because risk is such a widely used term in our language that subtle differences in meaning will be inevitable without some effort to agree explicitly on the meaning intended. There is enormous potential for misunderstanding and error when parties are using the same word to mean substantially different things, yet the differences may seem too subtle to allow either party to recognize the inconsistencies.

The core of the risk management approach itself is *risk assessment*. This exercise can be highly technical, beginning in the basic sciences of chemistry, biology, and physics, and then running through the applied disciplines of toxicology, epidemiology, engineering, medicine, pharmacology, and many others, depending on the depth of evidence available for assessment. In many cases, a more pragmatic qualitative risk assessment may be necessitated by the absence of substantial evidence. What comes out is a *hazard characterization*, which seeks to provide a comprehensive understanding of exactly what kinds of harm can result, to humans, other species, or the environment generally, with respect to the impacts of a natural hazard or a technology. Here, the most important guide is the *dose-response relation*. Since everything in the world is harmful at some level (including the staples of life, water and oxygen), it is essential to understand what is the harmful dose, and this estimate is what distinguishes hazard (the potential to cause harm) from risk (the chance of harm occurring).

Now we add *exposure*, another key ingredient. If a harmful dose is present somewhere, but you are not, then you are not at risk. Yet often we do not know whether or not this is the case – all we know is that there is a certain *probability* that we may encounter a harmful dose. This is risk, namely the chance of harm. For example, we know that all long-term smokers are "at risk" of contracting lung cancer (and hundreds of other types of harms to health), but only 12-17 percent of them will get this particular deadly disease in Canada (Villeneuve and Mao 1994). The catch is that we will not know which smokers have fallen into that group until the body count is done! This notion of risk is a prediction or expectation that involves

- a hazard (the source of danger)
- uncertainty of occurrence and outcomes (expressed by the probability or chance of occurrence)
- adverse consequences (the possible outcomes)
- a time frame for evaluation
- the perspectives of those affected about what is important to them.

In summary, risk is the predicted or expected chance that a set of circumstances over some time frame will produce some harm that matters (Hrudey 1997).

Uncertainty pervades our estimates of risk. We should have differing levels of confidence in our estimates of probability depending on the quality of the evidence relied upon. We can often express our level of confidence with numerical confidence intervals, much like those reported for opinion polls. For example, we might hear that 58 percent, plus or minus 5 percent, of Canadians would favour Leslie Nielsen for prime minister, nineteen times out of twenty – an expression that the 95 percent confidence interval (nineteen out of twenty) on the response is between 53 and 63 percent. Greater uncertainty in our estimate will be reflected by a wider confidence interval. These confidence intervals reflect only the survey sampling error, but they offer no insight about response bias (for example: Does the question influence the answer? Are the answers meaningful for judging actual voting intentions?).

The existence of uncertainty in probability estimates of risk is unavoidable, even if it is not commonly expressed. This fact creates an interesting dilemma for risk ranking, as illustrated in Figure 1.1. Which risk has a greater probability, Risk A or Risk B? Figure 1.1 shows the central estimate (mean or median) of the magnitude of each risk with the circle. The bars represent the confidence intervals (typically 95 percent) as an expression of the uncertainty that bounds the best estimate for each risk. The large size of the confidence intervals shown may seem pessimistic, but such wide confidence intervals are very common for estimated low-level risks. This observation raises the challenge that we should really be ranking probability distributions rather than point estimates of probability. If we demand higher confidence (such as 99 percent), the size of the confidence interval and the potential for greater ambiguity created by overlapping confidence intervals will inevitably increase. A technocrat might not see a dilemma in this choice because she/he would regard the central point of each distribution as the best estimate of the risk magnitude and use that for ranking. However, someone inclined towards avoidance of the largest likely disaster could logically argue that Risk B has potentially worse consequences than Risk A, because the upper bound of the confidence interval for Risk B is higher than the upper bound for Risk A, making it the larger risk to be avoided. The choice for ranking risks in this case is a matter of values: do we prefer to rank risks on the basis of central ("best") estimate of risk, or do we rank based on the plausible worst case? There is no scientific or strictly objective answer to which of these choices is "correct." In summary, ranking risk on strictly objective grounds is not possible given the true character of risk numbers.

A key aspect is the quantitative character of risk since we regard numbers as being more verifiable than qualitative characteristics. As noted earlier, a

Figure 1.1

Risk comparisons considering uncertainty (confidence) intervals for two different risks A and B

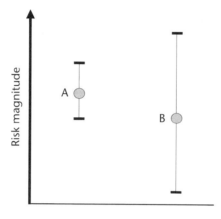

key element of the numerical character of risk is the probability estimate. We might expect that probability, being a mathematical concept, is free of debate about its meaning or interpretation. P.L. Bernstein (1996) has documented the evolution of our modern concepts of probability, including the debates that have raged about the meaning and interpretation of probability. P.R. Kleindorfer, H.C. Kunreuther, and P.J.H. Schoemaker (1993) have described three different schools of probability (classical, frequency, and subjective). The classical school is amenable to theoretical analysis because it defines probability as the number of specified outcomes divided by the total number of possible outcomes. This definition requires that both the numerator and denominator be known completely. Classical analysis is commonly applied to games of chance. The probability of an event (for example, in cards, a one in thirteen chance of selecting any ace from a full deck) can be predicted strictly from a theoretical analysis of the circumstances. More complicated outcomes can then be calculated using the mathematical laws of permutations and combinations without actually performing the action. The conditions necessary to satisfy the requirements for classical analysis are very specific and are generally too hypothetical to be applied to any meaningful health risk estimation. An artificial health risk example would be that the probability of drawing the bullet in Russian roulette, with a six-chamber revolver, would be one in six.

The frequency school establishes probability estimates based on observations of repeated events or trials. This perspective is widely used in actuarial work (for example, in insurance, frequency evidence is based on the analysis of prior outcomes such as life tables). The difficulty with the frequency view is that it applies well to stable and repetitive processes only. The advantage of the frequency approach is that it can be applied to any situation that can be observed through many repetitions, including those cases amenable to classical analysis. Unfortunately, many events cannot be measured this way simply because they are rare or cannot be repeated a sufficient number of times to allow for a meaningful determination of relative frequency. Accordingly, one can estimate future probability of motor vehicle fatalities in a given area based upon historical data for that area, provided that future causative conditions remain unchanged. In this example, the causal connection between the motor vehicle incidents and the resulting fatalities is usually clear enough so that the issue of causation is a minor source of uncertainty.

The subjective school holds that probability estimates for real events cannot be measured in a strictly objective sense. Rather, probability estimates reflect a degree of belief or confidence that a specified event will occur. The confidence of the estimator may be based upon classical analysis and/or substantial frequency evidence, so the subjective label does not imply purely emotive or irrational judgments. However, the nature of the prediction demands some elements of judgment and the subjective belief of the individual who is making the prediction. As such, the subjective school holds that probability is not strictly objective, even if the supporting frequency evidence is substantial. Uncertainty will arise because experience is usually limited and the causal connection is often not clear. So, you can be very certain about the motor vehicle fatality risk estimates where the causal mechanism for the fatality is not in question, but you can be much less certain about whether your probability of getting brain cancer from using cell phones is greater or less than one in one million, since at present we have no confidence about there even being a causal mechanism.

We should recognize varying levels of confidence in subjective probability estimates, depending on the amount, quality, coherence, and relevance of evidence upon which the belief or inference is formed. However, we cannot escape the premise that risk probability predictions usually have most in common with the subjective school. For example, we may have a high level of confidence in predicting the probability of a random motor vehicle fatality in Canada next year, based upon our access to substantial empirical evidence to support a frequency-based estimate. However, suppose we asked an expert team of physicists, automotive engineers, and emergency room physicians to estimate the same risk, but restricted their evidence to a detailed road map of Canada, a list of motor vehicle registrations, and any of their basic, discipline-specific knowledge. The experts could even perform experiments using rodents in miniature vehicles and robots in full-size vehicles. Their prediction, regardless of its objectivity or expert pedigree, would be far less reliable than one derived primarily from an analysis of frequency statistics. Yet, the expert opinion scenario, with its higher uncertainty, is usually much closer to most health and environmental risk assessments than the former. So, while the probability prediction may be based upon substantial relevant experience, the composite notion of risk for any real environmental health circumstance will always involve substantial inference and judgment, such that assessed risk probabilities are inevitably statements of belief.

The problem with risk management is that being "at risk" is partly just the luck of the draw. No matter how well substantiated the link between some contributing risk factor and the population frequency of any particular outcome, the resulting population-based frequency-probability estimate cannot be determinative for a specific individual. Only when the risk factor has been transformed into a reliable indicator for the outcome (for example, the appearance of a tumour) can a more meaningful prognosis be made for an individual. For each beginning smoker who asks, "Will *I* get lung cancer from smoking?" the appropriate answer is "Maybe – but you should also realize that, as health risks go, this is a high-consequence, well-characterized risk." One can see why this answer may not be persuasive to a young person who is surrounded by intense peer pressure to take up the habit. The meaning of risk is hard enough to convey to people where health risks are concerned, but even harder in the case of environmental risks, where the cause-effect chains are much more complex and difficult to pin down. Ten years later, some people still dispute what caused the collapse of the Atlantic cod fishery, which was once one of the most prodigiously productive natural resources on the planet.

Finally, we seek to manage risks by exploring options for risk reduction once we have the risk assessment in hand – because it is only the risk assessment that tells us which factors of hazard and exposure we should manipulate if we want to reduce risk. For example, when we discovered that heavy metals (lead, cadmium, and so on) are potent neurotoxins and that neurotoxins are especially harmful to developing brains, risk managers lowered the allowable exposures of young children to these substances.

Essays

In his essay "Use of Risk Assessments by Canadian Judges in the Determination of Dangerous and Long-Term Offender Status, 1997-2002," David MacAlister writes: "The Canadian criminal justice system's first large-scale experiment with actuarial risk assessment occurred in the context of assessing risk for failure if released on parole." It is easy to see why the risk assessment approach might be useful in these contexts, because a predictive judgment is sought and the uncertainties in the possible outcomes are massive – for instance, what is the "likelihood" of re-offence? (As MacAlister notes, "likelihood" is interpreted to mean "a probability of greater than 50 percent.") Of course, clinical profiles of the specific individuals before the court, made by qualified experts, have long had a role in the making of such judgments. And even the advocates of the risk assessment approach can recognize the inherent problem with this process – in the assessment of risk, the individual "points" along the probabilistic spectrum are irrelevant and only the overall population statistics can be defended. However, in the criminal justice context, these "points" are real individuals, and our system places a fundamental value on securing justice in the circumstances prevailing for each individual case.

Once a hazard is well characterized, we can "screen" for its rate of occurrence in a specific population. Thus, we have screening technologies for detecting breast cancer in women. There is no panacea, however, because no technology is perfect, and, hence, there arises the inherent problems of "false positives" and "false negatives" (in the second case, we miss the evidence when it is actually there, and, in the first, we think we detect it when it is actually absent). MacAlister is well aware of this difficulty as it arises with respect to the rich variety of risk assessment tools employed in evaluating the risk of re-offence.[3]

False positives and false negatives are a serious, inescapable problem wherever the risk assessment approach is utilized in both health and environmental risk domains (Hrudey and Leiss 2003). It cannot be eliminated, no matter how sophisticated our screening technologies become. The lower the true incidence of a hazard is, the more likely that false positives will predominate over true positives. The only solution is to apply a series of screening tests and to avoid relying on only one. This would appear to be even more important when the risk assessment approach is utilized in the criminal justice system. The ability to provide predictive evidence for new cases, based on a population of cases where evidence is available (the results over time of offenders actually released in the past) is a legitimate tool of evaluation. However, where the imperative is to be just in every specific case, it can never be sufficient. The risk profile must be supplemented with other evidence. The practical limitations of DNA evidence and the potential for the prosecutor's fallacy effectively demonstrate this imperative. D.J. Balding and P. Donnelly (1994) illustrate the problem for a hypothetical case in which a defendant who is innocent of a crime does nonetheless have a one in a million chance of matching the DNA of the true perpetrator, given that he or she was really innocent. If this was accepted as the only evidence (that is, no other supporting evidence) and the accused was drawn at random from a population of potential perpetrators of 500,000, this seemingly determinative match probability, by itself, would actually correspond to a 33 percent probability of innocence. This example tells us that, if the apparent gold standard of DNA evidence can be so limited when used as a source of evidence, anything drawn from the uncertain world of risk assessment must be supported by other types of evidence.

MacAlister concludes with the need for a very important additional safeguard, namely that the judgment of "likelihood to re-offend" must be tested against any evidence of systematic bias in the criminal justice system (for example, racial or ethnic bias). It should never be forgotten that, like every other human technique, risk assessment is, in the final analysis, an exercise in human judgment. Only when the test of possible systemic bias has also been explicitly applied and passed are we safe in using the risk assessment approach in the criminal justice arena. We should be *exceedingly precautionary* in this domain (see the next section of this essay) for a specific reason: the coming of genetic profiling. It is possible that authorities will want, someday, to try to predict criminality on the basis of an individual's genetic profile and to pre-emptively restrain individuals with certain types of profiles. The potential for abuse of the criminal justice system using genetic profiling is enormous, and we should be ready to head it off.

The attention to the "precautionary principle" (PP) has been by far the most interesting issue within risk management in the last decade. We have heard passionate commentary pro and con, which is a clue that a high-stakes game is being played. The European Union has moved more quickly to use the precautionary principle explicitly in regulatory decision making, whereas North America has not, and, as a result, this concept is being "contested" and has become a chess piece in the struggles over genetically modified foods, for example.

Some of those on each side, adherents and detractors, have sought to frame the debate about PP in terms of "burden of proof," and this aspect is what Dayna Nadine Scott focuses on in her essay "Shifting the Burden of Proof: The Precautionary Principle and Its Potential for the 'Democratization' of Risk." Some proponents of the precautionary principle claim that it "shifts" the burden of proof in a specific sense, namely, requiring *proof of safety* rather than *evidence of no unacceptable harm when specific tests are applied*, which is what now prevails as a regulatory requirement. Detractors seize upon this move as a demonstration of the intrinsic absurdity of the precautionary principle, since "safety" is too often interpreted to mean "no harm (whatsoever)," which could never be proved. The resulting impasse is detrimental for the future of the precautionary approach. Scott's essay does us all a huge service in examining the issue thoroughly and systematically, providing an admirable abundance of references and commentary.

Scott summarizes one of the dominant perspectives on this point as follows: "The precautionary principle seeks to shift the burden of proof onto those who create the hazard, benefit from the hazard, or advocate for the hazard." Indeed, this contention has become a commonplace in much of the advocacy literature about the precautionary principle. However, somewhat more precise language would be helpful. The issue is not just who bears the burden of proof but also what kind of burden it is – that is, "heavy" or "light."[4] This can be seen in the case of pesticides regulation, because pesticides are one of the few industrial products that, since the 1930s, have been subject to regulatory pre-approval before being allowed on the market (Bosso 1987). In order to win approval (registration), the manufacturer currently must submit huge quantities of data, mostly from toxicological studies using laboratory animals, followed by elaborate studies pertinent to extrapolation of effect from animal to human pharmacokinetics, in order to demonstrate that the product is within certain thresholds of anticipated harm, or negligible risk, to humans. Dozens of other studies on environmental impacts (degradation rates in soil and water, for example) are also required. It is abundantly clear that in this elaborate process the burden of proof, to demonstrate what is called "safety" in everyday language, is squarely on the shoulders of the manufacturer. There is nothing to "shift" here.[5] Most of the public controversies over pesticides and other products causing environmental harms have not been about burden of proof (that is, the question, "Who has to make the case for safety?") but rather about what *standard of proof* the proponents must satisfy (the other question, "How confident are the rest of us that the case for safety has been made adequately?").

Mistakes happen, and, more important, the scientific knowledge base changes. The history of pesticides regulation shows that, over time, the required number and types of scientific studies to be submitted by manufacturers in support of product registration have increased enormously. Yet irrespective of how many studies are required, the regulatory system converts a preliminary scientific assessment of acceptable risk into a property right (the product registration). Mistakes still happen, and, when they do, it is the legal system that causes a switch to occur, not only in the *burden* of proof but also in the *type* of proof required. First, when alleging new evidence showing unacceptable risk against a registered product, the burden of proof falls upon the complainant – a worker or farmer or public-interest group. Second, the product registration, which has vested a property right, cannot be taken away again without "sufficient" proof that the original decision was mistaken – according to legal (not scientific) conceptions of proof. Sometimes a long and costly battle must be fought before one side or the other triumphs.[6] Moreover, as indicated earlier, some of these battles over environmental risk management are fought out, quite inappropriately, in the context of criminal law, where the threshold of adequate proof is onerous.[7]

Who bears the burden of proof under the law is always an important issue. What is equally important is the standard of proof, especially where new and untried technologies, which may entail entirely new and unfamiliar types of risk factors, are introduced into the marketplace.[8] It is quite appropriate for the standard of proof (or threshold) to be raised regularly, because our capacity to detect potential harms (through better instrumentation and novel types of tests, for example) increases steadily. What citizens cannot have, however, is proof of safety in any kind of "absolute" sense. There is in principle no conceivable way to predict in advance every type of harm, however small or distant in time and space. There is only a range of estimated outcomes and judgments with respect to the acceptable or unacceptable levels of risk.

In this context, it is important to realize that the risk management approach at least strives to be inherently precautionary. Through risk assessment, we try to predict the patterns of possible harm and proactively reduce future harms to the lowest possible level. Prevention is surely precautionary. It is what we try to do with the assessment of prescription drugs, industrial chemicals (in the workplace and for the public), and radio-frequency fields (cellular telephones) – quite literally, for thousands of technologies and many natural hazards. In this perspective, the precautionary principle is an important supplementary guideline for special types of risks, namely for those where there are "serious or irreversible adverse effects" and unusually high levels of uncertainty.

The best example is global climate change. We can characterize this risk only by using elaborate computer models to predict possible futures. In other words, there is no "evidence" in the conventional sense – that is, proof of (potential) harm – that can possibly be adduced at this time. And it is a reasonable supposition that, if we wait for such "proof," it will be too late to act to prevent the harm. Therefore, we must adopt a precautionary approach to this risk and take actions long before "scientific certainty" can ever be attained. From this perspective, using the risk management approach is never a case of deciding whether to be precautionary or not. Rather, it is only a matter of deciding how precautionary to be under specific circumstances.

Towards the end of her essay, Scott quite correctly calls attention to one of the most problematic aspects of risk management, namely the pervasiveness of risk/risk trade-offs, mentioning two current cases raised by the emergence in North America of a new infectious disease pathogen, the West Nile virus. Risk management strategies to suppress the incidence of this disease focus on mosquito population control, for which the most effective tool is the application of larvicides in standing-water locations within municipalities. Larvicides are pesticides, and the risk/risk trade-off is a balance between the health risk of the West Nile virus versus some presumptive level of risk from exposure to the pesticide itself (Leiss 2003).[9] A second trade-off is the one made by the Canadian Blood Services, which suspended donor collection and withdrew some stockpiled blood supplies in areas (such as southern Saskatchewan) where testing revealed the existence of donated blood infected with the West Nile virus (Canadian Blood Services 2005). Scott is absolutely right in pointing to such cases as evidence of the serious practical matters of judgment involved in applying the precautionary principle to real-life situations.

Finally, the discussion about the promise of considering wider use of statistical power as a means of understanding and avoiding false negative errors is very important. The apparent bias of science towards avoiding false positives in preference to false negatives has been the subject of frequent controversy (Cranor 1993). The difference in hypothesis-acceptance probabilities is a valid consideration when there is an equal likelihood of the hypothesis being either true or false. Presumption of equal probability is not the starting point in a criminal trial, where the accused is presumed innocent until proven guilty. In the case where the hazard being judged is often rare, which is common in environmental issues, there is not an equal probability that any given attempt to detect the hazard will yield a true positive result. If the occurrence of a true hazard is only one in three cases, the scientific convention of allowing a 5 percent chance of a false positive error and a 20 percent chance of allowing a false negative error will yield an equal chance of false positives and false negatives (Hrudey and Leiss 2003).

In their essay "Legal Knowledges of Risks," Mariana Valverde, Ron Levi, and Dawn Moore include some fascinating case studies that allow the reader to appreciate both the complexity and the variability in applications of risk-based thinking to legal frameworks. Their study of "risk and the constitution of expertise in Megan's Law" is especially instructive. "Megan's Law" encompasses the US community notification statutes regarding the release of sexual offenders.[10] The authors comment: "The most recent governance strategy ... is premised on the expert identification and assessment of risk factors, while encouraging individual residents, not experts, to manage that risk in their daily lives." The authors show that these statutes set up a three-part interplay between expert knowledge and the law:

- First, experts use formal risk assessment tools (such as the ones listed in note 3 of this chapter) to make analyses on behalf of the judicial system, for example, assigning offenders to one of the "three tiers" for risk of re-offending – no risk, moderate risk, high risk.
- Second, prosecutors are responsible for assimilating these assessments into the judicial process, utilizing what the authors call "a hybrid form of expertise, a translation of risk expertise from actuarial and clinical prognostications to a format that is said to be the preserve of prosecutors and judges."
- Third, community members must interpret the information they receive from police as to the implications, for them and their children, of the presence in their midst of convicted sexual offenders who have been assigned certain "probabilities" of re-offending.

The case study illustrates, for the authors, the fact that the relationship between law and expertise (in this case, expertise in risk assessment) is a dynamic process, not a simple matter of "transfer" from one context to another – a process of ongoing "negotiation" of the uses of non-judicial expertise in a legal setting.

There are some interesting affinities between parts of the Valverde, Levi, and Moore chapter, on the one hand, and Danielle Pinard's "Evidentiary Principles with Respect to Judicial Review of Constitutionality: A Risk Management Perspective," on the other hand. Pinard, defining risk as "the possibility of experiencing a harmful, dangerous, or otherwise undesirable event," starts from the presupposition that risk has two essential components, "the factual aspect, or uncertainty with respect to the event's occurrence, and the normative aspect, or its undesirable nature." The first is the realm of objectivity, involving both empirical observations and mathematical-statistical manipulations of the resultant data. The second is "the social, political world, the world of value judgments with respect to desirability, undesirability, reasonableness, beneficial effects, and prejudice." What essentially concerns Pinard, in discussing how risk discourse enters the realm of law, is the transfer of "the illusion of certainty" from the objectivist side to the normative domain.

This point is very important and valid, and it is explored through an analysis of four Supreme Court of Canada judgments – on social assistance (the most extensive discussion), the possession of child pornography, tobacco advertising, and marijuana possession.[11] The first judgment was decided in 2002 in *Gosselin* c. *Québec (P.G.)*,[12] and as Danielle Pinard notes later in this book:

> The risk identified by legislators may be understood in the following way. In difficult economic times, most notably marked by a significant unemployment rate, there is a risk that people under thirty who receive social assistance and who are not compelled in some way to acquire useful ways of joining the labour market will become dependent upon social assistance over the long term.

Pinard sees, in the judgment of the (narrow) majority of the court in this case, a confounding of the two distinct domains, which were elucidated earlier, the normative and the factual. The petitioner had alleged that, in arbitrarily singling out a particular group – persons under thirty years of age – for separate (and prejudicial) treatment under the law governing eligibility for social assistance, the law was violating the human dignity of this group and preventing its members from their right to full participation in society. The majority replied: "But again, there is no evidence to support this claim."[13] Pinard quite rightly finds this assertion to be astonishing because the reference to a requirement of "proof" in this context seems so self-evidently inappropriate. Surely the point is a matter of normative reasoning, not proof in the ordinary sense of this term. Does the discrimination between classes of persons in this law offend what we mean by the *concept* of "human dignity"?

We cannot do justice to the long and closely reasoned analysis in this essay of the majority's reasoning in *Gosselin*. Suffice it to say that Pinard's examination raises very important issues – the refusal to re-examine relevant facts that bear directly on the allegation of prejudicial treatment and its consequences; the refusal to examine critically the validity of the underlying assumptions on which the legislation is based; and the affirmation of certain "facts of everyday life," which are simply assumed to be true. The examination of this case is complemented by three others (on child pornography, tobacco advertising, and marijuana possession), which are discussed more briefly.[14] Pinard shows that in the child pornography case (*R. v. Sharpe*),[15] for example, the majority based its reasoning on a phrase, "reasoned apprehension of harm," which is an inherently probabilistic or risk-based conception, and, in effect, substituted this concept for the requirement of proof of harm – that is, factual evidence of "actual damage." Pinard draws a most interesting conclusion from the analytical approach applied to these recent cases. "Conceptualizing tests of constitutionality as risk management exercises enables better discernment of their factual aspects. This process clarifies the strategies generated by the courts to develop the factual reasoning that is essential to their conclusions of law." This idea is intriguing and warrants further development.

The essay by Duff R. Waring and Trudo Lemmens, "Integrating Values in Risk Analysis of Biomedical Research: The Case for Regulatory and Law Reform," is an important contribution to an area of great concern, where new structures of rights and responsibilities are needed. Waring and Lemmens identify three types of risks associated with the participation of persons in clinical trials for biomedical research, namely "risks of physical and psychological harm to participants, risks to the objectivity and integrity of science that are posed by conflicts of interest, and risks to other social values, for example, public trust in the ethical conduct of research." The essay is rich with extensive citations and relevant examples.

The authors dissect the serious shortcomings in the prevailing institutional oversight of medical research, which is managed by local research ethics boards based at universities and other research institutions. In a nutshell, this type of oversight mechanism provides a form of ethics review that is convenient and efficient from the standpoint of the institutions, but which is also radically defective from the standpoint of the research subjects. The defects include various levels of risks associated with the possibilities of an insufficient disclosure of conflict of interest, particularly financial interests; a lack of full characterization of the hazards in clinical trials, particularly new types of hazards associated with gene transfer; a lack of consistency across institutions; and a lack of due attention to social values. Waring and Lemmens are especially concerned, and rightly so, with these shortcomings with respect to the new types of biomedical research, especially gene transfer and stem cell research.

The authors' recommendations, as well as the core principle on which these recommendations are based, are well argued. They explain: "We want the law to ensure that the value frameworks of the participants who might assume the risks are given equal weight [to those of the researchers and sponsors] in the process of research review." In other words, there should be a legislated framework for research review, with a detailed regulatory structure to determine how the review must be conducted. The authors call for a new legal structure to enshrine and enforce the core principle, including the following recommendations:

- federal legislation to govern the oversight of biomedical research in Canada
- the creation of an independent national agency for research review, which would have a branch that would gather, collate, and analyze data relevant to the risk assessments of new biomedical interventions.

There is no question that the university-based research enterprise is coming under increasing pressure from economic interests. Many well-published basic scientists in Canada complain about excessive reliance on "matching" industry money in too many granting council programs. Medical research especially appears to be headed for recurrent scandals about the influence of sponsors on research strategies and outcomes. Meanwhile, senior government officials and ministers pretend that all is well in the academic gardens – that industry sponsorship demonstrates the "relevance" of research (a good thing) and is a driver of economic development (a very, very good thing).

Waring and Lemmens cite the high-profile cases where extreme risks to participants in research trials on gene transfer and stem cell research have led to injury and death. And this is only the beginning in terms of the human health benefits that are going to be sought in the sequencing of genes and our ability to manipulate gene functions. The authors are right in emphasizing the factor of "social values" in the evaluation of biomedical research, for the new powers sought in completing our command over the genomes of all living things go to the very heart of the values of civilization – the autonomy of the individual and the family, personal identity, freedom, and so on (Tyshenko and Leiss 2004). One can guess that the resultant social conflicts could get very ugly in this domain. Thus, there is no time to lose. The creation of the independent regulatory agency advocated by Waring and Lemmens is essential if we are to have a reasonable chance of managing these social risks effectively and fairly.[16]

In conclusion, it is instructive to note the many intersecting themes about law and risk contained in this collection of essays, a few of which have already been mentioned. Can the interest in "precaution" be useful in the context of evaluating the risk of re-offence posed by dangerous and sexual offenders? Could the legal system benefit from examining in close detail the different ways in which probability has been described in the field of risk assessment? Is there a mismatch between the need for new policy perspectives to be enshrined in law and regulation, on the one hand, and the capacity of our law-making system to deliver what we need in a timely manner, on the other hand? Should Canadian scholars and judges set out more clearly the implications of using DNA evidence in the prosecution of serious crimes? Finally, is there an adequate home for risk-based approaches in Canadian constitutional law? These and other topics could provide a basis for further studies in the interplay of law and risk.

Notes

1 Only a few references can be given here: Cranor (1993); Foster (1993); US National Research Council (1994). For current cases, see the website of the Risk Science and Law Specialty Group of the Society for Risk Analysis, "a group of scientists, lawyers, and others interested in the interface between risk assessment and laws, regulations, and courtroom proceedings," and follow the links to the casebooks: <http://www.riskworld.com/Profsoci/SRA/RiskScienceLawGroup/homepage.htm>.

2 *Canadian Charter of Rights and Freedoms,* Part I of the *Constitution Act, 1982,* being Schedule B to the *Canada Act 1982* (U.K.), 1982, c. 1, s. 1.

3 His list includes the Hare Psychopathy Checklist – Revised, the Violence Risk Assessment Guide, the Sex Offender Risk Appraisal Guide, the Rapid Risk Assessment for Sex Offender Recidivism, the Violence Prediction Scheme, the Historical/Clinical/Risk Management guide, the Spousal Assault Risk Assessment guide, and the Sexual Violence Risk guide.

4 In the environmental regulatory policy field, one often encounters the phrase "regulatory burden," which refers to the overall scope of the command-and-control type of regulation, in which there is an explicit (prescribed) response specified by the regulator for each type of environmental harm. On the other hand, it is possible to substitute different types of policy instruments, e.g., market-based ones, which do not change the targets, such as emissions targets, but which provide more flexibility to the firm in deciding how best to meet those targets; this flexibility itself can be seen as a reduced burden (see Gunningham and Grabosky 1998). These are two usages of "burden" which are quite different from what is meant by a legal burden of proof.

5 To be sure, only a relatively few classes of products (notably pesticides, pharmaceuticals, and medical devices) require a formal process of regulatory pre-approval. Another prominent case is the certification of airworthiness for aircraft. On the other hand, most other products are required to meet various types of performance standards; for something like the automobile, there are separate standards for many of its component parts. In all such cases it is incumbent on the manufacturer to meet these standards. Of course, if failure is alleged in this regard (as in the recent high-profile case of automobile tires), those making the allegations do bear the burden of proof. The purpose of this note is only to point out some of the many complexities in the allocation of burden of proof, where product performance is at issue.

6 See the "alar" case study in Chapter 6 in Leiss and Chociolko (1994).

7 See the case study of the *Canadian Environmental Protection Act* in Leiss (2001), chapter 8, including the commentary on *Canada* v. *Hydro-Québec* (1997). Because "environmental protection" is not a specified power in constitutional law terms, it has been derived by judges from the authority over natural resources, which is a power assigned to the provinces (the exception being fisheries, which is a specified federal jurisdiction). Being thus excluded from most areas of environmental management, the very tightly circumscribed federal power in this domain has had to be derived from its criminal law power. The result is that federal prosecutions must meet the criminal-law test of proof, which makes federal environmental legislation (except for the *Fisheries Act*) largely impotent.

8 Environmental risk management standards have always lagged far behind those for human health, for many reasons, including common-property issues, long lag times between exposure and evidence of injury, and greater difficulty in establishing cause-effect relationships (thus certain types of uncertainties are more difficult to resolve here). One way of summarizing these difficulties is to say that societies have shaved the margin for error too closely, in their desperate search for resources to extract for human benefit. Here again, increased precaution is not so much a matter of shifting the burden of proof as it is one of allowing a significantly greater margin for error in our impositions on the environment and other species.

9 Since the article cited here was written, an aggressive program of larviciding in the larger Ontario municipalities appears to have been a major factor in reducing mosquito populations and the expected incidence of human cases of infection with the virus in the 2003 mosquito season.

10 Their discussion of this case therefore should be read in conjunction with the MacAlister chapter, which deals with similar themes in a Canadian context.
11 For another discussion of the issues in the tobacco litigation see Leiss (1999).
12 *Gosselin* v. *Québec (Attorney General)*, 2002 S.C.C. 84.
13 *Ibid.* at para. 64.
14 The controversies around the so-called decriminalization regime (Bill C-38) for possession of small amounts of marijuana show once again how difficult it is, in some cases, to take a simple risk-based approach to health issues in Canada – although it must be said that, in anything having to do with "drugs," the tendentious and unhelpful sorties from US-based figures are a primary obstacle to reasoned discussion.
15 *R.* v. *Sharpe*, [2001] 1 S.C.R. 45.
16 The trials and tribulations of the *Assisted Human Reproduction Act* (2004, c. 2, <http://laws. justice.gc.ca/en/A-13.4/text.html>) do not inspire optimism about other new regulatory legislation that may be required in the future, especially where genetic manipulation is concerned. The social policy issues addressed by this act were first identified in the late 1980s. A Royal Commission (1993) was appointed in 1989 and reported four years later, with an "urgent" call for new federal legislation. More than a decade passed, with drafters regularly stuffing new provisions into successive versions of the proposed legislation to deal with new technologies (such as mammalian cloning) that appeared during the act's leisurely progress through the system of law-making.

References

Balding, D.J., and P. Donnelly. 1994. "How Convincing Is DNA Evidence?" Nature 368: 285-86.
Bernstein, P.L. 1996. *Against the Gods: The Remarkable Story of Risk* (New York: J. Wiley).
Bosso, Christopher. 1987. *Pesticides and Politics: The Life Cycle of a Public Issue* (Pittsburgh: University of Pittsburgh Press).
Canada, House of Commons. 2002. "An Act Respecting Assisted Human Reproduction." <http://www.parl.gc.ca/37/2/parlbus/chambus/house/bills/government/C-13/C-13_1/C-13_cover-E.html>.
Canadian Blood Services. 2005. <http://www.bloodservices.ca> under "West Nile Virus."
Cranor, C.F. 1993. *Regulating Toxic Substances: A Philosophy of Science and the Law* (New York: Oxford University Press).
Foster, K.R., *et al.*, eds. 1993. *Phantom Risk: Scientific Inference and the Law* (Cambridge, MA: MIT Press).
Gunningham, N., and P. Grabosky. 1998. *Smart Regulation: Designing Environmental Policy* (Oxford: Clarendon Press).
Hrudey, S.E. 1997. "Current Needs in Environmental Risk Management." Environmental Reviews 5: 121-29.
–, and W. Leiss. 2003. "Risk Management and Precaution: Insights on the Cautious Use of Evidence." Environmental Health Perspectives 111: 1577-81.
Kaplan, S. 1997. "The Words of Risk Analysis." Risk Analysis 17: 407-17.
–, and B.J. Garrick. 1981. "On the Quantitative Definition of Risk." Risk Analysis 1: 11-27.
Kleindorfer, P.R., H.C. Kunreuther, and P.J.H. Schoemaker. 1993. *Decision Sciences: An Integrated Perspective* (Cambridge, UK: Cambridge University Press).
Leiss, W. 1993. Review of the 1992 English translation of Ulrich Beck, *Risk Society*. Canadian Journal of Sociology. <http://www.ualberta.ca/~cjscopy/articles/leiss.html>.
–. 1999. "The Censorship of Political Speech, with Special Reference to Tobacco Product Advertising." In K. Petersen and A.C. Hutchinson, eds., *Interpreting Censorship in Canada*, 101-28 (Toronto: University of Toronto Press).
–. 2001. *In the Chamber of Risks: Understanding Risk Controversies* (Montreal: McGill-Queen's University Press).
–. 2003. "West Nile Virus: Yet Another Risk Communication Fiasco." <http://www.leiss.ca/chronicles/122>.
–, and C. Chociolko. 1994. *Risk and Responsibility* (Montreal: McGill-Queen's University Press).

Renn, O. 1992. "Concepts of Risk: A Classification." In S. Krimsky and D. Golding, eds., *Social Theories of Risk*, 53-79 (Westport, CT: Praeger).

Royal Commission on New Reproductive Technologies (Patricia Baird, Chairperson). 1993. *Final Report: Proceed with Care*. 2 volumes. Ottawa: Minister of Government Services Canada.

Tyshenko, M., and W. Leiss. 2004. "Life in the Fast Lane: An Introduction to Genomics Risks." In W. Leiss and D. Powell, *Mad Cows and Mother's Milk: The Perils of Poor Risk Communication*, 296-340. 2nd ed. (Montreal: McGill-Queen's University Press).

United States, National Research Council. 1994. *Science and Judgment in Risk Assessment* (Washington, DC: National Academy Press).

Villeneuve, P.J., and Y. Mao. 1994. "Lifetime Probability of Developing Lung Cancer, by Smoking Status, Canada." Canadian Journal of Public Health 85: 385-88.

2
Use of Risk Assessments by Canadian Judges in the Determination of Dangerous and Long-Term Offender Status, 1997-2002

David MacAlister

While the Canadian criminal justice system incorporates a blending of values, sentencing has recently come to focus on desert – punishment is imposed, ostensibly as a deserved response to past behaviour, at least to the extent that the offender can be held responsible for his or her actions.[1] Exceptions to this general principle are found in rare instances, such as when an individual's liberty is restricted through the use of a peace bond[2] or when an offender is detained after having been found not criminally responsible on account of mental disorder.[3] Such individuals are restricted due to concern over the risk of their future behaviour resulting in harm to others. Sentencing to imprisonment is frequently asserted to combine the goals of deterrence, denunciation, and incapacitation. However, the only sentencing options that utilize risk of future behaviour as a principal criterion are the long-term supervision offender (LTSO) and the dangerous offender (DO) designations.[4] It may be said that the current LTSO and DO provisions reflect a cautious acceptance of a "community protection" model of criminal justice.[5]

Sentencing offenders as dangerous, rather than sentencing them for a specific past offence, appears to have been on the increase in recent decades. This development may be viewed as an adoption of a "new penology"[6] or "actuarial justice,"[7] whereby individuals with certain earmarked characteristics are identified as part of a group that must be regulated as an aspect of society's danger management strategy. Recent years have witnessed a turn away from the utilization of "dangerousness" terminology in the mental health sciences and an adoption of "risk" discourse. This shift has accompanied a switch from reliance on clinical assessments of dangerousness to actuarial prediction models for assessing risk. While this change has rapidly unfolded in the academic and mental health practitioner arenas, the legal arena continues to operate under a legislative scheme that embodies an approach to risk for violence that is now over fifty years old. Canada's dangerousness provisions are a product of the 1940s. Minor amendments in 1997 produced changes to the legislative scheme, although the substance of the DO law remains intact. However, the provision for imposing a long-term offender designation with a concomitant post-release period of supervision lasting up to ten years provides a significant alternative to the previous legislative scheme.

This chapter looks at recent changes to the law governing DOs as it has been unfolding through the judicial interpretation of the law of risk, as decided in cases since the enactment of the 1997 amendments to the *Criminal Code*.[8] It will briefly review the history of the DO legislation in Canada to provide the context within which the current legislative scheme came into being. It will also briefly outline the distinction between different methods of assessing risk for violence that are encountered today, noting the rise of actuarial risk assessment methodology in recent years. It will then review the recent case law to ascertain what major developments pertaining to risk assessment are being encountered in our criminal courts today.

Given the significant developments in the area of law and risk that have arisen over the last several decades, it is time to determine whether the DO scheme allows courts to inquire into issues that contemporary mental health professionals feel comfortable addressing. Have courts traditionally deferred to mental health professionals in assigning the dangerousness label? Do they continue to do so? Do courts appear to have problems with fitting current assessments of "risk" into a paradigm of "dangerousness" mandated by the *Criminal Code*? Have courts accepted the risk discourse? Are courts growing more wary of the ability of mental health experts to assess risk?

A review of sentencing reasons for judgment in cases involving dangerous and long-term offender applications between 1997 and 2002 should reveal preliminary answers to these questions. This chapter looks at decisions handed down across all Canadian jurisdictions.[9] This time frame was chosen for various reasons. First, the *Criminal Code* provisions were amended to come into their latest iteration in 1997. While the changes to the DO provisions were fairly minor, they are significant in some regards. Accordingly, looking at cases decided since these amendments were brought about should reveal contemporary approaches to the dangerousness issue, rather than historical views that may no longer prevail. Second, an important issue to be addressed is whether a judge's view of risk assessments affects the decision to withhold a DO declaration and instead use a long-term supervision order designation. The LTSO designation has been available only since the legislative amendments of 1997. Third, the historical use of DO designations primarily on sexual offenders, as opposed to non-sexual violent offenders, has caused some concern about whether the provisions are being used against all target groups for whom the legislation was designed. One of the objectives of this research is to assess whether the DO provisions are being used more widely now than in the past. It is hoped that this essay will fill a void in the literature by inquiring into the use of the long-term offender designation over the past several years. It will also add to the literature on law and risk, which has experienced considerable attention in recent years.

Brief History of the Legislation

Habitual Offender and Criminal Sexual Psychopath Provisions, 1947-60

Canada first attempted to develop a scheme of preventive detention for offenders in 1947, with the passage of habitual offender legislation.[10] The habitual offender amendments to the *Criminal Code* dealt only with offenders who had lengthy criminal records, at least three indictable offence convictions carrying possible penalties of five years or more. It provided a means through which they could be removed from society indeterminately. If the Crown could establish that the offender was leading a persistently criminal lifestyle and an indeterminate sentence would be expedient for public protection, the court could declare the offender to be "habitual" and sentence him or her to an indefinite term of imprisonment.

In 1948, the *Criminal Code Amendment Act* introduced criminal sexual psychopath provisions into the code:

> Criminal Sexual Psychopath (1948) – a person who "by a course of misconduct in sexual matters had evidenced a lack of power to control his sexual impulses and who as a result is likely to attack or otherwise inflict injury, loss, pain or other evil on any person."[11]

This act had a different focus from the habitual offender legislation, permitting the Crown to apply for a special sentencing hearing to assess whether the offender was a criminal sexual psychopath. The Crown could apply for the designation of an accused as a criminal sexual psychopath if he or she was convicted of one of the sexual offences identified in the provision.

An assessment was made by at least two psychiatrists, at least one of whom was nominated by the Crown. If the court accepted an assessment that the person was sexually dangerous, the offender would be subject to the special sentencing provisions in the act. The sentence given was a combination of a determinate term followed by indeterminate incarceration. The determinate sentence required a minimum of two years' imprisonment. The indeterminate sentence immediately followed the determinate portion of the sentence. It was to be reviewed by the justice minister every three years to determine suitability for parole and, if parole was deemed suitable, under what conditions it should be granted.

Change to Dangerous Sexual Offender, 1960-77

In 1958, J.D. McRuer identified several problems with the 1948 legislation.[12]

The term "criminal sexual psychopath" was criticized as being vague and unscientific. The vagueness of the term made the criminal standard of proof beyond a reasonable doubt difficult to meet, resulting in very few indeterminate sentences. Since the term "criminal sexual psychopath" was viewed by McRuer as being part of the problem, a recommendation was made to change the designation from "criminal sexual psychopath" to "dangerous sexual offender." A minor modification to the definition was built into the new legislative provision adopted in 1960:

> Dangerous Sexual Offender (1960) – a person who "by his conduct in any sexual matter, has shown a failure to control his sexual impulses, and who is likely to cause injury, pain or other evil to any person through failure in the future to control his sexual impulses or is likely to commit a further sexual offence."[13]

Cyril Greenland notes that the intended effect of the 1960 changes was to ease the process of adjudication.[14] A finding of dangerousness required only one conviction, and it could include the one on which the dangerous sexual offender application was based, provided the personal history and circumstances of the case led to a conclusion of dangerousness. The phrase "lack of power to control sexual impulses" was altered to require only the proof of actual "failure" to do so. Additionally, the requirement that the offender "inflict" injury was changed to require only that the offender "cause" the injury in question. The determinate portion of the sentence was dropped. Offenders designated as dangerous sexual offenders who were subject to an indeterminate sentence were to be reviewed every year.

The dangerous sexual offender provisions and the criminal sexual psychopath provisions that preceded them have been described as an "experiment that failed."[15] The problems associated with predicting future dangerousness, the failure to provide treatment, the lengthy detention of offenders, and the targeting of homosexual offenders were all identified as matters for concern regarding the application of the legislative scheme during the early era.

Dangerous Offender Provisions, 1977-97

In 1969, the Ouimet Committee on Corrections made several major recommendations regarding the habitual offender and dangerous sexual offender provisions.[16] The habitual offender legislation was viewed as ineffective and found to be used inconsistently across Canada. Offenders held under the habitual offender provisions were often repeat nuisance offenders or property offenders, not dangerous criminals who posed a threat to the public. In addition, the dangerous sexual offender law was used inconsistently across the country, sometimes for non-violent sexual offenders. The committee also noted that the provisions did not address dangerous persons whose offences were not sexual but still very dangerous. The committee called for the continued use of a clinical method of identifying offenders to be subject to indeterminate detention.[17] Reliance on psychiatry for assessing, diagnosing, and treating DOs prevailed.[18]

As a result of the Ouimet Committee on Correction's recommendations, new legislation was enacted in 1977,[19] coming in the form of yet another amendment to the *Criminal Code*. The new provisions repealed the habitual offender and dangerous sexual offender provisions[20] and were formulated so as to apply to both sex offenders and those who had committed acts of a violent, but non-sexual, nature. The 1977 changes adopted a model that is still found in similar form today. It applied to those offenders who were found to have committed a "serious personal injury offence," defined to include many violent offences carrying a heavy penalty and several sexual offences. The court could entertain an application only where the Crown had applied for such a hearing, following conviction, and where the attorney general consented to the application. The offender could be remanded for evaluation prior to the hearing. The court was required to hear from at least two psychiatrists, one nominated by the Crown and one nominated by the offender. In addition, the court could hear other evidence it considered relevant to the dangerousness inquiry. The *Criminal Code* allowed judges to choose between imposing indeterminate and determinate sentencing options on offenders found to be dangerous. Parole eligibility was available for offenders after serving three years. Those who were denied parole became eligible after each subsequent two years.

Despite continued criticisms and calls to change the DO legislation, the legislation survived the advent of the *Canadian Charter of Rights and Freedoms*[21] era, including an attack on the legislative scheme that made its way to the Supreme Court of Canada. In *R. v. Lyons*,[22] the top court rejected claims that the dangerous provisions contravened sections 7, 9, and 12 of the *Charter*.[23] The court found that the legislative provisions at the time were constitutionally permissible, finding no fault with the court entertaining psychiatric predictions of dangerousness or with the indeterminate period of detention. The availability of parole, although rarely accessible to declared DOs, was seen to be crucial in allaying any concerns about the legitimacy of the scheme.

In the mid-1990s, proposals were circulated that would have amended the DO provisions by allowing for post-sentence detention for non-declared offenders nearing sentence expiration who were believed to be a threat to community safety. The possibility of *Charter* infringements appears to have discouraged adoption of this approach.[24] An alternative approach that would have used post-release civil commitment for those offenders who still posed a risk at the end of their sentence was criticized because of the inability of provincial mental health legislation to provide prolonged detention and the concern that the federal government was attempting to convert a criminal justice matter into a mental health issue.[25]

Current Dangerous and Long-Term Offender Provisions, 1997 to Present
In the mid-1990s, the federal government came under pressure to respond to high-profile cases reported in the media involving released offenders who subsequently committed violent or sexual offences.[26] In late 1996, the federal government announced the latest series of amendments to the DO provisions in the *Criminal Code*. The changes came into force over the summer of 1997.[27] The current regime retains much from the 1977 legislation but with some obvious changes. The most obvious change is that where a DO declaration is not warranted, the court may now declare an offender to be a long-term offender, sentencing the individual determinately and subjecting them to a lengthy community supervision order after their eventual release, provided the statutory criteria for a long-term supervision order are met.

The Crown must apply for a DO hearing after an offender has been convicted for a "serious personal injury offence" (SPIO or predicate offence). As before, this category of offences includes sexual assaults and violent offences carrying a maximum penalty of ten years or more.[28] Before the DO hearing, the judge will remand the offender for up to sixty days to have a behavioural assessment completed, provided there are reasonable grounds for believing the offender might be found to be a dangerous or long-term offender. This single assessment is filed with the court and used as evidence at the subsequent dangerous and/or long-term offender hearing. No longer must the Crown and defence provide their own competing experts for the hearing.[29] However, the parties may supplement the court-ordered assessment with their own experts' testimony, so long as the court considers the evidence relevant.[30] The idea behind mandating a single, court-ordered assessment derives from an acceptance of the Dutch model, which uses a multidisciplinary neutral assessment team rather than competing experts who may offer divergent views.[31] The new scheme envisions the use of a single overarching assessment, ideally by a team of experts, to aid the court in assessing dangerousness. Presumably, this method seeks to adopt a less contentious approach to risk assessment than is found when each side proffers experts who battle it out in the adversarial setting of a courtroom, as predominated in the pre-1997 dangerousness hearings.

In addition to proving a SPIO, the Crown must establish the offender's dangerousness as outlined in section 753(1) of the *Criminal Code*. The test for dangerousness will vary depending on the type of SPIO that is proven to have occurred. Two branches exist. The first pertains to section 752(a) offences – the violent offences that carry a maximum penalty of ten years or more in prison. In such cases, the Crown must go on to prove that the offender is a "threat to the life, safety or physical or mental well-being of other persons," based upon evidence that establishes: (1) "a pattern of repetitive behaviour ... showing a failure to restrain his or her behaviour and a likelihood of causing death or injury to other persons, or inflicting severe psychological damage on other persons, through failure in the future to restrain his or her behaviour"; (2) "a pattern of persistent aggressive behaviour by the offender ... showing a substantial degree of indifference on the part of the offender respecting the reasonably foreseeable consequences to other persons of his or her behaviour"; or (3) "any behaviour by the offender, associated with the offence for which he or she has been convicted, that is of such a brutal nature as to compel the conclusion that the offender's behaviour in the future is unlikely to be inhibited by normal standards of behavioural restraint."[32]

The second branch for establishing dangerousness applies to those individuals whose predicate offence is a conviction for a listed sexual assault offence in section 752(b). In such cases, the Crown must prove that the offender "by his or her conduct in any sexual matter ... has shown a failure to control his or her sexual impulses and a likelihood of causing injury, pain or other evil to other persons through failure in the future to control his or her sexual impulses" exists.[33] The consequences of a DO finding now require an indeterminate sentence. The option to sentence the offender to a determinate period has been taken away.[34] In addition, the period of time that must be served before parole eligibility arises has been increased to seven years.[35] However, the 1997 amendments introduced a new form of disposition: the long-term offender designation. Under the pre-1997 scheme, it had been held that a sentencing judge had no discretion to withhold a DO declaration once the statutory criteria for the designation were made out.[36] The only discretion was whether to impose a determinate or an indeterminate sentence. However, under the new legislative scheme, it may be arguable that discretion to withhold a DO declaration does arise, even when the statutory criteria for the designation have been made out. The new legislative scheme takes away the judge's discretion with regard to the determinate sentencing option. This could be said to mandate discretion for the judge to withhold a DO declaration even where the Crown has made out its case, but the indeterminate disposition would be inappropriate on the facts of the case.[37] In such cases, the long-term offender designation would seem to be appropriate.

The long-term offender designation is obtainable as a result of a stand-alone application[38] or as a default position for the Crown in a failed DO application.[39] Offenders who meet the statutory criteria for a long-term offender are sentenced to a determinate period of incarceration of at least two years and are subjected to up to ten years of supervision in the community upon their eventual release. When being pursued as the intended disposition, the long-term offender provisions are targeted only towards sexual offenders rather than all serious violent offenders.[40]

History of Risk Assessment for Violent Offending

Early Clinical Approaches

The ability to predict future behaviour has long been an elusive goal. Since at least the mid-1970s, critics of violence prediction have identified a host of problems associated with this type of risk assessment.[41] John Monahan's review of the early research on violence prediction was less than encouraging, but it pointed a potential way forward, by calling for the incorporation of statistical concepts in the assessment of risk for violence.[42] Leading up to the late 1980s, dangerousness assessments tended to be based upon the clinical judgment of the mental health practitioner. Typically, a mental status exam of the subject and a review of file data led an assessor to identify the behavioural and psychological dynamics present in the individual. These findings would often result in a clinical diagnosis over which assumptions regarding dangerousness prevailed.

The process of psychiatric diagnosis was fraught with reliability problems.[43] With the passage of time, techniques for diagnosis increased in reliability.[44] However, concerns remain about the reliability of clinical diagnosis of mental and behavioural disorders.[45] Of course, clinical assessments of risk for future violence involve more than diagnostic classification. Clinicians take a host of factors into account in determining whether they believe an offender will manifest violence in the future. However, there are no professional standards in psychology or other mental health disciplines for the assessment of risk for violence.[46] In addition to citing low reliability of clinical judgment, critics have focused on low validity and an inability to specify or articulate the basis upon which decisions were being made.[47] Clinical decisions are not as transparent and intuitively understandable as actuarial methods. However, the real problem seems to have been their inferior predictive validity when compared to actuarial approaches.[48] In the 1990s, the limitations of unaided clinical risk assessment were widely recognized in the literature, giving rise to alternative approaches.

Actuarial Risk Assessment

John Monahan's 1981 call for the continued use, but need to improve the techniques, of risk assessment in criminal justice came to fruition. Nowhere has the development of risk assessment tools been more prolific than in this country. The Canadian criminal justice system's first large-scale experiment with actuarial risk assessment occurred in the context of assessing risk for failure when an offender was released on parole. Joan Nuffield developed a statistical tool (the Statistical Information on Recidivism or SIR scale) to predict general recidivism among federal inmates on conditional release, which came into use in the 1980s.[49] However, it was the development of the Dangerous Behavior Rating Scheme (DBRS) in 1983 that appears to have signalled the beginning of a new era in risk assessment in Canada.[50] While the predictive validity of this instrument was quite weak,[51] it marked the beginning of what was to become a long line of theoretically based and reliable dangerousness-assessment tools.

In the early 1990s, a group of Ontario researchers developed the Violence Risk Appraisal Guide (VRAG),[52] which has become one of the most widespread actuarial methods for assessing risk for violence. This assessment device has been repeatedly tested and has shown strong predictive validity for violent recidivism among certain forensic populations[53] and for sex offender recidivism.[54] However, recent evidence appears to indicate that this device lacks predictive efficacy with non–mentally disordered populations.[55] Since most dangerous and long-term offender cases involve non–mentally disordered offenders, this calls into question the widespread use of the VRAG as a primary tool for assessing dangerousness.

A key component of the VRAG, and the most heavily weighted component in the appraisal, is the Hare Psychopathy Checklist score for the offender (PCL-R).[56] This twenty-item assessment tool, which scores individuals on a three-point scale (0, 1, or 2), has a maximum possible score of forty. According to R.D. Hare, the cut-off for a prototypical psychopath is a score of thirty.[57] The checklist has a stable factor structure, breaking down into two component factors. Factor 1 taps into interpersonal/affective traits, while factor 2 taps into the behavioural components of psychopathy.[58] A growing number of studies illustrate the device's utility as a risk assessment tool in determining general recidivism and violent recidivism.[59] Indeed, it has been asserted that the PCL-R is "unparalleled" and "unprecedented" in its value as a tool to predict violence.[60]

Recent research suggests that the PCL-R may be overblown as a risk assessment tool. One recent study suggests other tools are as good, or better, at predicting offender risk.[61] Another indicates that while the PCL-R may be the best risk assessment tool on the market, the high rate of false positives[62] makes it unsuitable for use as a device to decide on the liberty of offenders.[63] However, it is widely used as a risk assessment tool itself and is incorporated into a multitude of other risk assessment devices.[64]

Structured Clinical Judgment

Structured clinical judgment involves combining actuarial methods with clinical or professional expertise to form a risk assessment. This approach appears to be the one that has come to dominate in most of Canada. Over the past decade, many assessment techniques have been developed with built-in actuarial elements, supplemented with a clinical judgment. The most frequently encountered assessment devices include the PCL-R,[65] the VRAG,[66] the Sex Offender Risk Appraisal Guide (SORAG),[67] the Rapid Risk Assessment for Sex Offender Recidivism (RRASOR),[68] and the STATIC-99.[69] Additionally, the following guides incorporate one or more of these assessment tools as part of their overall assessment: the Violence Prediction Scheme (VPS),[70] the Historical/Clinical/ Risk Management guide (HCR-20),[71] the Spousal Assault Risk Assessment guide (SARA),[72] and the Sexual Violence Risk guide (SVR).[73]

Current Risk Assessment Approaches

At the present time, considerable debate exists in the academic literature on the subject of risk assessment.[74] Problems with early clinical approaches to assessing dangerousness led to an increased use of actuarial methods. Relying on more objective assessments, such as actuarial devices, has its advantages. Lending an air of mathematical precision to the dangerousness assessment is intuitively desirable for mental health experts, judges, and lawyers alike. The statutory scheme for DO declarations requires a judge to determine a "likelihood" of future risk to re-offend. To most of us, likelihood is a mathematically linked concept. Something is "likely" if it is "probable" that it will occur. Probability speaks to mathematical chance or certainty, which is typically a greater than even chance that something will occur.[75]

However, many behavioural scientists are uncomfortable with including factors in risk assessment instruments that are known to be irrelevant to the case at hand. In such cases, there is a tendency to want to sidestep the actuarial tool and use one's own good sense in determining the likelihood of futur'e violence. A considerable body of literature indicates that actuarial predictions are better than clinical predictions.[76] It tends to show that any deviation from the actuarial assessment leads towards decreased ability to accurately assess future risk for violence. This has led to a situation where some experts stick to the actuarial tools, no matter what, while others use the tools as a jumping-off point, from which clinical judgment makes the real determination.

Dangerous or Long-Term Designations: What Affects the Determination?

The current study reviewed cases decided under the 1997 dangerous and long-term offender scheme. In total, over 700 dangerous and long-term offender reports were identified in this database for the six years under review. Many of these cases dealt with the same offender, looking at a variety of issues arising from the pre-trial stages through to appeal. In the end, 148 actual separate cases were identified as providing sufficient information for analysis. Additionally, it should be noted that although many of the cases dealt with applications of the DO law predating the 1997 amendments, they were included since they typically addressed the long-term offender issue.[77]

Which Law to Apply to Transitional Cases?

In British Columbia and Alberta, the determination of dangerous and long-term offender status has been significantly affected by recent Court of Appeal case law. The Supreme Court has delivered judgment on five major dangerous/long-term offender cases arising out of British Columbia and the appeals were dismissed.[78] In the meantime, BC trial courts are applying the Court of Appeal reasoning from these cases in resolving issues dealing with the application of the new provisions. Alberta courts are doing the same, applying an Alberta Court of Appeal case to similar effect.[79] These cases address whether the pre-1997 amendment law should apply to DO cases arising from facts occurring before the effective date of the new provisions. Since the *Criminal Code* amendments did not include transitional provisions, the *Charter*[80] and general principles of criminal law require that the offender get the benefit of a lesser penalty if the law has changed between the time of the offence and the time of sentencing. General principles also dictate that procedural law in place at the time of the court hearing should apply at that hearing; however, the substantive law in place at the time of the offence should apply at the hearing. The amendments may be viewed as incorporating both substantive and procedural changes to the law. Additionally, it is unclear whether the law has been altered to produce a lesser penalty.[81] BC courts have been applying the Court of Appeal's rationale that the new LTSO provisions must be available, if applicable on the facts, even if the facts of the case predate the 1997 amendments coming into force. In essence, the LTSO provisions are regarded as a lesser penalty. However, if there is no reasonable prospect of eventual control in the community, the old DO rules are applied, including the allowance for the possibility of a determinate sentence and the possibility of parole arising after only three years. As a result of this approach, the LTSO designation has been applied with a fair degree of regularity over the last two years, particularly in British Columbia.

Role of Risk Assessment

In the rest of Canada outside of British Columbia and Alberta, the case law convincingly indicates that a large proportion of judges view a high score on the PCL-R, or an assessment of "high risk to offend" on an actuarial tool or other assessment device, as mandating a declaration of dangerousness, provided the minimum statutory criteria are otherwise met. In British Columbia and Alberta, the transitional cases and the post-1997-amendment cases tell a different story. In such cases, even where the DO criteria are met, courts may not declare an offender to be dangerous, even if there is a high assessment of risk and experts appear to be confident that violent re-offending is likely to occur, provided there is some prospect of treatability in the community in the future. This action arises from the lower courts taking direction from the British Columbia Court of Appeal's ruling in *R. v. Johnson* and similar cases.[82] Justice Catherine Anne Ryan indicated that the long-term supervision order should be considered in cases where the offender is not pathologically intractable and is amenable to future control in the community:

> As I read them, what distinguishes the long-term offender provisions from the dangerous offender provisions is the absence of the requirement that the pattern or conduct of the offender be substantially or pathologically intractable, and that if the offender has any treatable condition it will be of such a kind that it must be, if not curable, at least eventually controllable in the community.[83]

This also appears to be true in Alberta, where the Alberta Court of Appeal strongly promoted the use of the LTSO provisions for cases that otherwise might have resulted in a DO declaration.[84] Since many mental health experts promise positive effects from treatment for a wide variety of offenders, it should come as no surprise that judges frequently find clinicians providing testimony supporting the reasonable possibility of treatment that could be carried over to the community in the future.

The cases in which a long-term supervision order is least likely to present itself as an obvious alternative for the court are those in which the offender has been diagnosed as a psychopath. There is an abundance of literature indicating psychopaths are particularly resilient to treatment.[85] In fact, a well-known study indicates that psychopaths who receive treatment may be more likely to recidivate violently than those left untreated.[86] Of the various DO applications in which the court refused the DO designation and found the offender to be a long-term offender, several involved judgments that specifically pointed out a low score on the PCL-R.[87] For example, in *R. v. D.R.M.*,[88] a DO application was rejected in favour of a long-term supervision order. The court made particular mention of the offender's PCL-R score (thirteen to fourteen or twenty-four, depending upon which expert was relied upon) in accepting treatability prospects. This conclusion was reached despite a SIR scale rating that showed the offender to be a high risk to reoffend. A low PCL-R score was also similarly referred to in *R. v. W.H.H.*,[89] where an offender, ostensibly meeting the DO criteria, was granted a five-year determinate sentence plus a ten-year long-term supervision order instead of a DO declaration. In *R. v. N.E.L.*, the correct PCL-R score was disputed by the experts, one rating the offender a twenty-five, while the other awarded a score of thirty-six. In this case, a long-term supervision order was applied since the Crown had failed to show that the offender could not be controlled in the community.[90]

Many judgments expressly note an offender's high PCL-R score in declaring dangerousness. In *R. v. J.F.H.*,[91] the court noted a PCL-R score of thirty, accepting that since the offender met the cut-off for diagnosis as a psychopath, he would not be treatable, thereby ruling out the LTSO option. Likewise, in *R. v. D.S.*,[92] the court noted a PCL-R score of thirty-four to thirty-five, plus actuarial assessments indicating virtual certainty of recidivism. The court declared the offender to be a DO, stating "there is no known, recognized or effective treatment for a psychopath."[93] Several other cases note the importance of a PCL-R score above the diagnostic cut-off of thirty as weighing negatively against the offender.[94]

While individual variation among judges exists, there does not appear to be any preference regarding risk assessment methodology among most judges. They appear equally happy with clinical judgments, actuarial assessments, or some combination in a structured clinical judgment. Some judges place considerable reliance on risk assessment findings, while others appear to be more influenced by the past record of the offender. In several cases, judges seemed to adopt a mathematical approach to the DO requirement of "likely" to re-offend violently. They appeared to equate likelihood to re-offend with "probability" or a greater than 50 percent chance.[95] The risk assessment tool that is most commonly encountered in courts in recent years has been the PCL-R. While this tool was not specifically designed as a risk assessment tool,[96] it has exhibited high levels of reliability and validity for the prediction of recidivism in general and violent recidivism in particular. A host of other assessment tools have been encountered, but it is the PCL-R that has received the most use in recent years. Most judges appear to be willing to work with whatever information is provided to them. Since the law does not require that judges identify whether risk assessment tools were used and, if so, which ones, it is very difficult to ascertain how assessments were performed in many cases. However, it should be noted that wherever risk assessment tools are mentioned, judges appear to have been influenced by them.

In Nova Scotia, a clear preference for actuarial assessment appears to be emerging among the judiciary. In *R. v. J.T.H.*,[97] the Nova Scotia Court of Appeal allowed an appeal from a DO finding, criticizing the sentencing judge for relying on clinical judgment when actuarial evidence indicated lesser risk to re-offend. Justice Gerald B. Freeman noted: "If predictions reflecting clinical judgments are little better than mere chance, little confidence can be placed in them by courts seeking to satisfy themselves as to whether there is a likelihood of re-offending." He went on to note that while actuarial tests are "still works in progress" and predictions based upon them are less than perfect, they appear to be the "best tools available."[98] Other judges have also expressed a preference for an actuarial approach.[99]

A problem that does not seem to have been foreseen in the application of the new legislation flows out of the increased use of the long-term offender designation. The use of a DO designation virtually compels inmates to take part in treatment programs. Offenders sentenced to an indeterminate period know that treatment participation will be a necessary prerequisite for assessment as an acceptable risk for parole. Their only hope for return to the community is participation in treatment programs to lessen the risk to the community to an acceptable level. However, such DO cases, where there is an indication that treatment might some day have a positive effect in allowing for control of the offender's behaviour, are now frequently getting a determinate sentence and a long-term supervision order. The problem is that there is no longer a strong incentive for the offender to participate in treatment programs while institutionalized. With a determinate sentence, the worst that can happen to offenders is that they will possibly have to serve their sentence to warrant expiry, at which point they must be returned to the community. It is difficult to envision any level of supervision that will allay concern about sexual and violent offenders returning to the community without treatment. The only reason they are not declared dangerous any longer is because of their apparent amenability to treatment – yet they may turn out to be the least likely to sign up for treatment. As of 7 July 2002, 154 long-term supervision orders had been awarded by the courts.[100]

Increasing the Use of Dangerous Offender Provisions?

In 1998, James Bonta and his colleagues found that the DO provisions were indeed being applied to high-risk offenders.[101] However, they noted that they were almost exclusively being used against sexual offenders.[102] Their research identified a comparable sample of federal offenders who were not predominantly sex offenders, who had been detained to warrant expiry, and who had recidivated violently upon release. This comparison group was found not to differ in any significant way from the detained DOs. The implication was clear. Dangerous offender applications could be used on a wider class of offenders, including those who heretofore had become detention failures.

In 1998, Isabel Grant speculated that there would be an increase in the use of the DO provisions, accompanying the 1997 revisions to the law.[103] This speculation has indeed turned out to be the case. Figure 2.1 shows that since 1997 the Correctional Service of Canada has experienced a robust increase in the annual number of admissions of declared DOs.[104] While the Correctional Service of Canada data, released in November 2002, cover a time period up to the end of June 2002, the data collected for the present study reveal that this trend has not abated, despite widespread use of the long-term offender provisions. In British Columbia, the number of successful DO applications varied from between four and ten per year between 1997 and 2002. Since the long-term offender provisions duplicate the DO requirements to a considerable degree, but offer a potentially less restrictive outcome over time, it may have been surmised that these provisions would be appropriate for those offenders who would otherwise have been DO cases. This does not appear to be the case. Rather than reducing the number of DO declarations, the provision of long-term offender status appears to supplement the use of DO designations. A net-widening effect appears to have occurred, whereby offenders who would have received ordinary determinate sentences in the past now receive such a sentence plus an extended period of post-release supervision. Indeed, the Correctional Service of Canada admits as much:

> LTSO's are somewhere between DO's and the general inmate population on a number of characteristics. Because the number of DO designations has not decreased, the LTSO's are likely comprised of those who may previously have been categorized with the general offender population.[105]

Figure 2.1

Number of dangerous offenders designated annually, 1978-2002

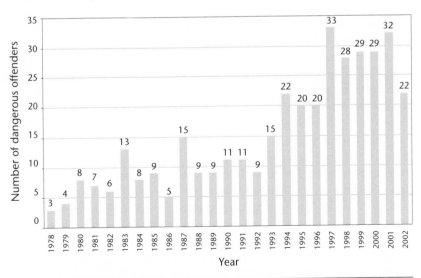

Sources: Solicitor General Canada, *Corrections and Conditional Release Statistical Overview* (Ottawa: Public Works and Government Services Canada, 2002) at 94; <http://www.sgc.gc.ca/publications/corrections/pdf/StatsNov2002_e.pdf>; and personal communication with Chris Molloy, Correctional Service of Canada.

As Table 2.1 shows, there were 142 DO applications identified in the Canadian case law between 1997 and 2003, where sufficient information was provided in the judgment to assess the issues under consideration in this study.[106] Of these 142 cases, 104 resulted in a declaration at trial that the offender was a DO, while 36 cases witnessed the application being rejected. When a DO application was rejected, the court imposed a long-term offender period of supervision on a determinate sentence 70 percent of the time. In 6 cases, the Crown applied directly for a LTSO order rather than a DO designation.[107] All 6 cases were successful.

Two major past trends in the use of the DO provisions persist. As has historically been the case, the majority of DO cases arise in the provinces of British Columbia (34 percent) and Ontario (33 percent). Additionally, of the 104 cases resulting in a DO declaration at trial, all but 12 cases involved a predicate offence that could be characterized as a sexual offence. This figure, which indicates that approximately 88 percent of declared DOs had a sexual offence as their predicate offence, appears to be consistent with the proportion of sexual offenders captured in DO proceedings in the past.[108] Preliminary analysis of the case law database appears to indicate that the increase in DO declarations may have peaked, at least for the time being.[109] This appears to be particularly true in British Columbia and Alberta, where the use of the long-term offender option is being strongly supported by the courts of appeal.

The 1997 amendments to the DO provisions appear to have come into operation at a time when significant developments are ongoing in the area of forensic risk assessment. In the past, judges typically had to pick between competing experts, at least one for the Crown and at least one for the defence. Judges often had to pick which one to believe or rely upon. Now, courts are in a position to remand offenders for assessment and to select who will be responsible for the assessment in some jurisdictions. The defence may assign their own expert to evaluate the offender, but these experts are frequently being rejected by the courts in favour of what is taken to be the court's neutral expert.

While the 1997 amendments envision the court-ordered assessment to be a neutral, multi-party examination of the offender, there appears to be some variability in the ability of the various provinces to muster a sophisticated multidisciplinary clinical assessment. Cases arising out of British Columbia often seem to reflect a team assessment, but this appears to happen less frequently in the prairie provinces. The considerable resources available through BC's Forensic Psychiatric Services Commission may play an important role in the availability of such assessments in this province.

Conclusion

Dangerous offender and long-term offender proceedings are infused with

Table 2.1

Dangerous offender case dispositions by jurisdiction, 1997-2002

	Applications of dangerous offender (DO)	Declaration at trial of DO	Declaration of DO upheld on appeal	Declaration of DO overturned on appeal	Application of DO rejected at trial	Declaration of long-term offender (LTO) upon rejection of DO	Rejection of DO overturned on appeal and declaration of DO made	Application of LTO
British Columbia	48	36	8	10	11	9	2	–
Alberta	8	7	2	2	–	1	–	1
Saskatchewan	12	11	2	–	1	–	–	1
Manitoba	4	3	3	–	1	1	–	–
Ontario	46	30	13	–	16	10	–	2
Quebec	8	7	1	1	1	1	–	2
New Brunswick	–	–	–	–	–	–	–	–
PEI	–	–	–	–	–	–	–	–
Nova Scotia	8	5	2	1	3	3	–	–
Newfoundland	4	3	1	–	1	–	1	–
Yukon	–	–	–	–	–	–	–	–
Northwest Territories	3	1	–	–	2	–	–	1
Nunavut	1	1	–	–	–	–	–	–
Total	142	104	32	14	36	25	3	6

contemporary risk discourse. The early years involving the clinical assessment of dangerousness have given way to multidisciplinary risk assessment strategies, combining actuarial assessment and structured clinical investigation. This development has reflected a shift in the literature from predicting "dangerousness" to assessing the offender's degree of "risk."[110] Concerns still exist about the civil liberty implications of these provisions. As Grant indicates:

> The language of risk may obscure some of the real problems in any predictive exercise. Labelling someone as high risk is not saying the person will re-offend. Rather, it is saying, with some degree of certainty, that the person is at high risk for re-offending. This does not mean that he will re-offend nor that the assessment of risk was necessarily wrong if no violent offences follow. Thus, an assessment that an offender is a high risk is unfalsifiable. The new language of risk obscures the false positive problem but does not remove it. It is still very likely that coercive measures will be utilized against offenders who would not actually have re-offended.[111]

The question that remains is what level of certainty society should require before permitting the long-term deprivation of liberty associated with the DO provisions. It is unclear whether forensic psychology has taken risk assessment to a level of certainty acceptable in the criminal law. The requirement that the Crown prove "likelihood" to violently re-offend beyond a reasonable doubt appears to be a disguised requirement that the Crown establish risk to re-offend as likely or on a balance of probabilities. The Crown does not have to prove beyond a reasonable doubt that the offender will re-offend – only a likelihood of re-offending must be proven. To prove beyond a reasonable doubt that an offender will re-offend is a standard that exceeds even the best actuarial risk assessment tools of today.

Courts avoid the dilemma created by DO provisions by asserting that offenders are not sentenced for what they might do in the future but rather for what they have done in the past – the predicate offence, usually combined with a pattern of similar behaviour. However, this finding is not entirely accurate. Assessment of future likelihood to re-offend is built into all aspects of the DO criteria. It is an essential element that supplements the past misdeeds of the offender and must be established for the legal criteria to be satisfied.

Canada's reformed DO provisions are a key component in its risk management strategy for violent crime. However, they may be viewed as an aspect of law and order expediency.[112] They cater to contemporary concern over the risk of sexual and other violence that is widespread in our society. They reflect an abandonment of principles of responsibility and an acceptance of risk assessment methodologies that aggregate people into groups with like characteristics for the purposes of penal disposition. This carries a number of risks itself.[113] It does nothing to alleviate the societal circumstances giving rise to dangerous behaviour. It is a crime prevention strategy that arises through incapacitation, not through addressing the causal origins of crime. It rejects legalism and due process in favour of "involuntary detention of individuals not for something they have done wrong but for something it is estimated they might do based on the previous behaviour of the group with which they are statistically associated."[114] Judges should remain vigilant to the potential dangers associated with the use of actuarial assessments in the context of the criminal law. The legislation should not be used to target already marginalized Canadians,[115] setting them up for harsher treatment.

Given the grave risk of false positive predictions of dangerousness, members of the judiciary must be cautious, particularly when faced with actuarial risk assessments, cloaked as they are in the terminology of mathematical precision. They must be careful not to lose sight of the fact that probabilistic assessments are being made based on group behaviour, while they are dealing with real individuals appearing before them. Our system of justice places high value on securing justice in each individual case by treating it individually, rather than on the basis of its characteristics that appear to be similar to others for which mathematical data are available. Given the serious repercussions attached to a finding of dangerousness, we must be careful not to foreclose avenues of knowledge. No matter how sophisticated our screening technologies become, we will always have difficulty predicting incidents that have a low level of frequency of occurrence. The only solution appears to be to rely on a series of tests or assessments rather than on just one. The risk profile provided through contemporary actuarial assessments must be supplemented with other evidence indicating the need for extreme measures in the case before the court.

Appendix: Relevant Current *Criminal Code* Provisions

Part XXIV: Dangerous Offenders and Long-Term Offenders

Definitions

752. In this Part,

"court" means the court by which an offender in relation to whom an application under this Part is made was convicted, or a superior court of criminal jurisdiction;

"serious personal injury offence" means

(a) an indictable offence, other than high treason, treason, first degree murder or second degree murder, involving
  (i) the use or attempted use of violence against another person, or
  (ii) conduct endangering or likely to endanger the life or safety of another person or inflicting or likely to inflict severe psychological damage on another person, and for which the offender may be sentenced to imprisonment for ten years or more, or

(b) an offence or attempt to commit an offence mentioned in section 271 (sexual assault), 272 (sexual assault with a weapon, threats to a third party or causing bodily harm) or 273 (aggravated sexual assault).

(R.S.C. 1970, c. C-34, s. 687; S.C. 1976-77, c. 53, s. 14; S.C. 1980-81-82-83, c. 125, s. 26.)

Application for Remand for Assessment

752.1 (1) Where an offender is convicted of a serious personal injury offence or an offence referred to in paragraph 753.1(2)(a) and, before sentence is imposed on the offender, on application by the prosecution, the court is of the opinion that there are reasonable grounds to believe that the offender might be found to be a dangerous offender under section 753 or a long-term offender under section 753.1, the court may, by order in writing, remand the offender, for a period not exceeding sixty days, to the custody of the person that the court directs and who can perform an assessment, or can have an assessment performed by experts. The assessment is to be used as evidence in an application under section 753 or 753.1.

(2) The person to whom the offender is remanded shall file a report of the assessment with the court not later than fifteen days after the end of the assessment period and make copies of it available to the prosecutor and counsel for the offender.

Application for Finding That an Offender Is a Dangerous Offender

753. (1) The court may, on application made under this Part following the filing of an assessment report under subsection 752.1(2), find the offender to be a dangerous offender if it is satisfied

(a) that the offence for which the offender has been convicted is a serious personal injury offence described in paragraph (a) of the definition of that expression in section 752 and the offender constitutes a threat to the life, safety or physical or mental well-being of other persons on the basis of evidence establishing
   (i) a pattern of repetitive behaviour by the offender, of which the offence for which he or she has been convicted forms a part, showing a failure to restrain his or her behaviour and a likelihood of causing death or injury to other persons, or inflicting severe psychological damage on other persons, through failure in the future to restrain his or her behaviour,
   (ii) a pattern of persistent aggressive behaviour by the offender, of which the offence for which he or she has been convicted forms a part, showing a substantial degree of indifference on the part of the offender respecting the reasonably foreseeable consequences to other persons of his or her behaviour, or
   (iii) any behaviour by the offender, associated with the offence for which he or she has been convicted, that is of such a brutal nature as to compel the conclusion that the offender's behaviour in the future is unlikely to be inhibited by normal standards of behavioural restraint; or
(b) that the offence for which the offender has been convicted is a serious personal injury offence described in paragraph (b) of the definition of that expression in section 752 and the offender, by his or her conduct in any sexual matter including that involved in the commission of the offence for which he or she has been convicted, has shown a failure to control his or her sexual impulses and a likelihood of causing injury, pain or other evil to other persons through failure in the future to control his or her sexual impulses.

(2) An application under subsection (1) must be made before sentence is imposed on the offender unless

(a) before the imposition of sentence, the prosecution gives notice to the offender of a possible intention to make an application under section 752.1 and an application under subsection (1) not later than six months after that imposition; and
(b) at the time of the application under subsection (1) that is not later than six months after the imposition of sentence, it is shown that relevant evidence that was not

reasonably available to the prosecution at the time of the imposition of sentence became available in the interim.

(3) Notwithstanding subsection 752.1(1), an application under that subsection may be made after the imposition of sentence or after an offender begins to serve the sentence in a case to which paragraphs (2)(a) and (b) apply.

(4) If the court finds an offender to be a dangerous offender, it shall impose a sentence of detention in a penitentiary for an indeterminate period.

(4.1) If the application was made after the offender begins to serve the sentence in a case to which paragraphs (2)(a) and (b) apply, the sentence of detention in a penitentiary for an indeterminate period referred to in subsection (4) replaces the sentence that was imposed for the offence for which the offender was convicted.

(5) If the court does not find an offender to be a dangerous offender,

(a) the court may treat the application as an application to find the offender to be a long-term offender, section 753.1 applies to the application and the court may either find that the offender is a long-term offender or hold another hearing for that purpose; or

(b) the court may impose sentence for the offence for which the offender has been convicted.

(6) Any evidence given during the hearing of an application made under subsection (1) by a victim of an offence for which the offender was convicted is deemed also to have been given during any hearing under paragraph (5)(a) held with respect to the offender.

Application for Finding That an Offender Is a Long-Term Offender

753.1 (1) The court may, on application made under this Part following the filing of an assessment report under subsection 752.1(2), find an offender to be a long-term offender if it is satisfied that

(a) it would be appropriate to impose a sentence of imprisonment of two years or more for the offence for which the offender has been convicted;

(b) there is a substantial risk that the offender will reoffend; and

(c) there is a reasonable possibility of eventual control of the risk in the community.

(2) The court shall be satisfied that there is a substantial risk that the offender will reoffend if

(a) the offender has been convicted of an offence under section 151 (sexual interference), 152 (invitation to sexual touching) or 153 (sexual exploitation), subsection 163.1(2) (making child pornography), subsection 163.1(3) (distribution, etc., of child pornography), subsection 163.1(4) (possession of child pornography), subsection 163.1(4.1) (accessing child pornography), section 172.1 (luring a child), subsection 173(2) (exposure) or section 271 (sexual assault), 272 (sexual assault with a weapon) or 273 (aggravated sexual assault), or has engaged in serious conduct of a sexual nature in the commission of another offence of which the offender has been convicted; and

(b) the offender

(i) has shown a pattern of repetitive behaviour, of which the offence for which he or she has been convicted forms a part, that shows a likelihood of the offender's causing death or injury to other persons or inflicting severe psychological damage on other persons, or

(ii) by conduct in any sexual matter including that involved in the commission of the offence for which the offender has been convicted, has shown a likelihood of causing injury, pain or other evil to other persons in the future through similar offences.

(3) Subject to subsections (3.1), (4) and (5), if the court finds an offender to be a long-term offender, it shall

(a) impose a sentence for the offence for which the offender has been convicted, which sentence must be a minimum punishment of imprisonment for a term of two years; and

(b) order the offender to be supervised in the community, for a period not exceeding ten years, in accordance with section 753.2 and the Corrections and Conditional Release Act.

Acknowledgment

The author would like to thank William Leiss for his thoughtful comments on an earlier draft of this chapter.

Notes

1 The fundamental sentencing principle, which is found in section 718.1 of the *Criminal Code*, R.S.C. 1985, c. C-46 [hereinafter *Criminal Code*], is that "[a] sentence must be proportionate to the gravity of the offence and the degree of responsibility of the offender."

2 See *ibid.* at section 810.

3 See *ibid.* at Part XX.1.

4 See *ibid.* at Part XXIV.

5 See M. Petrunik, "The Hare and the Tortoise: Dangerousness and Sex Offender Policy in the United States and Canada" (2003) 45 Canadian Journal of Criminology and Criminal Justice 43-72.

6 M.M. Feeley and J. Simon, "The New Penology: Notes on the Emerging Strategy of Corrections and Its Implications" (1992) 30 Criminology 449-74.

7 M. Feeley and J. Simon, "Actuarial Justice: The Emerging New Criminal Law" in D. Nelken, ed., *The Futures of Criminology* (London: Sage, 1994).

8 *Criminal Code, supra* note 1.

9 All post-1996 cases found in the territorial collection database of Quicklaw for British Columbia, Alberta, Saskatchewan, Manitoba, Ontario, Quebec, New Brunswick, Prince Edward Island, Nova Scotia, Newfoundland and Labrador, the Yukon Territory, the Northwest Territories, and Nunavut containing the terms "dangerous offender," "délinquant dangereux," and "long-term offender" were retrieved and analyzed. Since the Quicklaw database for academic subscribers excludes the Ontario Reports, these were analyzed from their print form.

10 *Criminal Code Amendment Act*, S.C. 1947, c. 55, s. 18.

11 *Criminal Code Amendment Act*, S.C. 1948, c. 39, s. 43.

12 J.D. McRuer (Chairman), *Report of the Royal Commission on the Criminal Law Relating to Criminal Sexual Psychopaths* (Ottawa: Queen's Printer, 1958).

13 *An Act to Amend the Criminal Code*, S.C. 1960-61, c. 43, s. 32.

14 C. Greenland, *Dangerous Sexual Offenders in Canada*, Studies on Imprisonment (Ottawa: Law Reform Commission of Canada, 1976).

15 C. Greenland, "Dangerous Sexual Offender Legislation in Canada, 1948-1977: An Experiment That Failed" (1984) 26 Canadian Journal of Criminology 1-12.

16 Canadian Committee on Corrections (Ouimet Committee), *Toward Unity: Criminal Justice and Corrections* (Ottawa: Queen's Printer, 1969).

17 M. Petrunik, *Models of Dangerousness: A Cross Jurisdictional Review of Dangerousness Legislation and Practice* (Ottawa: Solicitor General, 1994).

18 J. Jakimec, F. Poporino, S. Addario, and C.D. Webster, "Dangerous Offenders in Canada, 1977-1985" (1986) 9 International Journal of Law and Psychiatry 479-89.

19 *Criminal Law Amendment Act, 1977*, S.C. 1976-77, c. 53, s. 14.

20 Nonetheless the detentions of those previously declared habitual or dangerous sexual offenders continued. It was not until the mid-1980s that each detained habitual offender's case came under close scrutiny. S.M. Leggatt, *Report of the Inquiry into Habitual Criminals in Canada* (Ottawa: Government of Canada, 1984).

21 *Canadian Charter of Rights and Freedoms*, Part I of the *Constitution Act, 1982*, being Schedule B to the *Canada Act 1982* (U.K.), 1982, c. 11 [hereinafter *Charter*].

22   *R. v. Lyons*, [1987] 2 S.C.R. 309.

23   *Charter, supra* note 21.

24   John Howard Society of Alberta, *Dangerous Offender Legislation around the World*, 1999, <http://www.johnhoward.ab.ca/PUB/C20.htm#exe>.

25   *Ibid*. Note, however, that the United States Supreme Court has recently upheld the use of involuntary commitment at the end of a sentence for "sexually violent predators" in both *Kansas* v. *Hendricks*, (1997) 521 U.S. 346 and *Seling* v. *Young*, (2001) 531 U.S. 250.

26   See I. Grant, "Legislating Public Safety: The Business of Risk" (1998) 3 Canadian Criminal Law Review 177.

27   *An Act to Amend the Criminal Code (High Risk Offenders), the Corrections and Conditional Release Act, the Criminal Records Act, the Prisons and Reformatories Act and the Department of the Solicitor General Act*, S.C. 1997, c. 17, ss. 4-8.

28   See appendix for the precise language of the current provisions.

29   This change comes as one of the key recommendations of the Federal-Provincial-Territorial Task Force on High-Risk Violent Offenders, *Strategies for Managing High-Risk Offenders* (Victoria: Federal-Provincial-Territorial Task Force on High-Risk Violent Offenders, 1995).

30   The 1997 provisions delete the requirement of two psychiatrists being heard in a dangerous offender hearing and appear to replace the requirement with the single court-ordered assessment. No mention is made of other experts testifying. However, it has become common practice for additional mental health experts to be called by the defence.

31   A. Manson, *The Law of Sentencing* (Toronto: Irwin Law, 2001) at 321.

32   See *Criminal Code, supra* note 1 at s. 753 (1)(a)(i)-(iii).

33   See *ibid*. at s. 753(1)(b).

34   This has been critiqued for depriving judges of a discretion that allows them to tailor the sentence to the circumstances of the offender. J. Soward, "Mandatory Indeterminate Sentence under Dangerous Offender Legislation" (1998) 7 Dalhousie Journal of Legal Studies 189-213. As of 30 June 2002, of the 313 active DOs in Canada, 13 had determinate sentences. Solicitor General Canada, *Corrections and Conditional Release Statistical Overview* (Ottawa: Public Works and Government Services Canada, 2002) at 91.

35   See *Criminal Code, supra* note 1 at s. 761(1).

36   *R. v. Moore* (1985), 16 C.C.C. (3d) 328 (Ont.C.A.).

37   A residual discretion to refuse to declare an offender dangerous, who met all of the statutory criteria, has been upheld in *R. v. Driver*, [2000] B.C.J. No. 63 (S.C.) at para. 25 and *R. v. Neve* (1999), 137 C.C.C. (3d) 97 (Alta.C.A.) at para. 227.

38   See *Criminal Code, supra* note 1 at s. 753.1.

39   See *ibid*. at s. 753(5).

40   See *ibid*. at s. 753.1(2).

41   See, for example, B.J. Ennis and T.R. Litwack, "Psychiatry and the Presumption of Expertise: Flipping Coins in the Courtroom" (1974) 62 California Law Review 693.

42   See J. Monahan, *The Clinical Prediction of Violent Behavior* (Rockville, MD: National Institute of Mental Health, 1981) and J. Monahan, *Predicting Violent Behavior: An Assessment of Clinical Techniques* (Beverly Hills: Sage Publications, 1981).

43   See D.L. Rosenhan, "On Being Sane in Insane Places" (1974) 179 Science 250-58. Psychiatrists in North America routinely use the *Diagnostic and Statistical Manual of Mental Disorders* (Washington, DC: American Psychiatric Association, 1952) [hereinafter *DSM*], now in its fourth edition, to diagnose subjects.

44   The development of the *DSM-III, supra* note 43, was hailed for its contribution to reliability in psychiatric diagnosis. See R.L. Spitzer, J.B.W. Williams, and A.E. Skodol, "DSM-III: The Major Achievements and an Overview" (1980) 137 American Journal of Psychiatry at 151-64. While the *DSM-III* published inter-rater reliability data from field trials with the instrument, the *DSM-IV* subsequently failed to do so. Data for inter-rater reliability on the Antisocial Personality Disorder field trial for *DSM-IV* are available elsewhere. See T.A. Widiger *et al.*, "DSM-IV Antisocial Personality Disorder Field Trial" (1996) 105 Journal of Abnormal Psychology at 3-16 that shows levels of reliability that appear to be acceptable in psychiatry.

45   S. Kirk and H. Kutchins, *The Selling of DSM: The Rhetoric of Science in Psychiatry* (New York: Aldine de Gruyter, 1992). See also T.W. Campbell, "Challenging the Evidentiary Reliability of DSM-IV" (1999) 17 American Journal of Forensic Psychology 47-68.

46   R. Borum, "Improving the Clinical Practice of Violence Risk Assessment: Technology, Guidelines, and Training" (1996) 51 American Psychologist 945-56.

47   J. Monahan and H.J. Steadman, eds., *Violence and Mental Disorder: Developments in Risk Assessment* (Chicago: University of Chicago Press, 1994).

48   C.W. Lidz, E.P. Mulvey, and W. Gardner, "The Accuracy of Predictions of Violence to Others" (1993) 269 Journal of the American Medical Association 1007-11 and D. Mossman, "Assessing Predictions of Violence: Being Accurate about Accuracy" (1994) 62 Journal of Consulting and Clinical Psychology 783-92.

49   J. Nuffield, *Parole Decision Making in Canada* (Ottawa: Communication Division, Solicitor General Canada, 1982). This finding was recently revalidated. J. Bonta, W.G. Harman, R.G. Hann, and R.B. Cormier, "The Prediction of Recidivism among Federally Sentenced Offenders: A Re-validation of the SIR Scale" (1996) 38 Canadian Journal of Criminology 61-79. A later tool developed by psychologists associated with the Correctional Service of Canada, which was designed to assess general risk for recidivism and treatment needs, is the Level of Service Inventory – Revised (LSI-R). D.A. Andrews and J. Bonta, *The Level of Service Inventory – Revised* (Toronto: Multi-Health Systems, 1995).

50   C.D. Webster and R.J. Menzies, "Supervision in the Deinstitutionalized Community" in S. Hodgins, ed., *Mental Disorder and Crime* (Newbury Park: Sage Publications, 1993).

51   R.J. Menzies and C.D. Webster, "Construction and Validation of Risk Assessments in a Six-Year Follow-up of Forensic Patients: A Tri-dimensional Analysis" (1995) 63 Journal of Consulting and Clinical Psychology 766-78.

52   Violence Risk Appraisal Guide, cited in G.T. Harris, M.E. Rice, and V.L. Quinsey, "Violent Recidivism of Mentally Disordered Offenders: The Development of a Statistical Prediction Instrument" (1993) 20 Criminal Justice and Behavior 315-35 [hereinafter VRAG].

53   See G.T. Harris, M.E. Rice, and C.A. Cormier, "Prospective Replication of the Violence Risk Appraisal Guide in Predicting Violent Recidivism among Forensic Patients" (2002) 26 Law and Human Behavior 377-94.

54   M.E. Rice and G.T. Harris, "Cross-Validation and Extension of the Violence Risk Appraisal Guide for Child Molesters and Rapists" (1997) 21 Law and Human Behavior 231-41.

55   W. Loza, D.B. Villeneuve, and A. Loza-Fanous, "Predictive Validity of the Violence Risk Appraisal Guide: A Tool for Assessing Violent Offenders' Recidivism" (2002) 25 International Journal of Law and Psychiatry 85-92.

56   R.D. Hare, *The Hare Psychopathy Checklist – Revised* (Toronto: Multi-Health Systems, 1991) (now in its second edition, 2003) [hereinafter PCL-R].

57   R.D. Hare, "Psychopathy: A Clinical Construct Whose Time Has Come" (1996) 23 Criminal Justice and Behavior 25-54.

58   *Ibid.* Note that Scottish researchers have recently argued that the psychopathy construct is best viewed as being composed of three factors. D.J. Cooke and C. Mitchie, "Refining the Construct of Psychopathy: Towards a Hierarchical Model" (2001) 13 Psychological Assessment 171-88.

59   R.D. Hare, "Psychopathy as a Risk Factor for Violence" (1999) 70 Psychiatric Quarterly 181-97; S.D. Hart, "Psychopathy and Risk for Violence" in D.J. Cooke, A.E. Forth, and R.D. Hare, eds., *Psychopathy: Theory, Research and Implications for Society* (Dordrecht: Kluwer Academic Publishers, 1998); S.D. Hart, "The Role of Psychopathy in Assessing Risk for Violence: Conceptual and Methodological Issues" (1998) 3 Legal and Criminological Psychology 121-37; J.F. Hemphill, R.D. Hare, and S. Wong, "Psychopathy and Recidivism: A Review" (1998) 3 Legal and Criminological Psychology 139-70; V.L. Quinsey, "The Prediction and Explanation of Criminal Violence" (1995) 18 International Journal of Law and Psychiatry 117-27; G.T. Harris, M.E. Rice, and C.A. Cormier, "Psychopathy and Violent Recidivism" (1991) 15 Law and Human Behavior 625-37; R.C. Serin, "Psychopathy and Violence in Criminals" (1991) 6 Journal of Interpersonal Violence 423-31; and R.C. Serin, "Violent Recidivism in Criminal Psychopaths" (1996) 20 Law and Human Behavior 207-17.

60   R.T. Salekin, R. Rogers, and K.T. Sewell, "A Review and Meta-analysis of the Psychopathy Checklist and Psychopathy Checklist-Revised: Predictive Validity of Dangerousness" (1996) 3 Clinical Psychology: Science and Practice 203-15.

61   P. Gendreau, C. Goggin, and P. Smith, "Is the PCL-R Really the 'Unparalleled' Measure of Offender Risk? A Lesson in Knowledge Cumulation" (2002) 29 Criminal Justice and Behavior 397-426.

62   False positives are cases where the device predicts future dangerousness, but the individual turns out not to be a danger.

63   D. Freedman, "False Prediction of Future Dangerousness: Error Rates and Psychopathy Checklist-Revised" (2001) 29 Journal of the American Academy of Psychiatry and Law 89-95.

64   R.D. Hare, "Psychopathy and Risk for Recidivism and Violence" in N. Gray, J. Laing, and L. Noaks, eds., *Criminal Justice, Mental Health, and the Politics of Risk* (London: Cavendish Publishing, 2002).

65   See PCL-R, *supra* note 56.

66   See VRAG, *supra* note 52.

67   The Sex Offender Risk Appraisal Guide is a variation on the VRAG, *supra* note 52, designed specifically for assessing risk of sex offender recidivism. See V.L. Quinsey, G.T. Harris, M.E. Rice, and C.A. Cormier, *Violent Offenders: Appraising and Managing Risk* (Washington, DC: American Psychological Association, 1998).

68   Rapid Risk Assessment for Sex Offender Recidivism, cited in R.K. Hanson, *The Development of a Brief Actuarial Risk Scale for Sexual Offender Recidivism*, User Report 1997-04 (Ottawa: Department of Solicitor General Canada, 1997).

69   STATIC-99, cited in R.K. Hanson and D. Thornton, *Static 99: Improving Actuarial Risk Assessments for Sex Offenders* (Ottawa: Solicitor General Canada, 1999).

70   Violence Prediction Scheme, cited in C.D. Webster, G.T. Harris, M.E. Rice, C. Cormier, and V.L. Quinsey, *The Violence Prediction Scheme: Assessing Dangerousness in High Risk Men* (Toronto: Centre of Criminology, University of Toronto, 1993) [hereinafter VPS], incorporating the VRAG into the instrument.

71   Historical/Clinical/Risk Management guide, cited in C.D. Webster, D. Eaves, K. Douglas, and A. Wintrup, *The HCR-20 Scheme: The Assessment of Dangerousness and Risk* (Burnaby, BC: Simon Fraser University and Forensic Psychiatric Services Commission of BC, 1995) [hereinafter HCR-20], incorporating the PCL-R into the instrument.

72   Spousal Assault Risk Assessment guide, cited in P.R. Kropp, S.D. Hart, C.D. Webster, and D. Eaves, *Manual for the Spousal Assault Risk Assessment Guide* (Vancouver: BC Institute on Family Violence, 1994). This is similar to the HCR-20, *supra* note 71, but designed for a narrower population and type of violence: spouse assault.

73   Sexual Violence Risk guide, cited in J.V. Boer, S.D. Hart, P.R. Kropp, and C.D. Webster, *Manual for Sexual Violence Risk 20: Professional Guidelines for Assessing Risk of Sexual Violence* (Vancouver: BC Institute on Family Violence, 1997); D.P. Boer, R.J. Wilson, C.M. Gauthier, and S.D. Hart, "Assessing Risk of Sexual Violence: Guidelines for Clinical Practice" in C.D. Webster and M.A. Jackson, eds., *Impulsivity: Theory, Assessment and Treatment* (New York: Guilford Press, 1997), incorporating elements from the PCL-R, VPS, and HCR-20 among others.

74   See, for example, J. Bonta, "Offender Risk Assessment: Guidelines for Selection and Use" (2002) 29 Criminal Justice and Behavior 355-79. Compare the critiques of actuarial prediction: T.R. Litwack, "Actuarial versus Clinical Assessments of Dangerousness" (2001) 7 Psychology, Public Policy, and Law 409-43 and E. Silver and L.L. Miller, "A Cautionary Note on the Use of Actuarial Risk Assessment Tools for Social Control" (2002) 48 Crime and Delinquency 138-61, with the staunch supporters of an actuarial approach: W.M. Grove, D.H. Zald, B.S. Lebow, B.E. Snitz, and C. Nelson, "Clinical versus Mechanical Prediction: A Meta-Analysis" (2000) 12 Psychological Assessment: A Journal of Consulting and Clinical Psychology 19-30 and W.M. Grove and P.E. Meehl, "Comparative Efficiency of Informal (Subjective, Impressionistic) and Formal (Mechanical, Algorithmic) Prediction Procedures: The Clinical-Statistical Controversy" (1996) 2 Psychology, Public Policy, and Law 293-323.

75   If actuarial predictions are indeed a step forward, their use in dangerousness assessments

seems particularly apt to many mental health experts: K. Heilbrun, J.R.P. Ogloff, and K. Picarello, "Dangerous Offender Statutes in the United States and Canada: Implications for Risk Assessment" (1999) 22 International Journal of Law and Psychiatry 393-415.

76 See, for example, Quinsey *et al.*, *supra* note 67.

77 While the 1997 amendments lacked any transitional provisions, many courts have allowed the use of the long-term supervision offender option in cases involving facts arising prior to the recent amendments.

78 *R. v. Johnson*, [2001] B.C.J. No. 2021 (C.A.) [hereinafter *Johnson*]; *R. v. Edgar*, [2001] B.C.J. No. 2022 (C.A.); *R. v. Smith*, [2001] B.C. J. No. 267 (C.A.); *R. v. Mitchell*, [2002] B.C.J. No. 122 (C.A.); and *R. v. Kelly*, [2002] B.C.J. No. 352 (C.A.) were all argued on appeal in the Supreme Court of Canada on 16 January 2003. All the appeals were dismissed. See the reasons in *R. v. Johnson* (2003) 177 C.C.C. (3d) 97 (S.C.C.).

79 *R. v. Neve*, [1999] A.J. No. 753 (C.A.) [hereinafter *Neve*].

80 *Charter*, *supra* note 21.

81 The old provisions provided the judge the option of sentencing a dangerous offender determinately (a lesser penalty) and carried an earlier parole eligibility period (three years versus seven under the 1997 law). However, the new provisions allow for the use of the long-term offender extended post-release supervision order to supplement a determinate sentence where the offender might in the past have been found to be dangerous, but cannot be so found under the new scheme because there is a "reasonable possibility of eventual control in the community" (possible to view as a lesser penalty).

82 *Johnson*, *supra* note 78, upheld on appeal to the Supreme Court of Canada.

83 *Ibid.* at para. 93.

84 See *Neve*, *supra* note 79.

85 See the summary of the research provided in R.D. Hare, "Psychopaths and Their Nature: Implications for the Mental Health and Criminal Justice Systems" in T. Millon, E. Simonsen, M. Birket-Smith, and R.G. Davis, eds., *Psychopathy: Antisocial, Criminal, and Violent Behavior* (New York: Guilford Press, 1998) at 201-2.

86 M.E. Rice, G.T. Harris, and C.A. Cormier, "An Evaluation of a Maximum Security Therapeutic Community for Psychopaths and Other Mentally Disordered Offenders" (1992) 16 Law and Human Behavior 399-412.

87 Hare asserts a score of thirty out of forty or above is his preferred cut-off for the prototypical psychopath for his research purposes. Hare, "Psychopathy: A Clinical Construct," *supra* note 57. This appears to be quite a widely accepted norm.

88 *R. v. D.R.M.*, [2002] B.C.J. No. 1171 (S.C.).

89 *R. v. W.H.H.*, [2000] B.C.J. No. 2852 (S.C.).

90 *R. v. N.E.L.*, [2002] B.C.J. No. 3045 (S.C.). In Ontario, see *R. v. Payne*, [2001] O.J. No. 146 (S.C.J.) and *R. v. Moser*, [2002] O.J. No. 1344 (S.C.J.), to the same effect.

91 *R. v. J.F.H.*, [2002] O.J. No. 362 (S.C.J.).

92 *R. v. D.S.*, [2001] O.J. No. 2589 (S.C.J.).

93 *Ibid.* at para. 284. In the recent case of *R. v. E.E.*, [2003] O.J. No. 1518 (S.C.J.) (outside the timeframe being analyzed in this study), the court noted that a PCL-R score of thirty-two "is, in and of itself, portentous of significant difficulties as regards recidivism" (at para. 30). It is noteworthy, however, that the court went on to combine scores on different assessment tools to minimize the risk of a false positive prediction.

94 See *R. v. S.M.R.*, [2002] O.J. No. 652 (S.C.J.); *R. v. Ferguson*, [2000] O.J. No. 3008 (S.C.J.); *R. v. Talbot*, [1997] O.J. No. 4549 (C.J.P.D.); *R. v. Chevrier*, [1999] O.J. No. 5213 (S.C.J.); *R. v. D.A.S.*, [2000] B.C.J. No. 2697 (S.C.); *R. v. Antonius*, [2000] B.C.J. No. 577 (S.C.), upheld [2003] B.C.J. No. 467 (C.A.); *R. v. Johnson*, [1998] B.C.J. No. 3216 (S.C.), appeal allowed [2001] B.C.J. No. 2021 (C.A.); *R. v. McPherson*, [1998] N.W.T.J. No. 123 (S.C.); and *R. v. Clyne*, [1999] M.J. No. 86 (Q.B.).

95 The following cases appeared to involve judges who were moved to declare an offender dangerous, at least in part because of a risk assessment showing a greater than 50 percent chance of violent re-offending: *R. v. L.C.W.*, [2000] S.J. No. 422 (Q.B.); *R. v. Berikoff*, [2000] B.C.J. No. 1373 (S.C.); *R. v. L.D.A.*, [1999] B.C.J. No. 1781 (S.C.); and *R. v. R.E.L.*, [1998] B.C.J. No. 1440 (P.C.).

96 The PCL-R was designed as a "research tool for operationalizing the construct of psychopathy." Hare, *supra* note 85 at 30.

97 *R. v. J.T.H.*, [2002] N.S.J. No. 476 (C.A.).

98 *Ibid.* at para. 30.

99 See, for example, *R. v. W.D.G.*, [1998] N.S.J. No. 517 (S.C.) and *R. v. S.S.*, [2002] O.J. No. 2825 (S.C.J.).

100 Solicitor General Canada, *Corrections and Conditional Release Statistical Overview* (Ottawa: Public Works and Government Services Canada, 2002) at 93.

101 J. Bonta, I. Zinger, A. Harris, and D. Carriere, "The Dangerous Offender Provisions: Are They Targeting the Right Offenders?" (1998) 40 Canadian Journal of Criminology 377-400.

102 Over 92 percent of their sample had been convicted of a sexual offence. *Ibid.* at 387.

103 I. Grant, "Legislating Public Safety: The Business of Risk" (1998) 3 Canadian Criminal Law Review 177-242 at 178.

104 Solicitor General Canada, *Corrections and Conditional Release Statistical Overview* (Ottawa: Public Works and Government Services Canada, 2002).

105 S. Trevethan, N. Crutcher, and J.-P. Moore, *A Profile of Federal Offenders Designated as Dangerous Offenders or Serving Long-Term Supervision Orders* (Ottawa: Research Branch, Correctional Service of Canada, 2002) at 33.

106 While section 726.2 of the *Criminal Code* requires the judge to provide reasons on the record when imposing sentence, not all cases make their way into the Quicklaw databases.

107 See *R. v. McDowell*, [2002] A.J. No. 1565 (P.C.); *R. v. McLean*, [2002] S.J. No. 597 (Q.B.); *R. v. Leblanc*, [2002] O.J. No. 4611 (S.C.J.); *R. v. Rae*, [1998] O.J. No. 3973 (C.J.P.D.); *R. c. Menard*, [2000] J.Q. No. 2632 (C.Q.); and *R. c. Raymond*, [1999] J.Q. No. 5307 (C.Q.).

108 The Correctional Service of Canada indicates that 83 percent of the 313 active dangerous offenders under its jurisdiction on 30 June 2002 had a sexual offence included on their current sentence. Solicitor General Canada, *supra* note 104 at 91.

109 As of September 2003, only nine successful DO applications were found in the Canadian case law for the current year: *R. v. Mousseau*, [2003] A.J. No. 933 (Q.B.); *R. v. L.E.T.*, [2003] B.C.J. No. 1797 (S.C.); *R. v. K.R.S.*, [2003] S.J. No. 189 (Q.B.); *R. v. Howdle*, [2003] S.J. No. 476 (Q.B.); *R. v. Kakakaway*, [2003] S.J. No. 362 (Q.B.); *R. v. M.O.*, [2003] O.J. No. 434 (C.J.); *R. v. Woodward*, [2003] O.J. No. 2216 (S.C.J.); *R. v. E.E.*, [2003] O.J. No. 1518 (S.C.J.); *R. v. Sirois*, [2003] J.Q. No. 5540 (C.Q.); and *R. v. B.W.N.*, [2003] N.B.J. No. 228 (Q.B.T.D.).

110 Grant, *supra* note 103 at 186.

111 *Ibid.* at 189-90. Grant has been a long-time critic of the use of preventive detention and the abandonment of fundamental civil liberties. See also I. Grant, "Dangerous Offenders" (1985) 9 Dalhousie Law Journal 347-82. Concerns about problems with reliance on forensic predictions in the context of Canada's dangerous offender law can be traced back at least to the 1970s. J.F. Klein, "The Dangerousness of Dangerous Offender Legislation: Forensic Folklore Revisited" (1976) 18 Canadian Journal of Criminology and Corrections 109-22.

112 See D. Stuart, "Time to Codify Criminal Law and Rise above Law and Order Expediency: Lessons from the Manitoba Warriors Prosecution" (2000) 28 Manitoba Law Journal 89-112.

113 E. Silver and L.L. Miller, "A Cautionary Note on the Use of Actuarial Risk Assessment Tools for Social Control" (2002) 48 Crime and Delinquency 138-61.

114 *Ibid.* at 155-56.

115 See the discussion of DO legislation being used to target already marginalized groups in M.G. Yeager, "Ideology and Dangerousness: The Case of Lisa Colleen Neve" (2000) 9 Critical Criminology 9-21. Renke's comment on *Neve*, *supra* note 79, is also illustrative in this regard. W.N. Renke, "Case Comment: Lisa Neve, Dangerous Offender" (1995) 33 Alberta Law Review 650.

Bibliography

Andrews, D.A., and J. Bonta. *The Level of Service Inventory – Revised* (Toronto: Multi-Health Systems, 1995).

Boer, D.P., R.J. Wilson, C.M. Gauthier, and S.D. Hart. "Assessing Risk of Sexual Violence: Guidelines for Clinical Practice." In C.D. Webster and M.A. Jackson, eds., *Impulsivity: Theory, Assessment and Treatment* (New York: Guilford Press, 1997).

Boer, J.V., S.D. Hart, P.R. Kropp, and C.D. Webster. *Manual for Sexual Violence Risk 20: Professional Guidelines for Assessing Risk of Sexual Violence* (Vancouver: BC Institute on Family Violence, 1997).

Bonta, J. "Offender Risk Assessment: Guidelines for Selection and Use" (2002) 29 Criminal Justice and Behavior 355-79.

–, W.G. Harman, R.G. Hann, and R.B. Cormier. "The Prediction of Recidivism among Federally Sentenced Offenders: A Re-validation of the SIR Scale" (1996) 38 Canadian Journal of Criminology 61-79.

–, I. Zinger, A. Harris, and D. Carriere. "The Dangerous Offender Provisions: Are They Targeting the Right Offenders?" (1998) 40 Canadian Journal of Criminology 377-400.

Borum, R. "Improving the Clinical Practice of Violence Risk Assessment: Technology, Guidelines, and Training" (1996) 51 American Psychologist 945-56.

Campbell, T.W. "Challenging the Evidentiary Reliability of DSM-IV" (1999) 17 American Journal of Forensic Psychology 47-68.

Canadian Committee on Corrections (Ouimet Committee). *Toward Unity: Criminal Justice and Corrections* (Ottawa: Queen's Printer, 1969).

Cooke, D.J., and C. Mitchie. "Refining the Construct of Psychopathy: Towards a Hierarchical Model" (2001) 13 Psychological Assessment 171-88.

Ennis, B.J., and T.R. Litwack. "Psychiatry and the Presumption of Expertise: Flipping Coins in the Courtroom" (1974) 62 California Law Review 693.

Federal-Provincial-Territorial Task Force on High-Risk Violent Offenders. *Strategies for Managing High-Risk Offenders* (Victoria: Federal-Provincial-Territorial Task Force on High-Risk Violent Offenders, 1995).

Feeley, M., and J. Simon. "Actuarial Justice: The Emerging New Criminal Law." In D. Nelken, ed., *The Futures of Criminology* (London: Sage, 1994).

–, and J. Simon. "The New Penology: Notes on the Emerging Strategy of Corrections and Its Implications" (1992) 30 Criminology 449-74.

Freedman, D. "False Prediction of Future Dangerousness: Error Rates and Psychopathy Checklist-Revised" (2001) 29 Journal of the American Academy of Psychiatry and Law 89-95.

Gendreau, P., C. Goggin, and P. Smith. "Is the PCL-R Really the 'Unparalleled' Measure of Offender Risk? A Lesson in Knowledge Cumulation" (2002) 29 Criminal Justice and Behavior 397-426.

Grant, I. "Dangerous Offenders" (1985) 9 Dalhousie Law Journal 347-82.

–. "Legislating Public Safety: The Business of Risk" (1998) 3 Canadian Criminal Law Review 177-242.

Greenland, C. *Dangerous Sexual Offenders in Canada*. Studies on Imprisonment (Ottawa: Law Reform Commission of Canada, 1976).

–. "Dangerous Sexual Offender Legislation in Canada, 1948-1977: An Experiment That Failed" (1984) 26 Canadian Journal of Criminology 1-12.

Grove, W.M., and P.E. Meehl. "Comparative Efficiency of Informal (Subjective, Impressionistic) and Formal (Mechanical, Algorithmic) Prediction Procedures: The Clinical-Statistical Controversy" (1996) 2 Psychology, Public Policy, and Law 293-323.

–, D.H. Zald, B.S. Lebow, B.E. Snitz, and C. Nelson. "Clinical versus Mechanical Prediction: A Meta-Analysis" (2000) 12 Psychological Assessment: A Journal of Consulting and Clinical Psychology 19-30.

Hanson, R.K. *The Development of a Brief Actuarial Risk Scale for Sexual Offender Recidivism.* User Report 1997-04 (Ottawa: Department of Solicitor General Canada, 1997).

–, and D. Thornton. *Static 99: Improving Actuarial Risk Assessments for Sex Offenders* (Ottawa: Solicitor General Canada, 1999).

Hare, R.D. *The Hare Psychopathy Checklist – Revised* (Toronto: Multi-Health Systems, 1991).

–. "Psychopathy: A Clinical Construct Whose Time Has Come" (1996) 23 Criminal Justice and Behavior 25-54.

–. "Psychopaths and Their Nature: Implications for the Mental Health and Criminal Justice Systems." In T. Millon, E. Simonsen, M. Birket-Smith, and R.G. Davis, eds., *Psychopathy: Antisocial, Criminal, and Violent Behavior* (New York: Guilford Press, 1998) at 201-2.

–. "Psychopathy as a Risk Factor for Violence" (1999) 70 Psychiatric Quarterly 181-97.

–. "Psychopathy and Risk for Recidivism and Violence." In N. Gray, J. Laing, and L. Noaks, eds., *Criminal Justice, Mental Health, and the Politics of Risk* (London: Cavendish Publishing, 2002).

Harris, G.T., M.E. Rice, and C.A. Cormier. "Psychopathy and Violent Recidivism" (1991) 15 Law and Human Behavior 625-37.

–, M.E. Rice, and C.A. Cormier. "Prospective Replication of the Violence Risk Appraisal Guide in Predicting Violent Recidivism among Forensic Patients" (2002) 26 Law and Human Behavior 377-394.

–, M.E. Rice, and V.L. Quinsey. "Violent Recidivism of Mentally Disordered Offenders: The Development of a Statistical Prediction Instrument" (1993) 20 Criminal Justice and Behavior 315-35.

Hart, S.D. "Psychopathy and Risk for Violence." In D.J. Cooke, A.E. Forth, and R.D. Hare, eds., *Psychopathy: Theory, Research and Implications for Society* (Dordrecht: Kluwer Academic Publishers, 1998).

–. "The Role of Psychopathy in Assessing Risk for Violence: Conceptual and Methodological Issues" (1998) 3 Legal and Criminological Psychology 121-37.

Heilbrun, K., J.R.P. Ogloff, and K. Picarello. "Dangerous Offender Statutes in the United States and Canada: Implications for Risk Assessment" (1999) 22 International Journal of Law and Psychiatry 393-415.

Hemphill, J.F., R.D. Hare, and S. Wong. "Psychopathy and Recidivism: A Review" (1998) 3 Legal and Criminological Psychology 139-70.

Jakimec, J., F. Poporino, S. Addario, and C.D. Webster. "Dangerous Offenders in Canada, 1977-1985" (1986) 9 International Journal of Law and Psychiatry 479-89.

John Howard Society of Alberta. *Dangerous Offender Legislation around the World,* 1999. <http://www.johnhoward.ab.ca/PUB/C20.htm#exe>.

Kirk, S., and H. Kutchins. *The Selling of DSM: The Rhetoric of Science in Psychiatry* (New York: Aldine de Gruyter, 1992).

Klein, J.F. "The Dangerousness of Dangerous Offender Legislation: Forensic Folklore Revisited" (1976) 18 Canadian Journal of Criminology and Corrections 109-22.

Kropp, P.R., S.D. Hart, C.D. Webster, and D. Eaves. *Manual for the Spousal Assault Risk Assessment Guide* (Vancouver: BC Institute on Family Violence, 1994).

Leggatt, S.M. *Report of the Inquiry into Habitual Criminals in Canada* (Ottawa: Government of Canada, 1984).

Lidz, C.W., E.P. Mulvey, and W. Gardner. "The Accuracy of Predictions of Violence to Others" (1993) 269 Journal of the American Medical Association 1007-11.

Litwack, T.R. "Actuarial versus Clinical Assessments of Dangerousness" (2001) 7 Psychology, Public Policy, and Law 409-43.

Loza, W., D.B. Villeneuve, and A. Loza-Fanous. "Predictive Validity of the Violence Risk Appraisal Guide: A Tool for Assessing Violent Offenders' Recidivism" (2002) 25 International Journal of Law and Psychiatry 85-92.

McRuer, J.D. (Chairman). *Report of the Royal Commission on the Criminal Law Relating to Criminal Sexual Psychopaths* (Ottawa: Queen's Printer, 1958).

Manson, A. *The Law of Sentencing* (Toronto: Irwin Law, 2001).

Menzies, R.J. and C.D. Webster. "Construction and Validation of Risk Assessments in a Six-Year Follow-up of Forensic Patients: A Tri-dimensional Analysis" (1995) 63 Journal of Consulting and Clinical Psychology 766-78.

Monahan, J. *The Clinical Prediction of Violent Behavior* (Rockville, MD: National Institute of Mental Health, 1981).

–. *Predicting Violent Behavior: An Assessment of Clinical Techniques* (Beverly Hills: Sage Publications, 1981).

–, and H.J. Steadman, eds. *Violence and Mental Disorder: Developments in Risk Assessment* (Chicago: University of Chicago Press, 1994).

Mossman, D. "Assessing Predictions of Violence: Being Accurate about Accuracy" (1994) 62 Journal of Consulting and Clinical Psychology 783-92.

Nuffield, J. *Parole Decision Making in Canada* (Ottawa: Communication Division, Solicitor General Canada, 1982).

Petrunik, M. *Models of Dangerousness: A Cross Jurisdictional Review of Dangerousness Legislation and Practice* (Ottawa: Solicitor General, 1994).

–. "The Hare and the Tortoise: Dangerousness and Sex Offender Policy in the United States and Canada" (2003) 45 Canadian Journal of Criminology and Criminal Justice 43-72.

Quinsey, V.L. "The Prediction and Explanation of Criminal Violence" (1995) 18 International Journal of Law and Psychiatry 117-27.

–, G.T. Harris, M.E. Rice, and C.A. Cormier. *Violent Offenders: Appraising and Managing Risk* (Washington, DC: American Psychological Association, 1998).

Renke, W.N. "Case Comment: Lisa Neve, Dangerous Offender" (1995) 33 Alberta Law Review 650.

Rice, M.E., and G.T. Harris. "Cross-Validation and Extension of the Violence Risk Appraisal Guide for Child Molesters and Rapists" (1997) 21 Law and Human Behavior 231-41.

–, G.T. Harris, and C.A. Cormier. "An Evaluation of a Maximum Security Therapeutic Community for Psychopaths and Other Mentally Disordered Offenders" (1992) 16 Law and Human Behavior 399-412.

Rosenhan, D.L. "On Being Sane in Insane Places" (1974) 179 Science 250-58.

Salekin, R.T., R. Rogers, and K.T. Sewell. "A Review and Meta-Analysis of the Psychopathy Checklist and Psychopathy Checklist-Revised: Predictive Validity of Dangerousness" (1996) 3 Clinical Psychology: Science and Practice 203-15.

Serin, R.C. "Psychopathy and Violence in Criminals" (1991) 6 Journal of Interpersonal Violence 423-31.

–. "Violent Recidivism in Criminal Psychopaths" (1996) 20 Law and Human Behavior 207-17.

Silver, E., and L.L. Miller. "A Cautionary Note on the Use of Actuarial Risk Assessment Tools for Social Control" (2002) 48 Crime and Delinquency 138-61.

Solicitor General Canada. *Corrections and Conditional Release Statistical Overview* (Ottawa: Public Works and Government Services Canada, 2002).

Soward, J. "Mandatory Indeterminate Sentence under Dangerous Offender Legislation" (1998) 7 Dalhousie Journal of Legal Studies 189-213.

Spitzer, R.L., J.B.W. Williams, and A.E. Skodol. "DSM-III: The Major Achievements and an Overview" (1980) 137 American Journal of Psychiatry 151-64.

Stuart, D. "Time to Codify Criminal Law and Rise above Law and Order Expediency: Lessons from the Manitoba Warriors Prosecution" (2000) 28 Manitoba Law Journal 89-112.

Trevethan, S., N. Crutcher, and J.-P. Moore. *A Profile of Federal Offenders Designated as Dangerous Offenders or Serving Long-Term Supervision Orders* (Ottawa: Research Branch, Correctional Service of Canada, 2002).

Webster, C.D., D. Eaves, K. Douglas, and A. Wintrup. *The HCR-20 Scheme: The Assessment of Dangerousness and Risk* (Burnaby, BC: Simon Fraser University and Forensic Psychiatric Services Commission of BC, 1995).

–, G.T. Harris, M.E. Rice, C. Cormier, and V.L. Quinsey. *The Violence Prediction Scheme: Assessing Dangerousness in High Risk Men* (Toronto: Centre of Criminology, University of Toronto, 1993).

–, and R.J. Menzies. "Supervision in the Deinstitutionalized Community." In S. Hodgins, ed., *Mental Disorder and Crime* (Newbury Park: Sage Publications, 1993).

Widiger, T.A., *et al.* "DSM-IV Antisocial Personality Disorder Field Trial" (1996) 105 Journal of Abnormal Psychology 3-16.

Yeager, M.G. "Ideology and Dangerousness: The Case of Lisa Colleen Neve" (2000) 9 Critical Criminology 9-21.

3
Shifting the Burden of Proof: The Precautionary Principle and Its Potential for the "Democratization" of Risk

Dayna Nadine Scott

> Ignorance is ignorance, and no right to believe anything can be derived from it.[1]
>
> Sigmund Freud, *The Future of an Illusion*

This sentiment captures the essence of the debate over what has been called the "defining principle" of the modern environmental movement.[2] Until recently, polluters, producers of toxic substances, and innovators of new technologies have claimed the right to believe that their discharges and products were "safe" until proven otherwise.[3] Ignorance, essentially, was on their side. The much-vaunted "precautionary principle," as many commentators predict, may change this perception.[4] For some, the precautionary principle promises a more effective way of managing environmental and health hazards than is provided by conventional scientific risk assessment.[5] It deals with suspected risks, not just "proven" risks. Thus, environmental and health advocates are currently pushing to have the precautionary principle recognized formally as a principle of customary international law.[6] In Canada, several statutes already make favourable reference to the precautionary principle or the "precautionary approach."[7] Current incarnations of the principle often take their form from the 1992 *Rio Declaration on Environment and Development*.[8] It states that "[w]here there are threats of serious or irreversible damage, lack of full scientific certainty shall not be used as a reason for postponing cost-effective measures to prevent environmental degradation."[9] Essentially, the precautionary principle mandates action in the face of scientific uncertainty to prevent potential harm to human health or the environment.

Since 1992, the push by advocacy groups to persuade courts and legislatures to adopt the precautionary principle has generated significant debate. Groups enjoying the *status quo*, a regime in which regulatory action is dictated by scientific proof, tend to argue that the principle is dangerous because it could be applied to force regulatory action on perceived risks for which there is no sound scientific basis for alarm, unnecessarily stifling innovation.[10] Further, critics contend that application of the principle could actually increase the harms facing society by impeding the development of new therapeutic products and technologies.[11] Thus, the principle has been labelled "anti-scientific," irrational, and unworkable.[12] One of the most contentious points of debate around the precautionary principle is the question of burden of proof. Is a substance, drug, or new technology safe until proven hazardous? Or is it hazardous until proven safe? This debate circles around the difficult concepts of uncertainty and indeterminacy. Who should be burdened by – and who should benefit from – the limits of our understanding? Ronnie Harding and Elizabeth Fisher describe the *status quo:*

> Where scientific uncertainty exists concerning possible harmful impacts of a development it has traditionally been left to those suggesting harm to demonstrate its likelihood convincingly, rather than those carrying out the development to demonstrate with a high level of confidence that harm will not occur.[13]

While most analysts agree that the precautionary principle calls for a shift in the burden of proof, there is considerable divergence of opinion over what this means and whether it is a good idea.[14] Those who object to the shift in burden argue that it is *never possible* to prove that an activity is "safe" or "harmless."[15] And among those who agree that a shifted burden is a good thing, there is an animated dispute over whether this shift should penetrate the "risk assessment" stage – or be constrained to the "risk management" stage – of analysis.[16]

Underlying any discussion of the precautionary principle is a conflict of authority: some would argue that all policy decisions should be based on "sound science," while others would defer to a moral authority, to democracy, or to ethics:

> The opposition between scientific and ethical authority seems to have played a dominant role in shaping the conflicts of modern discourse. It has fostered a contemporary drama in which scientific reason comes under periodic scrutiny from a purportedly higher normative tribunal. As part of their adversarial confrontation in the twentieth century, both science and ethics have increasingly modelled themselves on judicial proceedings.[17]

It is interesting that when the conflicting authorities of science and ethics fail to resolve difficulties, we often turn to law. This trend is reflected in the adoption of rhetorical strategies that call for a shift in the burden of proof. Just as today's skilled legal advocates "have perfected the art of shifting the burden of proof onto their opponents," advocates for the environment and public health have recognized and seized the power of the tacit strategy of burden shifting.[18] The warning from Richard Gaskins's 1992 book *Burdens of Proof in Modern Discourse* is that "a burden of proof which is *for* you one day and which seems as though it must always be for you, can come to be *against* you the next."[19] Volatility in proof burdens, I will argue, holds democratic promise. Yet, while effecting a precautionary shift in the burden of proof is a significant step, and one that will carry consequences, it is not the monumental and unnatural change it is sometimes made out to be.[20] The repercussions of a shifty burden will be more subtle.

I will look at burden-shifting strategies as they apply both in environmental law and inside the institution of science itself.[21] To the question, "is it possible to shift the burden of proof in science?" I answer yes. To the question, "is it desirable?" I answer a more equivocal "it depends." I conclude that the precautionary principle's potential for democratization derives from its tendency to expose the trade-offs inherent in risk analysis. My examination of the concept of burdens of proof in law, and in science, foreshadows this conclusion.

Burden Shifting as a Rhetorical Strategy

As Gaskins's work makes clear, "weighty" rhetorical burdens are borne by everyone engaged in public discourse. Talk of the significance of "presumptions" and "burdens of proof" is increasingly turning up in contemporary debates on a range of topics. This trend is related to the concept of "indeterminacy."[22] The more obvious it becomes how little we know or understand, the more critical it becomes to talk about who should bear the burden of this ignorance.[23] "Indeterminacy," as it turns out, is an important impetus behind the precautionary principle. Dissatisfaction with risk assessment models over the past two decades has stimulated a rejection of "the idealistic notion that all scientific certainties can be accounted for and controlled" because the "view premised on a world that is determinate (ultimately knowable) and probabilistic (calculable)" has been largely discredited.[24] Many have argued that the precautionary principle emerged logically in response to a convergence of practical and theoretical rejections of the way scientific knowledge was being applied to environmental problems.[25] Dissatisfaction in practice stems from the recognition that scientific concepts, such as the "assimilative capacity model," have failed to preserve ecosystems and their functions and that legal systems have not adapted effectively to the challenges of complex chains of causation in cases of environmental and health harm.[26] Others would trace the principle's origins to various theoretical movements that have permeated popular thinking such as Ulrich Beck's concept of a "risk society."[27] In this conception of modernity, wealth production is systematically and necessarily tied to risk production.[28] Beck emphasizes the socially constructed nature of knowledge and embraces the ideal of "ecological democracy." His work has fostered a new political scepticism of the inherent value of technological "progress" and a distrust of scientific experts.[29]

Advocates started to openly challenge the *status quo* – if we are ignorant, why should it always count against the environment and health? Keeping in mind these influences, it is easy to see how the burden-shifting strategy was conceived:

> Perhaps [the failure of our environmental management regimes] demonstrates the poverty of our science and the danger of lodging final authority in scientific experts. On appeal to a different kind of court – one in which the whole scientific enterprise is compelled to prove its exclusive jurisdiction over truth claims – [any] argument might easily be reversed.[30]

It has long been recognized that, in any decision-making setting, there is always the "possibility that the decider, or the trier of fact, may at the end of his deliberations be in doubt on the question submitted to him."[31] Our answer to this dilemma has been to assign one party the "burden of proof" and the other party the "benefit of the doubt":

> Burden of proof and benefit of the doubt are opposite sides of the same coin; both refer to a technique for selecting between mutually exclusive alternatives, a technique that guarantees that a choice can be made, even in the closest cases.[32]

In the context of environmental and health controversies where significant and perhaps unknowable uncertainties persist, the allocation of the burden of proof essentially determines the substantive outcome of the dispute.[33] Accordingly, the question of shifting the burden of proof is critical: Is it possible? And is it desirable? At this point, I turn to examine law and its justifications for shifting proof burdens.

Law's Shifty Burdens

A close look at burdens of proof in law quickly exposes how contingent and ephemeral the placement of the burden can be. As burden-shifting strategies have become crucial to the success of campaigns to effect social change, understanding how law rationalizes these shifts is critical. It is also hoped that the legal justifications for shifting the burden of proof will provide insight into judging whether (and in what situations) the precautionary shift in burden mandated by the precautionary principle is warranted.

How Does the Law Decide When to Shift the Burden of Proof?

Both common law and civil law systems distinguish between two aspects of the burden of proof. They are the *burden of going forward* (the obligation to produce some kind of evidence) and the *risk of non-persuasion* (the risk that inconclusive findings will count against you).[34] Courts assign the burden of proof, and, accordingly, the benefit of the doubt, with "an instructive variety of implicit and explicit techniques."[35] I will review these techniques briefly and return to them later in this analysis with the aim of determining whether the same justifications for shifting the burden of proof in law can be applied under the precautionary principle.[36]

In law, there are generally three justifications for the allocation of burdens of proof:[37]

1. Those who want a change from the status quo *should bear the burden of proof*
Traditionally, the burden of proof lies with those who propose a change to the *status quo*.[38] This systematic bias towards existing authority, which is known as "conservative presumptionism,"[39] is thought to instil consistency and stability in law.[40] Richard Whately, in his 1846 *Elements of Rhetoric*, states that in deliberation, as in law, there is a presumption favouring established institutions, generally accepted beliefs, and prevailing plans and policies; accordingly, the burden of proof falls to advocates of change.[41] More recently, Canadian law professor Steve Wexler states that "[l]aw, being conservative, puts hurdles in the way of anyone who seeks a change in the legal status quo. The burden of proof is one such hurdle."[42]

2. Those with the best access to relevant information or knowledge should bear the burden of proof
It has also been recognized for many years that the party who bears the burden of proof should be the one who has the best access to the relevant facts.[43] Edmund Morris Morgan, in 1956, noted that one judicial justification for allocating the proof burden was to place it on the "party who has peculiar knowledge of a fact or peculiar means of access to evidence of its existence."[44] In addition, where the act of the alleged perpetrator would make it difficult for the "victim" to gain the relevant information in order to meet the burden on him or her, the law may shift the burden to the accused.[45] Morgan, however, quickly retreats from this "reason of convenience" as implying a hard-and-fast rule. He concedes that, in reality, where the burden of proof should rest is a question of policy and fairness based on experience and the particular situation.[46] John Sopinka, Sydney Lederman, and Alan Bryant concur. The answer, they state, "does not lie in a mechanical formula or rule of construction but rather in our traditional notions of justice."[47]

3. Equity considerations, such as resources and power, should determine which party bears the burden of proof
Traditional notions of justice in Canada are presumed to be reflected in the *Canadian Charter of Rights and Freedoms'*[48] entrenchment of the "presumption of innocence." The Crown, with its great resources and power, is contrasted against the vulnerable accused criminal. Some "strict liability offences" or "reverse onus" statutory schemes also apply the broad considerations of policy and fairness to justify the allocation of proof burdens.[49] However, any certainty or general rule as to when these "notions" should warrant a shift in the burden of proof is elusive. Fleming James commented in 1961 that "[s]ubstantive considerations may also be influential" in the allocation of burdens. "For real or supposed reasons of policy," he continued, "the law sometimes disfavors claims and defences which it nevertheless allows."[50] Here, burdens of proof are in a sense used as "handicaps" against the disfavoured contention.

Still, while the justifications employed by the law to shift burdens of proof – the concepts of deviance from the *status quo,* access to information, and fairness – seem to offer some guidance for judging when a shifted burden may be warranted under the precautionary principle, their universality is put into question by the observation in a leading evidence text that "rules relating to the burdens of proof are largely governed by the substantive law."[51] Yet instead of lessening the importance of these factors to the question of whether the burden to prove harm should be transformed into a burden to prove safety, this observation, in my view, indicates that these three factors may be applied to a class of problems – like genetically engineered crops or new drugs or synthetic pesticides – and a determination on the appropriateness of burden shifting may be applied to whole classes of substantive law. In fact, as will be explored in the next section, this is already the case in many areas of environmental and health regulation.

Implementing Precaution through a Shifted Burden
If law is to provide instruction, then, on when a shifted burden of proof may be warranted, the lesson must be that it is, at least in part, a matter of policy and fairness. Law does not seem to provide any warning of the immense or profound implications that many of the precautionary principle's opponents have predicted. On the surface, there's no reason the burden of proof cannot or should not shift. If a shift in the burden of proof does stimulate a "monumental change," it can only be because there is a real benefit accruing to those interests that now hold the presumption in their favour. This section explores the practical issues involved in actually implementing precaution through a shifted burden of proof.

Can "Harmlessness" Be Proven?

One of the most strident criticisms of the idea of burden shifting to implement the precautionary principle is the argument that "safety" or "harmlessness" can never be proven.[52] A.R.D. Stebbing, for example, has argued that harmlessness cannot be proven since any number of observations of harmlessness cannot eliminate the possibility that harmful effects may occur somewhere at some time.[53] Aaron Wildavsky argues along the same line, emphasizing that "proof of a negative" is logically impossible.[54]

The precautionary principle, however, does not demand absolute proof of safety.[55] While admitting that "absolute safety can never be proven," D. Kriebel *et al.* identify a key distinction: "[T]he *absence of evidence of harm* is not the same thing as *evidence of the absence of harm.*"[56] The precautionary principle, in shifting the burden of proof, demands the latter – evidence of the absence of harm. For example, the "absence of evidence of harm" could mean that no scientific testing has been conducted, while "evidence of the absence of harm" would imply that "rigorous and intensive scientific investigation" has failed to show any potential for harm.[57] When advocates for the precautionary principle speak of a shifted burden, they need not, in my view, call for scientific proof of safety but instead for scientific evidence of the absence of harm. A look at several examples of how a shifted burden operates in environmental law, in my opinion, dismisses the notion that the precautionary principle demands proof of safety in the logically impossible sense.

Examples of Shifted Burdens in Environmental Law and Policy

Some international agreements have already been operating under a regime employing a shifted burden for many years. I will mention briefly three examples. First, the Oslo Commission of 1972 established a "prior justification procedure" under which the permission for aircraft and ships to dump wastes at sea is granted only after a determination has been made that a particular harm threshold has not been exceeded.[58] Second, prior to the 1979 moratorium on commercial whaling, whalers demanded sound evidence that whales were endangered to justify interference with their activities.[59] Since the moratorium was called, whaling has not been permitted unless sound evidence is presented that whaling can resume without harm.[60] Third, changes to the international law of the sea had the effect of reversing the burden of proof with respect to driftnet fishing in 1989.[61] Legal commentary noted that "contrary to the normal sequence of events, the assumption underlying this action is that driftnets have undesirable impacts on stocks unless otherwise shown."[62] Furthermore, "reverse listing" is becoming a widespread domestic policy mechanism for implementing a shift in the burden of proof. It requires proponents of potentially harmful substances or activities to apply for permits to operate or enter the market. In fact, only those proponents who can demonstrate "safety" according to some pre-determined threshold will be allowed to proceed.[63] Many nations, including Canada, apply "reverse listing" mechanisms to new substances, such as pesticides. They are prohibited from introduction to the market until they are proven to be "safe."[64] The American regulatory regime also incorporates several "reverse listing" or "precautionary" mechanisms.[65] For example, under the *Food, Drug and Cosmetic Act*,[66] the controversial "Delaney clause" prohibits all substances to enter commerce that have been found to cause cancer in laboratory animals.

Far from demanding the impossible, the precautionary principle, as these examples have shown, can stimulate positive practical solutions. The existence of these schemes, such as the pre-market approval regime for pesticides, prompts Leiss and Hrudey, in the introduction to this book, to conclude that the risk management approach taken in Canada is "inherently precautionary."[67] As C.F. Cranor points out, however, these regulatory solutions are limited. While they work well for substances in products deliberately introduced onto the market, they are not effective at addressing risks from toxic pollution or the unanticipated by-products of industrial processes.[68] Further, before many of these schemes were implemented, policy makers had to be convinced that there was some reason to suspect harm. This point brings me to the troubling question of threshold.[69]

The Question of "Threshold"
It is agreed that the precautionary principle applies only in situations of scientific uncertainty. Some divergence of opinion, however, has emerged over the question of threshold. In other words, just how "possible" does the alleged harm have to be before the principle can be invoked? Is the mere allegation of harm sufficient? The "weight, measure, or degree of persuasion required of any party is closely related to the allocation of the burden of proof."[70] In law, we know this concept as the "standard of proof." By "standard of proof," Cranor states that he means "the degree of certainty required to substantiate a claim, as established by scientific evidentiary norms and practices," that the party bearing the burden of proof would have to meet.[71] International agreements adopting the precautionary principle have not taken a unified approach. For example, the *Final Ministerial Declaration* of the third International Conference on the Protection of the North Sea pledges ministers to "take action to avoid potentially damaging impacts of substances that are persistent, toxic and liable to bioaccumulate even when there is *no scientific evidence* to prove a causal link between emissions and effects."[72] At the other extreme, some so-called precautionary language still places the bar very high for those alleging harm. For example, James Cameron's analysis reveals that "most international legal fora" have recognized the need for an altered burden of proof only to a limited extent.[73]

They allow that "completely certain scientific evidence of harmfulness" is not required in order to justify regulatory action.[74] In this case, the nod to precaution is symbolic – no meaningful shift in the burden of persuasion occurs. Activities and substances may be regulated or banned that would not have otherwise been restricted, but the party coming forward with the "evidence" is still the party alleging harm.

A recent "communication" on the precautionary principle issued by the European Commission takes an intermediate position. It states that action is justified when "reasonable suspicion" of an unacceptable environmental risk exists but the causal relationship is unclear.[75] Others have suggested that a standard analogous to the civil law standard of proof – a "balance of probabilities" – is appropriate. This standard, "in conjunction with a burden of proof to the promoter of a technology, would mean that the promoter would have the burden of establishing that at least the weight of evidence does not support a *prima facie* case of serious risk."[76] Sometimes, however, the scheme will allow the proponent to come forward with evidence that rebuts the alleged harm in order to avoid the regulatory action. This is the case with respect to the *Convention on Biological Diversity:*[77]

> Once those advocating measures to prevent environmental degradation have satisfied the threshold test (i.e. they have shown the existence of a *threat* of a significant reduction or loss of biological diversity, falling short of "full scientific certainty"), decision-makers must assume that the threat is a reality. The burden of showing that this threat does not in fact exist effectively reverts to those engaging or wishing to engage in the activity.[78]

In this case, the burden of persuasion has shifted in an explicit way. However, as David Farrier points out, "the burden of proof is reversed only in relation to one input into the decision-making process – the question of environmental damage."[79] "Damage" or harm is taken to be proven, and then the decision maker must decide how to proceed, giving due consideration to social and economic factors. Brian Wynne and Sue Mayer agree. While the burden to prove *harm* may have shifted, the "onus is still on environmentalists to prove that a *threat* exists."[80]

It Does Not Have to Be "All or Nothing"
The concept of "apportioning" the burden is promising. Henk van den Belt and Bart Gremmen conclude that "it is not logically necessary that we put the whole of this so-called 'burden' on the shoulders of one party or the other; it turns out that we may divide this 'burden' in parts and assign them to different parties."[81] The same effect may be accomplished through "rebuttable presumptions," as explored in the previous section. It may also be

accomplished, in a sense, by choosing particular standards of proof – a lower standard of proof lessens the relative burden on a party.[82] Joel Tickner, in arguing that a key function of the precautionary principle is a shifted burden of proof, suggests that the burden should be on the proponent to "demonstrate that no harm would occur and that there were no safer alternatives."[83] This burden could be "lightened" in appropriate situations to require the proponent only to demonstrate the lack of a safer alternative.[84]

Possibilities for implementing precaution by creating shifty burdens in law and policy instruments seem to be limited only by our imaginations. Manipulation of the concepts of standard of proof and burden of proof can overcome the perceived problems with the precautionary principle such as proving "harmlessness" and determining an appropriate "threshold." The next section explores the proposition that to fully implement precaution in our management of environmental and health risks we have to extend our burden-shifting strategies further – into the sacred realm of scientific experimentation.

In Law, in Policy ... but in Science?

This section will confront the possibility of a shifted burden of proof within the practice of science itself. You can tell a critic of the precautionary principle by his or her vehement defence of "sound science." In theory, science aspires to "openness, impartiality and self-criticism."[85] Yet each narrow field of scientific inquiry is characterized by its particular methods, models, and associated assumptions. What becomes institutionalized as "sound science" within each of these intellectual communities is as much a product of culture as of principle.[86] Tied up in the debate over whether it is possible to shift burdens of proof in science are discourses on the nature of uncertainty, the difference between risk assessment and risk management, and the concept of "error burdens," which draws a parallel between the practice of statistics and the operation of law.

Characterizing Uncertainty

Scientific uncertainty has been invoked by industry and governments increasingly over the past two decades as an excuse for inaction on environmental and health threats.[87] Brian Wynne's important 1992 work characterized several types of uncertainty. He emphasized the key distinction between conventional conceptions of uncertainty and the concept of indeterminacy.[88] Uncertainty is conventionally described as a lack of data. It arises when a situation has never been monitored or when the effect has been judged to be too expensive to measure. Perceptions that this type of uncertainty is dominant have fuelled the conventional view that risk is "amenable to resolution by the production of 'more science' to fill the gaps."[89] In fact, the precautionary principle, in its earliest conception, was viewed simply as a tool to "buy time" – to bridge that "uncomfortable and temporary" period until further scientific research could resolve the dispute.[90]

Conventional risk assessment methods tended to "treat all uncertainties as if they were due to the incomplete definition of an essentially determinate cause-effect system."[91] It is now clear that more distressing forms of uncertainty prevail. Indeterminacy, for example, involves the "recognition of the essentially open-ended and conditional nature of all knowledge and its embeddedness in social contexts."[92] Conventional science predictably falters when complex systems under study operate according to processes that cannot be captured by its methods.[93] When nutrients accumulate in shallow waters, or when toxic chemicals bioaccumulate in tissues, systems approach a phase-change threshold where conditions can suddenly and dramatically change. This chaotic, inherent unpredictability in natural processes, combined with the conditional and erratic influences of social behaviour, creates contingency in all scientific assessment.

Appreciation for uncertainty and indeterminacy has forged a sharp divergence of views as to the appropriate role for science under the precautionary principle. Some would seek to have science continue to operate undisturbed, with precaution applied only after "sound science" has identified all the risks – essentially as an exercise in risk management. The more radical approach is to force precaution directly into the core of science, to penetrate the institution of risk assessment, and to challenge the way science is conducted.[94] Since neither risk assessment nor risk management are "neutral," "objective" processes, the argument is that there is no reason to presume that burden shifting should occur at the latter stage only.

Reconciling Risk Assessment and Risk Management

A movement gathered momentum through the 1980s for a structural "divorce" between the concepts of risk assessment and risk management.[95] Proponents of this divorce contended that risk assessment is value-neutral, consisting of objectively performed scientific analysis, while risk management involves the processing of hard data into social policy.[96] J.S. Gray, for example, has generated significant controversy with his view that "the precautionary principle is entirely an administrative and legislative matter and has nothing to do with science."[97] While he believes the precautionary principle is a "laudable" step forward, he states that "[s]cience should continue to be objective and there is no place for using arguments in the scientific literature that do not have the required objectivity and statistical validity."[98] Ellen Silbergeld takes the opposite view. "Values," from her perspective, "influence the resolution of uncertainty issues."[99] Even the scientific component of expert findings and recommendations necessarily drags along its value component because experts cannot be separated from their own views and perspectives.[100] A "diversity of values," then, will "lead individual scientists to different conclusions concerning phenomena that are uncertain."[101] Therefore, while most commentators agree that the precautionary principle applies properly to risk management, this line of thinking would similarly problematize risk *assessment*.

The "ideal" relationship between science and politics informs how many people view risk assessment and risk management. "[K]nowledge – generated by competent truth-seeking scientists working in accordance with stringent professional standards – is communicated, undistorted, to decision-makers who then utilize it as factual premises for policy decisions."[102] As Sheila Jasanoff notes, this "ideal type" is artificial:

> The negotiated and constructed model of scientific knowledge, which closely captures the realities of regulatory science, rules out the possibility of drawing sharp boundaries between facts and values or claims and context ... proceedings founded on the separatist principle frequently generate more conflict than those which seek, however imperfectly, to integrate scientific and political decision-making.[103]

The values and beliefs of scientists come into play where public policy must address unknown but possibly significant threats to the environment and health. For example, it is often lamented by opponents of the precautionary principle that risk assessors routinely adopt "worst-case" assumptions when data are unavailable or insufficient.[104] However, as van den Belt and Gremmen ask, "can the choice of such assumptions be justified solely on scientific grounds? Doesn't the scientific risk analyst thereby anticipate and pre-empt the decision that was understood to be the preserve of the [risk manager], namely to decide on whether a given risk is 'acceptable' to society?"[105]

Exposing Burdens of Proof in Science

Many opponents of the precautionary principle, however, refuse to acknowledge that values come into play in the generation of scientific knowledge.[106] It is often stated that policy should be based on "objective evidence" obtained through the scientific method. Richard Levins points out that "working scientists know that there is no such thing as 'THE scientific method.'"[107] There are many methods, and many of them are aimed at avoiding the most obvious kinds of errors. He notes the use of controlled comparisons; double blinds; matching of populations for age, sex, income, and so on; replication and statistical analysis; mathematical models; and hypothesis testing.[108] My focus is on hypothesis testing because it is the procedure by which science assigns its proof burdens. Scientific rationality, according to Kristen Shrader-Frechette and Earl McCoy, is all about applying theory to "assess the *probability* associated with various competing *hypotheses* and their consequences."[109] In the current hypothetical-deductive scientific paradigm, she argues, "rationality" is seen as being purely scientific – ethical and other values are to be kept out.[110] Yet scientific rationality, particularly ecological rationality, breaks down in situations of uncertainty.

Distribution of "Error Burdens"
Structuring statistical tests involves the implicit allocation of a burden of proof through the distribution of probabilities of error.[111] As Katherine Barrett and Carolyn Raffensperger complain, it is "considered 'better' science to erroneously claim there is no effect than to erroneously claim there is an effect."[112] Thus, conventional scientific experiments are designed to avoid false positives.[113] Yet as "every elementary handbook of statistics will tell you," guarding against false positives necessarily increases the likelihood of false negatives.[114] A null hypothesis would typically be construed in the following way: there is no adverse health effect. A Type I error would reject this null hypothesis when it is actually true, thus producing what is called a "false positive." Consequences could include an unwarranted public health scare, severe and potentially permanent damage to industry, and the loss of profits and jobs. A Type II error would accept the null hypothesis when it was actually false – a so-called false negative. The result would probably post-pone damage to industry and consumer confidence, but it may cost lives.

This outcome has prompted many to reflect that the burdens of proof followed in science, since they are specifically designed to protect against false positives, tend to "protect" potentially toxic substances (and those with an interest in these substances).[115] It happens because "good science," in the sense of science that does not sound false ecological alarms, is pur-chased at a cost – the cost of overlooking some toxic effects and failing to prevent harm.[116] Rachelle Hollander raises the question: Is this what "good regulation" looks like?[117] It seems to me that there are ethical and moral justifications for the opposite conclusion, namely that "good regulation" would purchase the peace of mind and security gained by preventing harms to the environment and public health at a cost of banning or slowing the development of harmless chemicals.[118] Each situation is going to raise unique moral choices and consequences. Given this variation, though, how can "standard practice" – the same rule, the same bias, the same error ratio – be fair? Will it always produce "good science"? In the words of Barrett and Raffensperger, "[w]hat may appear 'good' for pure science, may prescribe disastrous policy, potentially resulting in serious harm to the environment and its inhabitants."[119]

Hollander argues that the decision to use a specific scientific test and to set the standards for this test are themselves moral choices.[120] Van den Belt and Gremmen would agree. They emphasize that while the probability of making a Type I error – the "so-called *significance level*" – is typically set at 0.05, these levels are simply convention.[121] There is nothing sacred about the level chosen:

> If, because of the environmental interests at stake, we would be extremely concerned about the possibility of failing to reject the null hypothesis of "no effect" when it is actually false, we would indeed devise our statistical tests so as to minimize the risk of this error.[122]

Of course, this move would carry a cost, namely an increased risk of Type I errors and the risk of false ecological alarms.

Relative Costs of False Positives and False Negatives
What strikes me from the preceding section is the clearly political nature of choices in risk assessment. As van den Belt and Gremmen illustrate, the appropriate statistical test for every experiment depends to a large extent on the balancing of costs and benefits associated with each of the two types of errors.[123] The answer is very peculiar to the situation at hand. And the answer is a political choice. Choosing the appropriate statistical test involves a determination of which is the more harmful mistake: interrupting business-as-usual to declare a substance harmful, when it is later shown to be safe, or carrying on business-as-usual when the substance is actually harmful. These are not technical questions.

In this way, routine and largely unchallenged methods in scientific experimentation, such as the use of standard significance levels in hypothesis testing, "implicitly embody a particular distribution of the burdens of proof."[124] For example, if a community is particularly concerned about the effects of genetically engineered foods on its health and it attaches a high value to avoiding these effects, a decision to reduce the probability of a Type II error in experimentation would effectively increase the burden of proof on the proponents of these technologies. As van den Belt and Gremmen conclude, "the 'politics' of risk management has already penetrated the core of the allegedly purely 'scientific' risk assessment."[125]

Seizing Statistical Power
Among those who agree that the precautionary principle should penetrate the very core of science, many are now arguing that precaution should be implemented by increasing the use of a tool called "statistical power analysis."[126] Statistical power analysis focuses on the risk of committing a Type II error. According to H. Sanderson and S. Peterson, "it is relatively easy, using power analysis, to test an ecological risk assessment's null hypothesis in an environmentally precautionary manner."[127] Typically, for the "power" of a statistical test to be high, the acceptable risk of committing a Type II error is

set four times higher than the acceptable risk of committing a Type I error.[128] The process of scientific peer review enforces this convention by demanding statistical significance at the 95 percent confidence level before research findings are considered robust enough for publication.[129] This means that "early warnings" are essentially precluded – a truly precautionary science would not wait to report until the risk of committing a Type I error was below the 5 percent convention.[130]

Advocates of using this tool to implement the precautionary principle emphasize the potential for regulators to negotiate these levels with scientists and assessors. While they note that it will be a major challenge for science to "break out" of its obsession with Type I error, they are optimistic about the prospects. It does not seem to me that there could be anything "unscientific" about rethinking the values inserted into mechanical formulae that determine the statistical power or significance of a study. "The choice of a threshold of statistical significance," in Ted Schrecker's words, "is 'an issue of pure policy'; in other words, there is no reason to demand a 95 percent confidence level for policy purposes rather than 90 percent or 80 percent or even 51 percent."[131] As Lene Buhl-Mortensen emphasizes, to "take precaution by avoiding Type II errors rather than Type I errors is therefore no threat to the objectivity of science."[132]

Implementing this shift in the burden of proof in scientific practice allows the precautionary principle to penetrate to the core of science. As Wynne has noted, it is not "natural" knowledge, "but it involves the possible reshaping of the 'natural' knowledge itself."[133] A call for "sound science," then, is a plea to maintain the current allocation of burdens, the *status quo*. Is the *status quo* fair? Can it really be considered neutral, objective, or balanced? Why is there a perception that the current placement of burdens is balanced when the whole concept of burden of proof dictates that it is specifically, and deliberately, asymmetrical? The question should be this: Does it favour the right interests?

Seeking Truth and Justice in the Burden of Proof
It has been remarked that science and law are fundamentally opposed – law is justice seeking, while science is truth seeking.[134] Trying to implement precaution in scientific practice, it could be argued, is looking for justice in all the wrong places. If we seek justice in science, where do we find truth? This final section attempts, modestly, to make some sense of this dilemma.

Giving Up on "Truth"
I conclude from the preceding section's analysis that it is possible to shift burdens of proof in science. Shining a light on the unquestioned reliance on standard statistical practice has revealed, as has been argued recently in the scientific literature, that the implementation of the precautionary prin-

ciple, in one sense, *is* a technical problem. It is only a matter of reconsidering some assumptions and manipulating some values inserted into a statistical formula that is rarely challenged.[135] And while *implementation* may be a technical matter, the preceding part hopefully also made clear that the reconfiguration of the structure of hypothesis testing in science is a decidedly political matter. The choice to move to a precautionary science is very much about values.

Many commentators have now come out in defence of the precautionary principle, arguing that it is not inherently antagonistic to science.[136] In fact, a lot of practical, innovative writing has surfaced to answer the question of what precautionary science would look like. A precautionary science, according to this literature, would employ statistical power analysis to arrive at reasoned levels for acceptable risks of both false negatives and false positives.[137] Current practice works contrary to precaution because early warnings are precluded by scientists waiting to report findings until the risk of committing a Type I error is low enough (a 5 percent convention). In Barrett and Raffensperger's conception of "precautionary science," it would be "better to claim there is an effect when there is none, than to falsely claim there is no effect."[138] They suggest that "following false positives may generate more research questions and ultimately yield more correct information than following false negatives."[139] A precautionary science would also explicitly confront the inherent uncertainties in complex systems. Acknowledging that these uncertainties are profoundly uncontrollable and largely irreducible need not be paralyzing, but it will have profound repercussions for the methods and role of science.[140] We should strive at all times to make the boundaries of our knowledge very explicit.[141]

Before totally overhauling the practice of science, Cranor warns, we should take care to preserve its strengths. Burdens of proof in science, he stresses, "aim to protect against mistakenly overturning the hard-earned epistemic status quo and mistakenly adding to the stock of scientific knowledge."[142] Yet, as I have shown, this inferential caution and scepticism intended to protect "progress" can have the result of protecting certain interests at the expense of others. There is no reason that the "epistemology implicit in scientific standards and burdens of proof," as Cranor puts it, should preempt our achievement of social goals in line with the values embodied by the precautionary principle.[143]

> If the status of scientific knowledge shifts from being the objective, final arbiter to a more conditional and consensus-seeking knowledge form, which allows other forms of knowledge equal standing (and there is evidence that this is occurring), then its legitimatory function may be re-affirmed through a more realistic, and less rhetorical, appreciation of what science can and cannot do with respect to environmental management.[144]

Is allowing precaution to penetrate the core of our "truth-seeking" institution an admission that we are "giving up on truth"? In my view, it is not. Burdens of proof are as inevitable in hypothesis testing as they are in law. The nature of a burden is that it is deliberately unbalanced – it is biased. Shifting the burden of proof, then, in science means being explicit about what values are favoured and why. We have not surrendered truth because what we were getting in the past was not "pure truth" but truth encompassing a hidden judgment – a measure of justice not disclosed.

But Seeking Justice

The precautionary principle seeks to shift the burden of proof onto those who create the hazard, benefit from the hazard, or advocate for the hazard. At this point, I want to return to the justifications employed by the law to allocate burdens of proof and ask whether these criteria would justify the shift in burden of proof mandated by the precautionary principle. I am asking, in other words, is it just?

Precautionary Shift in Burden: Is It Just?

It has been suggested that the precautionary principle "appears to violate rules of presumption" that govern the criminal law.[145] I disagree. It is true that where the null hypothesis is – the accused is not guilty – the criminal law most dreads a Type I error (the conviction of the innocent). A Type II error would be preferred: "[B]etter that 10 guilty persons go unpunished than that 1 innocent person be convicted."[146] However, I focus on what the law does to implement this ethical preference. The law places the burden of proof on the Crown (the party alleging guilt) and employs a strict standard of proof. Thus, the law responds to the ethical judgment of which is the more dreaded type of error and adjusts the burdens and standards of proof accordingly. To apply the same rule of presumption to toxic chemical regulation would mean that we should judge it to be "better that 10 toxic chemicals go unregulated than 1 harmless chemical be banned." To put it mildly, I would argue that this is not the basis on which members of the public understand the regulatory system to be working. In this sense, I think a shifted burden under the precautionary principle is entirely consistent with the rules of presumption in law. The allocation of the burden to the Crown in criminal matters is based entirely on an *ethical judgment* about what is fair and justified in the circumstances. Making the judgment transparent, I believe, is the key to implementing the precautionary principle, regardless of where the burden is assigned in any particular case.

At this point, I want to return to the three criteria employed by the law to assign burdens of proof. For each, I ask whether it would justify the shifted burden implicit in the precautionary principle.

1. Those who want a change from the status quo *should bear the burden of proof*
In law, you will recall, the burden typically falls on the party who submits that we are mistaken about what is currently known – the party who seeks to change the *status quo*. However, James Olson argued in 1990 that a misplaced burden of proof is perpetuating harm to the environment. "A respect-based approach," in his view, "would presume an unpolluted or less polluted environment."[147] A rule of law under this approach would require persons seeking to "alter the status quo" to show that the proposed conduct would not degrade the environment. Olson argued that the traditional concept of burden of proof in Anglo-American jurisprudence has been fundamentally but unintentionally misapplied to pollution and environmental claims. In his view, the "status quo" should be measured from the perspective of a change in the environment, not a change in human activity. Misapplication of the burden of proof in this way, Olson urges, "institutionalizes the polluting activity as the status quo."[148]

Tim O'Riordan and James Cameron have argued that the precautionary principle reflects the fact that society is becoming more risk-averse. In their view, this change in outlook is "inevitably shifting the burden of proof onto those who propose to alter the status quo."[149] By this statement, they mean shifting the burden of proof onto those who would *introduce* a new risk. Obviously, what constitutes the *status quo* is a matter of perspective. Yet as Leiss predicts, allocating the burden of proof under this rule, so as to impose a burden on those who seek to introduce new risks but not "old" risks that are already part of the *status quo,* will be counterproductive.[150] Why should it matter whether the risky behaviour is one currently seeking introduction or one that has managed to slip by and enter the marketplace before we started watching? New technologies, even risky ones, generally seek to replace established practices, employing often-outdated technologies with known – not just suspected – risks.[151]

"Conservative presumptionism," many assume, is a formal rule – a rule of convenience.[152] However, the *status quo* is a matter of perspective, and this rule is not an ethically neutral doctrine. The problem with employing this justification is that the values embedded in it are not explicit, which makes it far too closed and inflexible to respond to the complexities of implementing the precautionary principle.

2. The party with the best access to relevant information or knowledge should bear the burden of proof
Law makes exception where access to relevant information, or the actions of the alleged "perpetrator," would make proof difficult. With respect to the precautionary principle, Cranor emphasizes several "asymmetries" of information. Much of what is known about potentially toxic substances, of course,

is, for new substances, their potential benefits, and, for old products, the benefits of keeping them on the market. What is uncertain about these potentially toxic substances are the health effects and the costs. He states:

> For example, firms develop products because they understand their potential benefits and believe that people will pay to have them, and they develop manufacturing processes in ways that benefit their goals and often their existing facilities. Thus, firms are well aware of the monetary costs of not having the products, changing the process, or being forced to reduce their pollutants. Firms do not appear to be as aggressive in identifying adverse health effects.[153]

This criterion, in my view, should properly influence the allocation of the burden of proof. Under a more precautionary approach, "those who have the economic incentive and information – those in control – would have the burden of proof."[154]

3. Equity considerations, such as resources and power, should determine which party bears the burden of proof
And finally, the law teaches that there is no magic in where we place the burden of proof. We should consider fairness and equity in particular situations. I am reminded that "the codification of probative responsibilities in law is a procedural expression of underlying principles of fairness."[155] As is illustrated by the following passage by Olson, these criteria will interact with each other to determine, in each situation, whether there is justification for a shifted burden:

> By hearkening back to the traditional purpose of burden of proof, maintaining the status quo ante, courts could effectively use the legal process and existing, well developed and widely accepted doctrine to protect the environment from polluting activities. Shifting the burden of proof in the context of toxic or hazardous chemicals is a truer expression of the purpose underlying that burden than allowing such pollution to continue in the guise of protecting the status quo. Shifting the burden of proof does nothing more than internalize the costs, risks and uncertainty of hazardous products or by-products to those who have the information, expertise, and control in the first instance.[156]

According to Cranor, one of the best advantages of a shifted burden is that "the agents who can do much to reduce such threats are those whose actions contribute to or pose the threats."[157] The onus to demonstrate safety would provide them with a "stake in reducing or an incentive to reduce the threats from their activities."[158] Society would benefit from their greater incentive to minimize damage than would be in place if they did not bear the burden of proof. Andre Nollkaemper agrees that "reversing the burden of proof can induce prevention" on the part of polluters.[159]

Burdens of proof, in my view, should be provisional and variable, fluid and shifty. Employing the law's criteria, particularly the considerations of access to information and equity, to the question of whether the precautionary principle mandates a shifted burden in particular situations will prove to be a fruitful and enriching experience. For many, the principle also promises to enhance democracy.

Does It Enhance "Democracy" in Risk Analysis?
Democratic ideals require that decisions affecting people's health be made in a manner that affords them a voice. Precaution, because it forces decision makers to regulate without recourse to the authority of formal science, sanctions the participation of a broad array of societal actors. Cameron has observed that, "by explicitly noting the limits of scientific determination," the precautionary principle legitimates the public, political determination of issues. In his words, the precautionary principle "thus allows for the democratisation of international environmental regimes."[160]

Silvio Functowicz and Jerome Ravetz, who introduced the concept of "post-normal science," argue that a science incorporating "mutual respect among various perspectives and forms of knowing" opens up the "possibility for the development of a genuine and effective democratic element in the life of science."[161] The problem with seeking only truth in science, as I have suggested, is that science does not deliver an objective truth. It delivers truth with a healthy dose of justice mixed in. The cost of blindly pretending that the determination of risk is a "truth-seeking" technocratic exercise is that the public cedes the power to influence critical political and value choices. They relinquish the power to seek justice in risk management. Jane Hunt's conception of the precautionary principle offers hope. She states that the principle

> implicitly recognizes and takes seriously the indeterminacy of scientific knowledge ... and thus opens up the normally closed-off connection between the intrinsically open question, how much harm might this discharge do? And the social question, how much do we need this process which causes this discharge?[162]

The promise of the precautionary principle, I believe, is in throwing open debate about risks and unleashing a spate of questions about what is at stake and for whom, and about what kind of place we want to live in and

how much control we want in shaping it. Precaution invites this explora-
tion because it fosters thoughtful, creative exchange between an activated
public and a wider, more inclusive, scientific community. Precaution is coming to define the modern environmental movement. It is building on the
momentum of a gentle revolution in science – from the "reductionist, analytical worldview that divides systems into smaller and smaller elements"
to a systems-focused science based on "unpredictability, incomplete control and a plurality of legitimate perspectives."[163] The precautionary principle is seen as a key catalyst in the renegotiation of the appropriate role for
science in public dialogue about risk.

Negotiating the Trade-Off Reveals Values

The values that underpin conventional science are not explicit. Procedures
promoted as objective and neutral are actually steeped in a very specific set
of values. Calls to "leave values at the door" and to "restrict discussions to
science," as Nancy Myers illustrates, simply serve to ensure that the values
currently upheld continue to reign.[164] Of course, when the "public" comes
to engage with questions of risk, there is unlikely to be any sense of "shared
values" that will determine without controversy where proof burdens should
rest. Yet the ensuing dialogue and deliberation, on the basis of explicitly
stated value assumptions associated with the allocation of proof burdens,
coupled with a transparent discussion of distributive impacts, will be critical to achieving democratic resolution of risk controversies.

Discussion of the burden of proof has figured prominently in the polem-
ics of the precautionary principle. Environmental and health regulation
will be effective, as van den Belt and Gremmen warn, only "within the
framework of an ethically defensible and socially acceptable distribution of
burdens of proof."[165] Focusing on the burden of proof has brought a great
strength to this work: it has underlined the pervasiveness of the "trade-
off." In law, this trade-off lies between the benefit of the doubt and the
burden of proof – between the risk of convicting the innocent and the risk
of freeing the guilty, and in science, it lies between a Type I error and a Type
II error – between the chance of a false alarm and the chance of a devastat-
ing tragedy.

Although I have looked favourably on many of their arguments, where I
differ from the advocates of the precautionary principle is on a practical
level. I agree that burden shifting is possible, and often desirable, but I cannot agree that it will present easy choices. Trade-offs rarely present themselves in practice as a choice between children's health and drug company
revenues or between clean water and corporate profits. More often, I predict,
the precautionary principle will be raised in contexts that present difficult
choices between the environment and public health (such as pesticide

applications to curb the West Nile virus) or between one health risk and another (such as the decision to reject blood from "risky" donors when the blood supply is dangerously low). It is these situations that will test the value of the precautionary principle. In the meantime, the concept of the burden of proof has proven useful for illuminating the pervasive trade-offs that surround all aspects of risk. Transparency in error burdens and proof burdens, and the values they uphold will be critical when we come to apply precaution in more difficult situations.

Conclusion

O'Riordan and Cameron contend that "precaution will not explode onto the environmental stage" but will "seep through the pores of decision-making institutions and the political consciousness of humanity by stealth."[166] If this happens, they state, "it will be because the tide of the times permits this permeation."[167] In my view, the placement of the burden of proof is as genuine a political question as exists. If we are to follow the lessons of law, its allocation and distribution is a matter of fairness. Wexler calls the burden of proof the "background of the law, the expression of our social attitudes."[168] Equally tellingly, Stephen Dovers and John Handmer characterize the precautionary principle as a "moral injunction."[169] By calling for action in the face of uncertainty, "by placing the onus on those who create the hazard, and by emphasizing alternatives and democracy, the precautionary principle promises to stimulate change."[170] A shifty burden, in the long run, will enhance democracy. Even as a rhetorical strategy, calls for a shifted burden under the precautionary principle may, paradoxically, serve to break through some of the rhetoric.[171] Established adversaries will be forced to renegotiate their places in public debate. Instead of seeing shifting burdens as sudden, revolutionary, or permanent change, we should approach them in the context of their reversibility, their contingency, and in the context of their circuitous tendencies. The transparency of values that results when error burdens are pried apart, when proof burdens are heaved onto new shoulders, and when trade-offs are revealed and struggled with can only be positive for democratic deliberation on risk.

Acknowledgments

The author would like to thank Professors Liora Salter and Roxanne Mykitiuk for their comments on an earlier draft of this essay. Similarly, the anonymous reviewers provided spirited and insightful feedback that contributed to an advancement of my thinking on several points, and the editors of this volume flattered me with their willingness to thoughtfully consider my arguments despite some divergence in our approaches to the concept of precaution. Finally, I am grateful to the Law Commission of Canada for the opportunity to participate in the competition that led to this volume.

Notes

1 Sigmund Freud, *The Future of an Illusion* (New York: Norton, 1975) at 66.
2 Ken Ogilvie, Executive Director, Pollution Probe, "Expert Consultation on Emerging Issues," speech at the International Joint Commission Workshop in Racine, Wisconsin, February 2003 [on file with author]. See also David Freestone, "The Precautionary Principle" in R. Churchill and D. Freestone, eds., *International Law and Global Climate Change* (London: Graham and Trotman, 1991) at 36; and David Freestone and Ellen Hey, "Implementing the Precautionary Principle: Challenges and Opportunities" in D. Freestone and E. Hey, eds., *The Precautionary Principle and International Law: The Challenge of Implementation* (The Hague: Kluwer Law International, 1996) 249 at 268.
3 James Cameron, "The Precautionary Principle: Core Meaning, Constitutional Framework and Procedures for Implementation" in Ronnie Harding and Elizabeth Fisher, eds., *Perspectives on the Precautionary Principle* (Leichhardt: Federation Press, 1999) 29 at 46 ("traditional legal standards in the environmental area have tended to privilege parties accused of degrading the environment. Until 'proven wrong,' such parties can continue the activity in question"). See also Andre Nollkaemper, "'What You Risk Reveals What You Value,' and Other Dilemmas Encountered in the Legal Assaults on Risks" in Freestone and Hey, eds., *supra* note 2, 73 at 85; James M. Olson, "Shifting the Burden of Proof: How the Common Law Can Safeguard Nature and Promote an Earth Ethic" (1990) 20 Environmental Law 891 at 894 ("under the current rights-based approach, humans can ... pollute or degrade earth or its species until 'proven wrong'").
4 For the opinion that the precautionary principle entails a "shift in the burden of proof," see Nollkaemper, *supra* note 3 at 84-85; David Farrier, "Factoring Biodiversity Conservation into Decision-Making Processes: The Role of the Precautionary Principle" in Harding and Fisher, eds., *supra* note 3, 99 at 108; D. Kriebel *et al.*, "The Precautionary Principle in Environmental Science" (2001) 109 Environmental Health Perspectives 871; and D. Kriebel and J. Tickner, "Reenergizing Public Health through Precaution" (2001) 91 American Journal of Public Health 1351.
5 For the argument that the precautionary principle should be adopted in the public health field, see B.D. Goldstein, "The Precautionary Principle Also Applies to Public Health Actions" (2001) 91 American Journal of Public Health 1358; and Kriebel and Tickner, *supra* note 4.
6 The proposition was recently put to the Supreme Court of Canada in *Spraytech* v. *Hudson (Town)*, 2001 S.C.C. 40, [2001] 2 S.C.R. 241, a case involving a municipality's banning of pesticide use for aesthetic purposes. The court accepted that there is a "good argument" that the precautionary principle is already a principle of customary international law and found it to be relevant to the interpretation of domestic law.
7 See, for example, the *Oceans Act*, S.C. 1996, c. 31, preamble; the *Canadian Environmental Protection Act, 1999*, S.C. 1999, c. 33, s. 2(1)(a).
8 A prevalent "alternative" statement of the principle comes from the 1998 Wingspread Conference: "When an activity raises threats of harm to human health or the environment, precautionary measures should be taken even if some cause-and-effect relationships are not fully established scientifically. In this context the proponent of an activity, rather than the public, should bear the burden of proof. The process of applying the precautionary principle must be open, informed and democratic and must include potentially affected parties. It must also involve an examination of the full range of alternatives, including no action" (Carolyn Raffensperger and Joel Tickner, *Protecting Public Health and the Environment: Implementing the Precautionary Principle* [Washington, DC: Island Press, 1999] at 353-54).
9 *Rio Declaration on Environment and Development*, United Nations Conference on Environment and Development, UN Doc. A/Conf.151/5/Rev.1 (13 June 1992), reprinted in 31 I.L.M. 874, 879 at Principle 15 [hereinafter *Rio Declaration*]. The principle has also been incorporated in numerous international treaties and declarations relating to the protection of the environment in recent years, including the *Montreal Protocol on the Substances That Deplete the Ozone Layer*, reprinted in 26 I.L.M. 1550 (1987); the *Convention on Biological*

Diversity, 5 June 1992, Rio de Janeiro, reprinted in 32 I.L.M. 818 (1992) [hereinafter *CBD*]; the *United Nations Framework Convention on Climate Change*, 9 May 1992, reprinted in 31 I.L.M. 848 (1992); and the *Agreement for the Implementation of the Provisions of the United Nations Convention on the Law of the Sea of 10 December 1982 Relating to the Conservation and Management of Straddling Fish Stocks and Highly Migratory Fish Stocks*, 4 August 1995, reprinted in 34 I.L.M. 142 (1995), among others.

10 See generally Gregory Conko of the Competitive Enterprise Institute in Washington, DC. G. Conko, "Throwing Precaution to the Wind: The Perils of the Precautionary Principle" Competitive Enterprise Institute Update, August/September 2000, <www.cei.org/gencon/ 005,01854.cfm>. In addition, a coalition of American manufacturing industries has stated that the precautionary principle, "if carried to the extreme," "threatens to stall global commerce, limit consumer choice, and slow technological progress," <http://www.wirthlin.com /industry/casefiles/416PUB_CASE01.phtml>, and Dr. Kenneth Green, chief scientist and director of the Risk and Environment Centre at the Fraser Institute, has stated that "for things like the production of chemicals," the precautionary principle "creates an insurmountable barrier to research in chemistry and biology," <http://www.fraserinstitute.ca/ shared/readmore.asp?sNav=ev and id=133>.

11 For a well supported articulation of the view that the precautionary principle is perverse in its implications for the environment and human welfare, see Frank Cross, "Paradoxical Perils of the Precautionary Principle" (1996) 53 Wash. and Lee L. Rev. 851.

12 *Ibid.* See also J.S. Gray, "Statistics and the Precautionary Principle" (1990) 21(4) Marine Pollution Bulletin 174 (for the view that the precautionary principle is "anti-scientific").

13 Ronnie Harding and Elizabeth Fisher, "Introducing the Precautionary Principle" in Harding and Fisher, eds., *supra* note 3, 2 at 3.

14 There is also a live debate as to which *types of risks* the precautionary principle should apply to. Leiss and Hrudey, for example, would limit its application to risks of "serious or irreversible adverse effects" (drawing on the *Rio Declaration* definition, *supra* note 9). Others would reserve the precautionary principle for substances known to be "toxic, persistent, and bioaccumulative." My position in this essay, and elsewhere, is that the scientific uncertainty surrounding the environmental toxicity of substances introduced to the environment is so pervasive that any confidence in our ability to predict accurately which substances will precipitate serious or irreversible harm is misplaced. As Jackson and Taylor remind us, chlorofluorocarbons (CFCs) were once classified as non-toxic and considered harmless; their persistence is now recognized for its capacity to cause "massive perturbation of the global ecosystem" (T. Jackson and P.J. Taylor, "The Precautionary Principle and the Prevention of Marine Pollution," paper presented at the first International Ocean Pollution Symposium, Puerto Rico, April 1991 at 35). Therefore, as explained in greater detail later in this chapter, the precautionary principle should apply not only in the regulation of substances of known toxicity but also in the regulation of all substances with the potential to cause harm (as determined through rigorous scientific testing and the application of statistical power analysis). My approach is consistent with that suggested by R. Michael M'Gonigle, T. Lynne Jamieson, Murdoch K. McAllister, and Randall M. Peterman, "Taking Uncertainty Seriously: From Permissive Regulation to Preventative Design in Environmental Decision Making" (1994) 32 Osgoode Hall L.J. 99 at 159-61.

15 For example, the late political scientist Aaron Wildavsky, a vocal critic of the precautionary principle, argued as early as 1995 that "proof of a negative" is logically impossible. Wildavsky, *But Is It True? A Citizen's Guide to Environmental Health and Safety Issues* (Cambridge: Harvard University Press, 1995) at 430.

16 For example, the recent "communication on the precautionary principle" issued by the European Commission takes the position that the principle is to be implemented by policy makers – not scientists. European Commission, *Communication from the European Commission on the Precautionary Principle* (2000), <http://europa.eu.int/comm/dgs/health_consumer/ library/pub/pub07_en.pdf>.

17 Richard Gaskins, *Burdens of Proof in Modern Discourse* (New Haven: Yale University Press, 1992) at xvi.

18 *Ibid.* at 21.
19 Steve M. Wexler, "Book Review: *Burdens of Proof in Modern Discourse* by Richard H. Gaskins" (1994) 73 Can. Bar. Rev. 286-87 [emphasis is added].
20 H.I. Miller and G. Conko, "The Science of Biotechnology Meets the Politics of Global Regulation," *Issues in Science and Technology Online* (2000), http://www.nap.edu/issues/17.1/miller.htm>; Wildavsky, *supra* note 15 at 430.
21 This analysis focuses on burdens of proof in the legal and policy instruments of environmental regulation. Burdens of proof in environmental *litigation* are another matter entirely. For a good introduction to the topic of burdens in a litigation context, see T.W. Koelling, "The Burden of Proof in Environmental and Public Health Litigation" (1981) 49 U. Mo. Kan. City L. Rev. 207.
22 Gaskins, *supra* note 17 at 20.
23 Speaking in terms of the philosophy of argumentation, Juha Raikka states: "The harder it is to prove how things really are, the more important it is to shift the burden to one's opponent" (Juha Raikka, "Burden of Proof Rules in Social Criticism" [1997] 11 Argumentation 463 at 463).
24 Katherine Barrett and Carolyn Raffensperger, "Precautionary Science" in C. Raffensperger and J. Tickner, eds., *Protecting Public Health and the Environment: Implementing the Precautionary Principle* (Washington, DC: Island Press, 1999) 106 at 113.
25 See, for example, Harding and Fisher, eds., *supra* note 3 at 9.
26 See M'Gonigle *et al.*, *supra* note 14 at 101.
27 Ulrich Beck, *Risk Society: Towards a New Modernity* (London: Sage Publications, 1992).
28 *Ibid.* at 19.
29 Frank Fischer, *Citizens, Experts, and the Environment: The Politics of Local Knowledge* (Durham: Duke University Press, 2000) at 48-51.
30 Gaskins, *supra* note 17 at 2.
31 Fleming James, "Burdens of Proof" (1961) 47 Va. L. Rev. 51 at 51.
32 Steve Wexler, "Burden of Proof Writ Large" (1999) 33 U.B.C. L. Rev. 75 at para. 2.
33 Daniel Bodansky, "The Precautionary Principle in U.S. Environmental Law" in Tim O'Riordan and James Cameron, eds., *Interpreting the Precautionary Principle* (London: Cameron May, 1994) 203 at 212.
34 Gaskins, *supra* note 17 at 21; James, *supra* note 31 at 51. The burden of going forward has also been called the "burden of evidence" and the "burden of adducing evidence." Juliane Kokott, *The Burden of Proof in Comparative and International Human Rights Law: Civil and Common Law Approaches with Special Reference to the American and German Legal Systems* (The Hague: Kluwer Law International, 1998) at 150-51. The finding that "there is evidence of a fact" can satisfy an evidential burden, or threshold, but the finding that "a fact has been proven on the evidence" is required to meet a burden of persuasion. In other words, the evidential burden can be discharged on the basis of evidence that "falls short of proof." John Sopinka, Sydney N. Lederman, and Alan W. Bryant, *The Law of Evidence in Canada*, 2nd ed. (Markham: Butterworths, 1999) at 55.
35 Gaskins, *supra* note 17 at xvi.
36 It must be pointed out that there exists some debate within legal commentary as to whether burdens of proof actually "shift." Sopinka, Lederman, and Bryant, *supra* note 34 at 71, for example, argue that except for presumptions of law or rebuttable statutory presumptions, burdens do not "shift" in a strict sense of the word. Burdens are simply assigned to different parties with respect to different issues or different facts. See also Rupert Cross and Colin Tapper, *Cross and Tapper on Evidence*, 9th ed. (London: Butterworths, 1999) at 125. Speaking perhaps more loosely, David Paciocco and Lee Stusser, *The Law of Evidence*, 2nd ed. (Toronto: Irwin Law, 2002) at 431, state that "the burden of proof can shift from party to party during the course of a trial, depending on the specific matter in issue." My sense of "burden shifting" is that a burden once "allocated" to one party may, in certain circumstances, be "allocated" to the other. It is this phenomenon that preoccupies the inquiry here.
37 These justifications have developed on a case-by-case basis, with no rule of law or formal framework to guide courts in their allocation of burdens. Sopinka, Lederman, and Bryant, *supra* note 34 at 77-80.

38 *Status quo ante* is Latin for "the postures, positions, conditions or situations that existed before." John A. Yogis, *Canadian Law Dictionary*, 4th ed. (Hauppauge: Barron's, 1998).
39 Raikka, *supra* note 23 at 467.
40 Gaskins, *supra* note 17 at 35.
41 Richard Whately, *Elements of Rhetoric: Comprising an Analysis of the Laws of Moral Evidence and of Persuasion, with Rules for Argumentative Composition and Elocution*, reprint edition by D. Ehninger (Carbondale: Southern Illinois Press, 1963).
42 Wexler, *supra* note 32 at para. 39.
43 James, *supra* note 31 at 60. For example, the "underlying rationale for allocating the legal burden to the defendant to disprove negligence in bailment actions" was stated by Lord Atkin in *The "Ruapehu"*: "The bailee knows all about it; he must explain. He and his servants are the persons in charge; the bailor has no opportunity of knowing what happened. These considerations, coupled with the duty to take care, result in the obligation on the bailee to show that that duty has been discharged" ((1925), 21 L1. L. Rep. 310 at 315). The Supreme Court of Canada in *Taylor Estate* v. *Wong Aviation Ltd.*, [1969] S.C.R. 481 at 189, held that these considerations must be met for the burden of proof to "shift" to the defendant to disprove negligence.
44 Edmund Morris Morgan, *Some Problems of Proof in the Anglo-American System of Litigation* (New York: Columbia University Press, 1956) at 75.
45 For example, a special report of the Global Environmental Change program in the United Kingdom notes that under UK law, where "the act of the perpetrator makes it difficult for the victim to prove causation," "it is morally acceptable to switch the burden of proof." This rule seems to reflect the information/knowledge justification for the allocation of the burden of proof. Economic and Social Research Council, Global Environmental Change Program, *The Politics of GM Food: Risk, Science and Public Trust*, Special Briefing no. 5, University of Sussex, October 1999, <http://www.gecko.ac.uk>.
46 *Ibid.* at 76.
47 Sopinka, Lederman, and Bryant, *supra* note 34 at 86.
48 *Canadian Charter of Rights and Freedoms*, Part I of the *Constitution Act, 1982*, being Schedule B to the *Canada Act 1982* (U.K.), 1982, c. 1, s. 1.
49 N.J. Stranz, "Beyond *R.* v. *Sault Ste. Marie*: The Creation and Expansion of Strict Liability and the 'Due Diligence' Defence" (1992) 30 Alta. L. Rev. 1233 at 1236.
50 James, *supra* note 31 at 61.
51 Sopinka, Lederman, and Bryant, *supra* note 34 at 53.
52 In the introduction to this book, for example, Leiss and Hrudey emphasize their view that "what citizens cannot have, however, is proof of safety in any kind of 'absolute' sense."
53 Leiss and Hrudey also echo this sentiment in the introduction to this book: "There is in principle no conceivable way to predict in advance every type of harm, however small or distant in time and space"; A.R.D. Stebbing, "Environmental Capacity and the Precautionary Principle" (1993) 24 Marine Pollution Bulletin 287.
54 Wildavsky, *supra* note 15 at 430.
55 Advocacy groups will, of course, stretch the principle to achieve its maximum rhetorical value in their campaigns. Gremmen and van den Belt, for example, show how Greenpeace employed what they call an "ultimate" version of the precautionary principle to demand proof of safety in its campaign against pesticide use. Bart Gremmen and Henk van den Belt, "The Precautionary Principle and Pesticides" (2000) 12 Journal of Agricultural and Environmental Ethics 197 at 198. An anonymous reviewer of this work, for example, is correct to point out that activists "in the real world of risk politics" will invoke the precautionary principle as a means to push for proof of safety with the aim of blocking the introduction of technologies they oppose. I think this is entirely in line with my treatment of the principle as a rhetorical instrument. Well-organized private interests similarly demand conclusive proof of *harm* as a precondition to regulation, and, in some sectors, have been successfully doing so for decades. My point is simply that the precautionary principle itself does not command an interpretation that requires absolute proof of safety.
56 Kriebel *et al.*, "Environmental Science," *supra* note 4 at 873.

57   Royal Society of Canada, *Elements of Precaution: Recommendations for the Regulation of Food Biotechnology in Canada. An Expert Panel Report on the Future of Food Biotechnology* (January 2001), <http://www.rsc.ca>.

58   *Convention for the Prevention of Marine Pollution by Dumping from Ships and Aircraft*, Oslo, 15 February 1972, 932 U.N.T.S. 3, Art.16.

59   The moratorium was established by the *Amendments to the Schedule of the International Convention for the Regulation of Whaling*, adopted by the 31st annual meeting of the International Whaling Commission, 13 July 1979 (Nollkaemper, *supra* note 3 at note 64).

60   *Ibid.*

61   *Resolution 44/255 on Large-Scale Pelagic Driftnet Fishing and Its Impact on the Living Marine Resources of the World's Oceans and Seas*, 22 December 1989, reprinted in (1990) 29 I.L.M. 241.

62   William T. Burke, "Regulation of Driftnet Fishing on the High Seas and the New International Law of the Sea" (1990) 3 Geo. Int'l Envtl. L. Rev. 265 at 276.

63   There is still plenty of room to disagree as to whether "safety" has been proven according to the threshold and as to whether the threshold is adequate. My point is simply that the regime operates under a shifted burden of proof without encountering insurmountable obstacles.

64   For a Canadian example, see the *Pest Control Products Act*, R.S.C. 1985, c. P-9 and the *Pest Control Products Act*, S.C. 2002, c. 28 (not yet in force). Both schemes prohibit the manufacture and distribution of any pest control product that is not registered by the minister of health (section 6(1) of the new act). Registration requires evaluation of a product during which the applicant "has the burden of persuading the Minister that the health and environmental risks" of the product are "acceptable" (section 7(6)(a) of the new act). For the European Community, see *EEC Directive 67/548 on the Approximation of Laws, Regulations, and Administrative Provisions of the Member States Relating to the Classification, Packaging, and Labelling of Dangerous Substances*, OJ 1967 L 196/1.

65   Under US pesticide regulation, the Environmental Protection Agency will only approve pesticides that do not pose "unreasonable risks to health or the environment" (*Fungicide, Insecticide and Rodenticide Act*, 7 U.S.C. s/s 136 et seq. (1996)). Yet another example is California's Proposition 65, which requires the state to list substances known to be reproductive or carcinogenic toxins. Any firm subsequently wishing to expose the public to a listed substance bears the burden of proving that the exposure does not pose a risk. See *Safe Drinking Water and Toxic Enforcement Act of 1986* (Chapter 6.6 added by Proposition 65 in the 1986 General Election), *California Health and Safety Code*, § 25249.5-25249.13 (1986).

66   *Food, Drug and Cosmetic Act*, 21 U.S.C. § 348(c)(3)(A) (1994).

67   An objective of this essay is to demonstrate that some regimes *do* employ shifted burdens and *are* in that sense precautionary, while others are not. A further objective is to point out that risk assessment, a critical component of the "risk management process" that Leiss and Hrudey consider to be "inherently precautionary," is deliberately and systematically skewed against precautionary action (see the fourth section of this chapter).

68   I should clarify at this point that where, in general, I have argued that "environmental regulation" in Canada operates in a way that spares polluters and innovators from demonstrating the "safety" of their products and discharges, the burden is in fact distributed differently for different regulatory regimes. The situation could be described as a spectrum ranging from a burden on innovators in the pre-market approval of pesticides and drugs, to a shared burden in environmental assessment, to a burden on the public with respect to toxic pollution. The important point to emphasize, however, is that with respect to toxic chemicals in Canada there is nothing "precautionary" about the regulatory regime. As David Boyd has noted, "although [the *Canadian Environmental Protection Act, 1999*] endorses the precautionary principle in theory, in practice toxic chemicals are allowed to be used in Canada until there is conclusive scientific evidence of their health or environmental impacts" (David Boyd, *Unnatural Law: Rethinking Canadian Environmental Law and Policy* [Vancouver: UBC Press, 2003] at 40); C.F. Cranor. "Asymmetric Information, the Precautionary Principle, and Burdens of Proof" in C. Raffensperger and J. Tickner, eds., *Protecting*

Public Health and the Environment: Implementing the Precautionary Principle (Washington DC: Island Press, 1999) 74 at 94.

69 The Royal Society of Canada, in a recent expert panel report, called the threshold question – "namely, the issue of what level of scientific evidence of potential harm is required to trigger the application of precaution" – "a central unresolved issue in national and international invocations of the [precautionary] principle." Royal Society of Canada, *supra* note 57.

70 Kokott, *supra* note 34 at 124.

71 Cranor, *supra* note 68 at 79.

72 *Final Ministerial Declaration*, The Hague, 8 March 1990, reprinted in (1990) 1 Y.B. Int'l Envtl. Law 658.

73 Cameron, *supra* note 3 at 46.

74 *Ibid.*

75 European Commission, *supra* note 16.

76 Royal Society of Canada, *supra* note 57 at 202.

77 *CBD, supra* note 9.

78 Farrier, *supra* note 4 at 108.

79 *Ibid.*

80 Brian Wynne and Sue Mayer, "How Science Fails the Environment" (1993) 138 New Scientist 32 at 32. This is in keeping with the origins of the precautionary principle. The *Ministerial Declaration* of the second International Conference on the Protection of the North Sea (regarded by many as the first official statement of the precautionary principle) stated that the principle would apply when there is "reason to assume" that harmful effects would occur (Ministerial Declaration Calling for the Reduction of Pollution, Nov. 25, 1987, 27 ILM 235).

81 Henk van den Belt and Bart Gremmen, "Between Precautionary Principle and 'Sound Science': Distributing the Burdens of Proof" (2002) 15 Journal of Agricultural and Environmental Ethics 103 at 111.

82 For example, consider the following image drawn from Douglas Walton, *Legal Argumentation and Evidence* (University Park: Pennsylvania State University Press, 2002) at 13-15. A balance of probabilities is a symmetrical distribution of the burden of proof (both sides bear similar "burdens"), beyond a reasonable doubt is a deliberately asymmetrical allocation (in order to tip the scales – one side would have to bring a lot more evidence than the other side would have to in order to win), and the standard "clear and convincing evidence," which is somewhere in between, is "somewhat asymmetrical."

83 Joel Tickner, "A Commonsense Framework for Operationalizing the Precautionary Principle," Wingspread Conference Paper, Racine, WI, 1998; <http://www.johnsonfed.org/conferences/precautionary/paplist.html>.

84 Hugh Benevides and Theresa McClenaghan for the Canadian Environmental Law Association, *Implementing Precaution: An NGO Response to the Government of Canada's Discussion Document* (April 2002), <http:// www.cela.ca> at 16.

85 Wynne and Mayer, *supra* note 80 at 33.

86 *Ibid.*

87 Ellen K. Silbergeld, "Risk Assessment and Risk Management: An Uneasy Divorce" in Deborah G. Mayo and Rachelle D. Hollander, eds., *Acceptable Evidence: Science and Values in Risk Management* (New York: Oxford University Press, 1991) 99 at 100.

88 Brian Wynne, "Uncertainty and Environmental Learning: Reconceiving Science and Policy in the Preventive Paradigm" (1992) Global Environmental Change 111 at 112.

89 Jane Hunt, "The Social Construction of Precaution" in Tim O'Riordan, ed., *The Social Construction of Precaution* (London: Cameron May, 1994) 117 at 118.

90 Wynne, *supra* note 88 at 118. See also Marielle Matthee and Dominique Vermersch, "Are the Precautionary Principle and the International Trade of Genetically Modified Organisms Reconcilable?" (2000) 12 Journal of Agricultural and Environmental Ethics 59 at 61.

91 Wynne, *supra* note 88 at 116.

92 Hunt, *supra* note 89 at 118. See also Barrett and Raffensperger, *supra* note 24 at 119.

93 Wynne and Mayer, *supra* note 80.
94 As noted by Nancy Myers, "The Precautionary Principle Puts Values First" (2002) 22 Bulletin of Science, Technology and Society 210 at 214, quantitative risk assessment, as a tool, has proven to be very effective in the battle against environmental regulations, especially in the trade setting.
95 Silbergeld, *supra* note 87 at 99. For a proponent of the divorce, see Wildavsky, *supra* note 15 at 431, who looks favourably on the "analytical purists" who would honour a strict distinction between risk assessment and risk management.
96 *Ibid.*
97 Gray, *supra* note 12 at 174. See also P. Johnston and M. Simmonds, "Letters: Precautionary Principle" (1990) 21(8) Marine Pollution Bulletin 402 and Gray's rejoinder in (1990) 21(12) Marine Pollution Bulletin 599.
98 *Ibid.*
99 Silbergeld, *supra* note 87 at 100.
100 This point has been forcefully made by Sheila Jasanoff, *The Fifth Branch: Science Advisors as Policymakers* (Cambridge, MA: Harvard University Press, 1989) at 9. See also Dinah Shelton, "The Impact of Scientific Uncertainty on Environmental Law and Policy in the United States" in Freestone and Hey, eds., *supra* note 2, 209 at 212.
101 Shelton, *supra* note 100.
102 Tora Skodvin and Arild Underdal, "Exploring the Dynamics of the Science-Politics Interface" in Steinar Andresen, Tora Skodvin, Arild Underdal, and Jorgen Wettstad, eds., *Science and Politics in International Environmental Regimes* (Manchester: Manchester University Press, 2000) 22 at 22.
103 Jasanoff, *supra* note 100 at 231.
104 See, for example, Stephen Breyer, *Breaking the Vicious Circle: Towards Effective Risk Regulation* (Cambridge, MA: Harvard University Press, 1993) at 48-49. Cross, *supra* note 11, also presents a critique of the "overly conservative" operation of regulatory agencies (at 856-58).
105 Van den Belt and Gremmen, *supra* note 81 at 115.
106 J.S. Gray, for example, would be among this group.
107 Richard Levins, International Summit on Science and the Precautionary Principle, University of Massachusetts at Lowell, <http://www.uml.edu/centers/LCSP/precaution/RTFs/levins.draft.paper.rtf>.
108 *Ibid.*
109 Kristen Shrader-Frechette and Earl D. McCoy, *Method in Ecology: Strategies for Conservation* (Cambridge: Cambridge University Press, 1993) at 150.
110 *Ibid.* at 151.
111 Van den Belt and Gremmen, *supra* note 81 at 117.
112 Barrett and Raffensperger, *supra* note 24 at 112.
113 *Ibid.* at 112. Ted Schrecker puts it like this: "The scientific enterprise, very much like an idealized version of the criminal justice system, is organized around minimizing the occurrence of false positives – that is, incorrect rejections of the null hypothesis." Ted Schrecker, "Using Science in Environmental Policy: Can Canada Do Better?" in Edward A. Parson, ed., *Governing the Environment: Persistent Challenges, Uncertain Innovations* (Toronto: University of Toronto Press, 2001) 31 at 42.
114 Van den Belt and Gremmen, *supra* note 81 at 118. See also Rachelle D. Hollander, "Expert Claims and Social Decisions: Science, Politics and Responsibility" in Deborah G. Mayo and Rachelle D. Hollander, eds., *Acceptable Evidence: Science and Values in Risk Management* (New York: Oxford University Press, 1991) 160 at 167; and M'Gonigle *et al.*, *supra* note 14 at 107.
115 Cranor, *supra* note 68 at 79. See also Barrett and Raffensperger, *supra* note 24 at 112.
116 This point is made effectively by Hollander, *supra* note 114 at 167.
117 *Ibid.*
118 For the ethical case that Type I errors should be preferred over Type II errors in situations with potentially serious consequences, see Kristen Shrader-Frechette, *Ethics of Scientific Research* (London: Rowman and Littlefield, 1994) at 111. The "classic formulation" of the

principle that there is an "asymmetry of consequences" between the types of error was developed by Talbot Page, "A Generic View of Toxic Chemicals and Similar Risks" (1978) 7 Ecology L. Q. 207. Cross's piece, *supra* note 11, attempts to disprove the "asymmetry of consequences" thesis.

119 Barrett and Raffensperger, *supra* note 24 at 112.

120 Hollander, *supra* note 114 at 168.

121 Graham McBride, "Statistical Methods Helping and Hindering Environmental Science and Management" (2002) 7 Journal of Agricultural, Biological, and Environmental Statistics 300 (arguing that very few environmental scientists are aware of the "arbitrariness" and "information sterility" of a single p-value. He also notes that "the interpretation to be made of the failure of a test to achieve such significance is not clear") at 300.

122 Van den Belt and Gremmen, *supra* note 81 at 118.

123 It is important to keep in mind, as pointed out by M'Gonigle *et al.*, *supra* note 14 at 114, that the costs associated with each of the two types of error are often incurred by different parties – the costs of false positives will be borne largely by industry and government, while the costs of false negatives will often be borne by individuals and by the natural environment.

124 *Ibid.* at 119.

125 *Ibid.*

126 For example, H. Sanderson and S. Peterson, "Power Analysis as a Reflexive Scientific Tool for Interpretation and Implementation of the Precautionary Principle in the European Union" (2002) 9 Environmental Science and Pollution Research 221-26, see this as the "first step towards increasing the reflexibility of science that Beck (1992) issued as a main precursor for future sustainable development." See also Anne Fairbrother and Richard S. Bennett, "Ecological Risk Assessment and the Precautionary Principle" (1999) 5 Human and Ecological Risk Assessment 943 (urging a "critical review of the default assumptions used in risk assessments" and advocating for increased attention to "reducing the Type II error of risk assessment studies").

127 *Ibid.*

128 *Ibid.* at 224.

129 Schrecker, *supra* note 113.

130 Sanderson and Peterson, *supra* note 126 at 226. See also McBride, *supra* note 121 at 301, who gives the example of a null hypothesis of "no association," stating that the experimental result would conclude that there is no association between the exposure and risk of illness "merely because the data did not (quite) result in the rejection of the null hypothesis."

131 Schrecker, *supra* note 113 at 43.

132 Lene Buhl-Mortensen, "Type II Statistical Errors in Environmental Science and the Precautionary Principle" (1996) 32 Marine Pollution Bulletin 528 at 531.

133 Wynne, *supra* note 88 at 111.

134 Liora Salter's work credits John Thibault and Laurens Walker, "A Theory of Procedure" (1993) 66 Cal. L. R. 541, with establishing the fundamental dichotomy between the objectives of truth and justice in dispute resolution procedures. Liora Salter, with the assistance of Edwin Levy and William Leiss, *Mandated Science: Science and Scientists in the Making of Standards* (Dordrecht: Kluwer Academic Publishers, 1988) at 174.

135 Sanderson and Peterson, *supra* note 126.

136 Barrett and Raffensperger, *supra* note 24 at 107; Wynne and Mayer, *supra* note 80 at 34 ("[w]hat is needed is a different, 'greener' culture of good science").

137 An anonymous reviewer of the Royal Society of Canada study on food biotechnology noted that many refereed ecological journals now demand that researchers perform a power analysis and that many biologists have now "advocated abandoning the slavish devotion to avoiding the Type I error." Royal Society of Canada, *supra* note 57 at 199.

138 Barrett and Raffensperger, *supra* note 24 at 117.

139 *Ibid.*

140 *Ibid.* at 119.

141 *Ibid.* at 120.

142 Cranor, *supra* note 68 at 79.
143 *Ibid.*
144 Hunt, *supra* note 89 at 125.
145 Royal Society of Canada, *supra* note 57 at 199.
146 *Ibid.*
147 Olson, *supra* note 3 at 894.
148 *Ibid.* at 899.
149 Tim O'Riordan and James Cameron, "The History and Contemporary Significance of the Precautionary Principle" in Tim O'Riordan and James Cameron, eds., *Interpreting the Precautionary Principle* (London: Cameron May, 1994) 12 at 16.
150 William Leiss, *Governance and the Environment*, Working Paper Series no. 96-1 (Kingston: Queen's University, 1996) at 19-20.
151 See Cross, *supra* note 11, who provides numerous examples. He argues that a conservative approach to *new* risks may increase the overall harm to public health because new products and facilities are "almost universally safer than existing ones" (at 876).
152 Raikka, *supra* note 23 at 467.
153 Cranor, *supra* note 68 at 78.
154 Olson, *supra* note 3 at 900.
155 Fred Kauffield, "Presumptions and the Distribution of Argumentative Burdens in Acts of Proposing and Accusing" (1998) 12 Argumentation 245 at 246.
156 Olson, *supra* note 3 at 915.
157 Cranor, *supra* note 68 at 86.
158 *Ibid.*
159 Nollkaemper, *supra* note 3 at 85.
160 Cameron, *supra* note 3 at 43.
161 Silvio Functowicz and Jerome Ravetz, "Uncertainty, Complexity and Post-Normal Science" (1993) 13 Environmental Toxicology and Chemistry 1881 at 1882.
162 Hunt, *supra* note 89 at 121.
163 Functowicz and Ravetz, *supra* note 161 at 1881.
164 Myers, *supra* note 94 at 215.
165 Van den Belt and Gremmen, *supra* note 81 at 105.
166 O'Riordan and Cameron, *supra* note 149 at 26.
167 *Ibid.* at 27.
168 Wexler, *supra* note 32 at para. 10.
169 Stephen R. Dovers and John W. Handmer, "Ignorance, Sustainability, and the Precautionary Principle: Towards an Analytical Framework" in Harding and Fisher, eds., *supra* note 3, 167 at 178.
170 Kriebel *et al.*, "Environmental Science," *supra* note 4 at 872.
171 Gaskins, *supra* note 17 at xvii.

Bibliography

Books and Articles

Barrett, K., and C. Raffensperger. "Precautionary Science." In C. Raffensperger and J. Tickner, eds., *Protecting Public Health and the Environment: Implementing the Precautionary Principle* (Washington, DC: Island Press, 1999) 106.

Beck, Ulrich. *Risk Society: Towards a New Modernity* (London: Sage Publications, 1992).

Benevides, Hugh, and Theresa McClenaghan (for the Canadian Environmental Law Association). *Implementing Precaution: An NGO Response to the Government of Canada's Discussion Document* (April 2002). <http://www.cela.ca>.

Bodansky, Daniel. "Scientific Uncertainty and the Precautionary Principle" (1991) 33 Environment 4.

–. "The Precautionary Principle in US Environmental Law." In Tim O'Riordan and James Cameron, eds., *Interpreting the Precautionary Principle* (London: Cameron May, 1994) 203.

Boyd, David. *Unnatural Law: Rethinking Canadian Environmental Law and Policy* (Vancouver: UBC Press, 2003).

Breyer, Stephen. *Breaking the Vicious Circle: Towards Effective Risk Regulation* (Cambridge, MA: Harvard University Press, 1993).

Buhl-Mortensen, Lene. "Type-II Statistical Errors in Environmental Science and the Precautionary Principle" (1996) 32 Marine Pollution Bulletin 528.

Burke, William T. "Regulation of Driftnet Fishing on the High Seas and the New International Law of the Sea" (1990) 3 Geo. Int'l Envtl. L. Rev. 265.

Cameron, James. "The Precautionary Principle: Core Meaning, Constitutional Framework and Procedures for Implementation." In Ronnie Harding and Elizabeth Fisher, eds., *Perspectives on the Precautionary Principle* (Leichhardt: Federation Press, 1999) 29.

Conko, Gregory. "Throwing Precaution to the Wind: The Perils of the Precautionary Principle," Competitive Enterprise Institute Update, August/September 2000. <www.cei.org/gencon/005,01854.cfm>.

Cranor, C.F. "Asymmetric Information, the Precautionary Principle, and Burdens of Proof." In C. Raffensperger and J. Tickner, eds., *Protecting Public Health and the Environment: Implementing the Precautionary Principle* (Washington DC: Island Press, 1999) 74.

–. "Learning from the Law to Address Uncertainty in the Precautionary Principle" (2001) 7 Science and Engineering Ethics 313.

–. "What Could Precautionary Science Be? Research for Early Warnings and a Better Future" (2002), Working Paper, University of Massachusetts Lowell.

Cross, Frank. "Paradoxical Perils of the Precautionary Principle" (1996) 53 Wash. and Lee L. Rev. 851.

Cross, Rupert, and Colin Tapper. *Cross and Tapper on Evidence*, 9th ed. (London: Butterworths, 1999).

Dovers, Stephen R., and John W. Handmer. "Ignorance, Sustainability, and the Precautionary Principle: Towards an Analytical Framework." In Ronnie Harding and Elizabeth Fisher, eds., *Perspectives on the Precautionary Principle* (Leichhardt: Federation Press, 1999) 167.

Earll, R.C. "Commonsense and the Precautionary Principle: An Environmentalist's Perspective" (1992) 24 Marine Pollution Bulletin 182.

Economic and Social Research Council, Global Environmental Change Program. *The Politics of GM Food: Risk, Science and Public Trust*, Special Briefing no. 5, University of Sussex, October 1999. <http://www.gecko.ac.uk>.

European Commission. *Communication from the European Commission on the Precautionary Principle* (2000). <http://europa.eu.int/comm/dgs/health_consumer/library/pub/pub07_en.pdf> (accessed 23 April 2003).

Fairbrother, Anne, and Richard S. Bennett. "Ecological Risk Assessment and the Precautionary Principle" (1999) 5 Human and Ecological Risk Assessment 943.

Farrier, David. "Factoring Biodiversity Conservation into Decision-Making Processes: The Role of the Precautionary Principle." In Ronnie Harding and Elizabeth Fisher, eds., *Perspectives on the Precautionary Principle* (Leichhardt: Federation Press, 1999) 99.

Fischer, Frank. *Citizens, Experts, and the Environment: The Politics of Local Knowledge* (Durham: Duke University Press, 2000).

Freestone, David. "The Precautionary Principle." In R. Churchill and D. Freestone, eds., *International Law and Global Climate Change* (London: Graham and Trotman, 1991) 36.

Freestone, David, and Ellen Hey. "Implementing the Precautionary Principle: Challenges and Opportunities." In D. Freestone and E. Hey, eds., *The Precautionary Principle and International Law: The Challenge of Implementation* (The Hague: Kluwer Law International, 1996) 249.

Functowicz, Silvio, and Jerome Ravetz. "Uncertainty, Complexity and Post-Normal Science" (1993) 13 Environmental Toxicology and Chemistry 1881.

Gaskins, Richard H. *Burdens of Proof in Modern Discourse* (New Haven: Yale University Press, 1992).

Giddens, Anthony. *The Third Way: The Renewal of Social Democracy* (London: Polity Press, 1998).

Goldstein, B.D. "The Precautionary Principle Also Applies to Public Health Actions" (2001) 91 Am. J. Public Health 1358.

Gray, J.S. "Statistics and the Precautionary Principle" (1990) 21(4) Marine Pollution Bulletin 174.

–. "Statistics and the Precautionary Principle – Reply" (1990) 21(12) Marine Pollution Bulletin 599.

Gremmen, Bart, and Henk van den Belt. "The Precautionary Principle and Pesticides" (2000) 12 Journal of Agricultural and Environmental Ethics 197 at 198.

Harding, Ronnie, and Elizabeth Fisher. "Introducing the Precautionary Principle." In Ronnie Harding and Elizabeth Fisher, eds., *Perspectives on the Precautionary Principle* (Leichhardt: Federation Press, 1999) 2.

Harremöes, Poul, *et al. The Precautionary Principle in the Twentieth Century: Late Lessons from Early Warnings* (London: Earthscan Publications, 2002).

Hollander, Rachelle D. "Expert Claims and Social Decisions: Science, Politics and Responsibility." In Deborah G. Mayo and Rachelle D. Hollander, eds., *Acceptable Evidence: Science and Values in Risk Management* (New York: Oxford University Press, 1991) 160.

Hunt, Jane. "The Social Construction of Precaution." In Tim O'Riordan and James Cameron, eds., *Implementing the Precautionary Principle* (London: Cameron May, 1994) 117.

Jackson, T., and P.J. Taylor. "The Precautionary Principle and the Prevention of Marine Pollution." Paper presented at the First International Ocean Pollution Symposium, Puerto Rico, April 1991.

James, Fleming. "Burdens of Proof" (1961) 47 Va. L. Rev. 51.

Jasanoff, Sheila. *The Fifth Branch: Science Advisors as Policymakers* (Cambridge, MA: Harvard University Press, 1989).

–. "Citizens at Risk: Cultures of Modernity in the US and EU" (2002) 11 Science as Culture 363.

Johnston, P., and M. Simmonds. "Letters: Precautionary Principle" (1990) 21(8) Marine Pollution Bulletin 402.

Kauffield, Fred. "Presumptions and the Distribution of Argumentative Burdens in Acts of Proposing and Accusing" (1998) 12 Argumentation 245.

Koelling, T.W. "The Burden of Proof in Environmental and Public Health Litigation" (1981) 49 U. Mo. Kan. City L. Rev. 207.

Kokott, Juliane. *The Burden of Proof in Comparative and International Human Rights Law: Civil and Common Law Approaches with Special Reference to the American and German Legal Systems* (The Hague: Kluwer Law International, 1998).

Kriebel, D., and J. Tickner. "Reenergizing Public Health through Precaution" (2001) 91 American Journal of Public Health 1351.

Kriebel, D., *et al.* "The Precautionary Principle in Environmental Science" (2001) 109 Environmental Health Perspectives 871.

Leiss, William. *Governance and the Environment*, Working Paper Series no. 96-1 (Kingston: Queen's University, 1996).

–. "Between Expertise and Bureaucracy: Risk Management Trapped at the Science-Policy Interface." In Bruce Doern and Ted Reed, eds., *Between Expertise and Bureaucracy: Risk Management Trapped at the Science-Policy Interface* (Toronto: University of Toronto Press, 2000) 49.

Levins, Richard. "Whose Scientific Method?" International Summit on Science and the Precautionary Principle, University of Massachusetts at Lowell, 2002. <http://www.uml.edu/centers/LCSP/precaution/RTFs/levins.draft.paper.rtf>.

McBride, Graham B. "Statistical Methods Helping and Hindering Environmental Science and Management" (2002) 7 Journal of Agricultural Biological and Environmental Statistics 300.

MacGarvin, Malcolm. "Precaution, Science and the Sin of Hubris." In Tim O'Riordan, ed., *Precaution, Science and the Sin of Hubris* (London: Cameron May, 1994) 69.

Matthee, Marielle, and Dominique Vermersch. "Are the Precautionary Principle and the International Trade of Genetically Modified Organisms Reconcilable?" (2000) 12 Journal of Agricultural and Environmental Ethics 59.

M'Gonigle, R. Michael, T. Lynne Jamieson, Murdoch K. McAllister, and Randall M. Peterman. "Taking Uncertainty Seriously: From Permissive Regulation to Preventative Design in Environmental Decision-Making" (1994) 32 Osgoode Hall Law Journal 99.

Miller, H.I., and G. Conko. "The Science of Biotechnology Meets the Politics of Global Regulation." Issues in Science and Technology Online, 2000. <http://www.nap.edu/issues/17.1/ miller.htm>.

Morgan, Edmund Morris. *Some Problems of Proof in the Anglo-American System of Litigation* (New York: Columbia University Press, 1956).

Myers, Nancy. "The Precautionary Principle Puts Values First" (2002) 22 Bulletin of Science, Technology and Society 210.

Nollkaemper, Andre. "The Precautionary Principle in International Environmental-Law – What's New under the Sun" (1991) 22 Marine Pollution Bulletin 107.

–. "'What You Risk Reveals What You Value,' and Other Dilemmas Encountered in the Legal Assaults on Risks." In David Freestone and Ellen Hey, eds., *The Precautionary Principle and International Law: Challenges and Implementation* (The Hague: Kluwer Law International, 1996) 73.

Ogilvie, Ken, Executive Director, Pollution Probe. "Expert Consultation on Emerging Issues." Speech at the International Joint Commission Workshop in Racine, Wisconsin, February 2003 [on file with author].

Olson, James M. "Shifting the Burden of Proof: How the Common Law Can Safeguard Nature and Promote an Earth Ethic" (1990) 20 Envtl. L. 891.

O'Riordan, T. "The History and Contemporary Significance of the Precautionary Principle." In Tim O'Riordan and James Cameron, eds., *Interpreting the Precautionary Principle* (London: Cameron May, 1994) 12.

–, and James Cameron. *Interpreting the Precautionary Principle* (London: Cameron May, 1994).

–, and A. Jordan. "The Precautionary Principle in Contemporary Environmental Politics" (1995) 4 Environmental Values 191.

Paciocco, David, and Lee Stusser. *The Law of Evidence*, 2nd ed. (Toronto: Irwin Law, 2002).

Page, Talbot. "A Generic View of Toxic Chemicals and Similar Risks" (1978) 7 Ecology L. Q. 207.

Raffensperger, C., and Joel Tickner. *Protecting Public Health and the Environment: Implementing the Precautionary Principle* (Washington, DC: Island Press, 1999).

Raikka, Juha. "Burden of Proof Rules in Social Criticism" (1997) 11 Argumentation 463.

Royal Society of Canada. *Elements of Precaution: Recommendations for the Regulation of Food Biotechnology in Canada. An Expert Panel Report on the Future of Food Biotechnology,* January 2001. <http://www.rsc.ca>.

Salter, Liora, with the assistance of Edwin Levy and William Leiss. *Mandated Science: Science and Scientists in the Making of Standards* (Dordrecht: Kluwer Academic Publishers, 1988).

Sanderson, H., and S. Peterson. "Power Analysis as a Reflexive Scientific Tool for Interpretation and Implementation of the Precautionary Principle in the European Union" (2002) 9 Environmental Science and Pollution Research 221.

Schrecker, Ted. "Using Science in Environmental Policy: Can Canada Do Better?" In Edward A. Parson, ed., *Governing the Environment: Persistent Challenges, Uncertain Innovations* (Toronto: University of Toronto Press, 2001) 31.

Shelton, Dinah. "The Impact of Scientific Uncertainty on Environmental Law and Policy in the United States." In David Freestone and Ellen Hey, eds., *The Precautionary Principle and International Law: The Challenge of Implementation* (The Hague: Kluwer International, 1996) 209.

Shrader-Frechette, Kristin S. *Risk Analysis and Scientific Method: Methodological and Ethical Problems with Evaluating Societal Hazards* (Boston: D. Reidel Publishing Company, 1985).

–. *Ethics of Scientific Research* (London: Rowman and Littlefield, 1994).

–, and Earl D. McCoy. *Method in Ecology: Strategies for Conservation* (Cambridge: Cambridge University Press, 1993).

Silbergeld, Ellen K. "Risk Assessment and Risk Management: An Uneasy Divorce." In Deborah G. Mayo and Rachelle D. Hollander, eds., *Acceptable Evidence: Science and Values in Risk Management* (New York: Oxford University Press, 1991) 99.

Skodvin, Tora, and Arild Underdal. "Exploring the Dynamics of the Science-Politics Interface." In Steinar Andresen, Tora Skodvin, Arild Underdal, and Jorgen Wettstad, eds., *Science and Politics in International Environmental Regimes* (Manchester: Manchester University Press, 2000) 22.

Sopinka, John, Sydney N. Lederman, and Alan W. Bryant. *The Law of Evidence in Canada*, 2nd ed. (Markham, ON: Butterworths, 1999).

Stebbing, A.R.D. "Environmental Capacity and the Precautionary Principle" (1993) 24 Marine Pollution Bulletin 287.

Stranz, N.J. "Beyond *R.* v. *Sault Ste. Marie:* The Creation and Expansion of Strict Liability and the 'Due Diligence' Defence" (1992) 30 Alta. L. Rev. 1233.

Thibault, John, and Laurens Walker. "A Theory of Procedure" (1993) 66 Cal. L. R. 541.

Van den Belt, Henk, and Bart Gremmen. "Between Precautionary Principle and 'Sound Science': Distributing the Burdens of Proof" (2002) 15 Journal of Agricultural and Environmental Ethics 103.

VanderZwaag, D. "The Precautionary Principle and Marine Environmental Protection: Slippery Shores, Rough Seas, and Rising Normative Tides" (2002) 33 Ocean Development and International Law 165.

Walton, Douglas. *Legal Argumentation and Evidence* (University Park: Pennsylvania State University Press, 2002).

Wexler, Steve M. "Book Review: *Burdens of Proof in Modern Discourse* by Richard H. Gaskins" (1994) 73 Can. Bar. Rev. 286.

–. "Burden of Proof Writ Large" (1999) 33 U.B.C. L. Rev. 75.

Whately, Richard. *Elements of Rhetoric: Comprising an Analysis of the Laws of Moral Evidence and of Persuasion, with Rules for Argumentative Composition and Elocution*, reprint edition by D. Ehninger (Carbondale: Southern Illinois Press, 1963).

Wildavsky, Aaron. *But Is It True? A Citizen's Guide to Environmental Health and Safety Issues* (Cambridge: Harvard University Press, 1995).

Wynne, Brian. "Uncertainty – Technical and Social." In H. Brooks and C.L. Cooper, eds., *Science for Public Policy* (Oxford: Pergamon Press, 1987) 95.

–. "Uncertainty and Environmental Learning – Reconceiving Science and Policy in the Preventive Paradigm" (1992) 2 Global Environmental Change: Human and Policy Dimensions 111.

–, and Sue Mayer. "How Science Fails the Environment" (1993) 138 New Scientist 32.

Yogis, John A. *Canadian Law Dictionary*, 4th ed. (Hauppauge: Barron's, 1998).

Jurisprudence

Spraytech v. *Hudson (Town)*, 2001 SCC 40.

Taylor Estate v. *Wong Aviation Ltd.*, [1969] S.C.R. 481.

The "Ruapehu" (1925), 21 Ll. L. Rep. 310.

Legislation

Canadian Environmental Protection Act, 1999, S.C. 1999, c. 33.

Food, Drug and Cosmetics Act, 21 U.S.C. § 348(c)(3)(A) (1994).

Fungicide, Insecticide and Rodenticide Act, 7 U.S.C. s/s 136 et seq. (1996).

Oceans Act, S.C. 1996, c. 31.

Safe Drinking Water and Toxic Enforcement Act of 1986 (Chapter 6.6 added by Proposition 65 in the 1986 General Election), *California Health and Safety Code*, § 25249.5-25249.13 (1986).

International Agreements

Convention for the Prevention of Marine Pollution by Dumping from Ships and Aircraft. Oslo, 15 February 1972, 932 U.N.T.S. 3, Article 16.

EEC Directive 67/548 on the Approximation of Laws, Regulations, and Administrative Provisions of the Member States Relating to the Classification, Packaging, and Labelling of Dangerous Substances. Doc. OJ 1967 L 196/1.

Final Ministerial Declaration. Third International Conference on the Protection of the North Sea, The Hague, 8 March 1990, reprinted in (1990) 1 Y.B. Int'l Envtl. Law 658.

Resolution 44/255 on Large-Scale Pelagic Driftnet Fishing and Its Impact on the Living Marine Resources of the World's Oceans and Seas. 22 December 1989, reprinted in (1990) 29 I.L.M. 241.

Rio Declaration on Environment and Development. United Nations Conference on Environment and Development. UN Doc. A/Conf.151/5/Rev.1 (13 June 1992), reprinted in 31 I.L.M. 874.

4
Legal Knowledges of Risk
Mariana Valverde, Ron Levi, and Dawn Moore

Theoretical Tools

In previous work, we have found that many practices of risk knowledge found in legal and quasi-legal sites are "hybrid," meaning that persons and institutions engaging with law, whatever their background and role, often mix expert and everyday knowledges of risky situations in such a way as to create new assemblages of risk information that are neither scientific nor anti-scientific (for example, Moore and Valverde 2000). We have also studied the persistence of common knowledge in legal decision-making processes in which expert evidence would be relevant but is not usually introduced, sometimes using intoxication and drink-related disorder as the empirical site (Levi and Valverde 2001; Valverde 2003a). Elsewhere, we have paid particular attention to what theorists working in science and technology studies (Latour 1987; Callon and Law 1997) call "translation" – that is, the dynamic process through which facts, concepts, and physical entities move from site to site and are either reinforced and solidified or else contradicted or undermined (Levi 2000; 2003; Valverde 2003b).

This chapter uses some of this existing work and some not-yet-published research to present a more fully developed theoretical framework. As is often the case, returning to the original research question (law and risk) after doing empirical research and reflecting on the limitations of available theoretical and methodological tools has the effect of suggesting a rephrasing of the question. First let us outline some key theoretically relevant findings that are found both in our own work and that of other sociolegal scholars of risk knowledges (for example, Ericson and Doyle 2004; O'Malley 2004):

1 *Risk is heterogeneous.* It is of doubtful use and it may be a real hindrance, both theoretically and empirically, to ask about risk in general. Even studies of a single site reveal a large number of heterogeneous, incompatible types of risks, dangers, and uncertainties.

2 *The adjective "legal" is more useful than the noun "law."* It is misleading to ask anything about law in general, not only because this erases key differences and contradictions between different functions and dimensions of law, and simultaneously isolates law from other regulatory and normative systems, but also – and this is a point not made by the legal pluralism literature – because theoretical inquiries into law have tended to generate static models. Static models of any kind, we will argue, are unhelpful, no matter what they substantively claim about law and society. Focusing on the dynamics of knowledge production and circulation is facilitated if one uses terms such as "legal network" or "legal actor" rather than the static term "law."

3 *The knowledge process is plural and heterogeneous.* Finally, we have found it highly fruitful to always use the plural form knowledges.[1] Existing literature on risk and law tends to counterpoise expert knowledge to law and legal reasoning, but we have found it useful to not assume that everything that goes in as "expert witness testimony" is epistemologically homogeneous ("science" or "expertise"). Similarly, we have found that prosecutors and judges, among others, can and do use not only extra-legal information but also the general authority of science to generate legally effective decisions. Who uses what knowledges, and how various combinations of knowledges are actually used, are questions whose answers cannot be deduced either from the provenance of the knowledge or from the actors' institutional location or credentials.

In keeping with these insights, our suggestion for a revised question that can be pursued in future research is no longer law and risk but rather the following: what kinds of risk knowledge moves are made by the various participants in particular legal networks and with what legal, social, and epistemological effects?

Pursuing this question in a variety of sites has been facilitated, to a greater or lesser extent, by methodological and theoretical insights borrowed or adapted from actor network theory (ANT) and from the overlapping field of science and technology studies (STS). Since we think these tools could be useful to other legal scholars, whether or not they are studying risk, we take the time to explain some key analytical tools we borrow from ANT (see discussion later in this chapter). The contribution that our essay makes is to a large extent theoretical and methodological, but not exclusively so. One substantive finding is that risk is by no means monopolized by scientists and other experts, as Ulrich Beck's influential work *Risk Society* (Beck 1992) tends to suggest. Risk assessments that were originally developed in a scientific context lose much of their scientificity as they are reworked into an assemblage whose logic is not scientific. This shift is clear in prosecutorial decisions about sex offenders (see discussion later in this chapter) as well as in other legal contexts, such as politically charged environmental impact determinations (Espeland 1998). It is also worth remembering that many effective tools of risk measurement and risk assessment do not use statistics or any expert information. Notable examples of this have been developed by two prominent American risk-and-law scholars, Tom Baker, in his analysis of the social/moral construction of responsibility in insurance law (Baker 2000; Baker 2002), and Jonathan Simon, in his study of how the risks of mountain climbing are allocated and managed (Simon 2002).

Another key finding of our case studies and our other work concerns the relation between the type of knowledge claim put forward and the credentials or the position of the person or group putting it forward. "Swapping knowledges" is predominantly studied in this essay in the second case study on the drug court, but it is a "knowledge move" that takes place in numerous other venues. This is theoretically important because debates about expertise in law (see, for example, Jasanoff 1995) tend to assume that scientists are the only authorized custodians of scientific information, so that if courts use scientific facts there is some kind of obligation to use these facts in a scientific manner, with creative uses being dismissed as incorrect. The correlate assumption, which is not so often voiced perhaps because it is so widely shared by the public and by scientists as well as by legal professionals, is that lawyers are the ones who authorize or deauthorize the use of legal knowledge resources such as case law and legal doctrine. Lay uses of legal doctrine and other legal resources tend to be dismissed as uninformed and inaccurate – as if lawyers owned not only the power to represent clients but also the intellectual machinery of law itself.[2] Just as scientists are fond of decrying the bastardization of their precious facts in courts of law, so too legal professionals assume that claims about rights, about crime, and even about justice that are made by non-professionals are uninformed opinions that can become effective only if subordinated to, or taken up in, the technical machinery of lawsuits and courts and transformed thus into "juridical capital" (Bourdieu 1987). Thus is "juridical capital," as a set of knowledge resources and of normative resources, not just a set of state institutions, monopolized by lawyers? And while scientists and lawyers have a great deal more symbolic capital and institutional authority than most other kinds of knowers, more marginalized groups also try to play this game of knowledge Monopoly (compare with feminist claims that "the right to choose" was originally a feminist invention that has been co-opted and bastardized by consumer capitalism).

We follow Nietzsche in thinking that it is not at all useful for scholarship to try to follow certain concepts, facts, or norms back to some "original" source.[3] Origins are always plural, muddied, and contested. Moreover, even in those unusual situations when a particular idea or doctrine or value can be actually traced to a single actor at a specific moment, it does not mean that the first use of a knowledge resource is somehow the true or authentic one. Justices in the United States Supreme Court may feel they have the duty to interpret the founders' original intentions, but scholars who are free from such institutional constraints have the opportunity of studying all uses of particular knowledge resources in the spirit of documentation rather than with the aim of judging. Later on, these studies can be put to normative legal or political uses by their own authors or by other users. We stress that what one could call "second-hand" knowledges – for example, judges' deployment of biomedical information that they have picked up either from expert witnesses or from other sources – are not necessarily illegitimate or improper. In keeping with ANT/STS methodology, our approach treats all uses and deployments of knowledge claims as equal, without making judgments about who should or should not be making these claims.

This approach is influenced by the nominalistic and agnostic perspective shared by Michel Foucault's influential genealogies of modern knowledge forms (Foucault 1973) and Bruno Latour's increasingly influential ethnographies of modern cultural forms, including law (Latour 1993; Latour 2002). From this perspective, knowledges do not "belong" to anyone or to any site. Knowledges are always circulating, changing, being taken apart, and reassembled in new shapes by new actors. The goal of scholarship, in this perspective, is not to discover that concept X or norm Y is originally, and hence truly, the property of this or that group or institution, but rather to try to capture this creative movement in our analyses. In this way, we can highlight the flexibility of knowledge resources, illuminating the byways of power/knowledge while refraining from the temptation to use our own texts to police how others use governance resources, including knowledge resources.[4]

The non-normative study of risk knowledges in law is, we believe, potentially very fruitful for a whole series of intellectual projects. For those interested in risk management and risk measurement, law is a very important site – legal sites often act as arenas in which constantly evolving assemblages of risk claims are made, using a variety of often hybridized information formats (Moore and Valverde 2000).[5] Studying risk monitoring and management practices is, in turn, essential for an understanding of contemporary shifts in legal governance (as countless risk scholars have pointed out, and here we do not hesitate to cite Beck [1992]). Thus, the question – a question that is political as much as epistemological – is not whether courts or other legal arenas are impervious to science or subordinated to science or something in between (Jasanoff 1995); the question is, we suggest, what are the different effects of particular circuits of risk information?

Not Law and Risk but Rather Legal Processes and Risk Knowledges

Some contemporary social theorists have made careers out of claiming that risk is a modern or postmodern preoccupation (for example, Castel 1991). However, anyone familiar with the history of law knows that monitoring and managing risk and uncertainty has been a very important dimension of law's work for centuries, in insurance, tort, and contract law in particular (compare Baker and Simon 2002; Baker 2000; and O'Malley 2000). If we take this longer-term view – a view that does not reduce risk as such to actuarial techniques and/or clinical and epidemiological tools and that re-members that "old" sociolegal tools, such as the seventeenth-century prac-tices of insuring ships and their cargoes, played an important role in the development of types of non-statistical risk thinking that are still very com-monly used today – it then becomes clear that legal institutions and legal conflicts are excellent sites on which to study the different forms that risk thinking and risk management take.

Conversely, studying diverse types of risks as they appear in legal con-texts reveals a great deal about law and about state technologies more gen-erally. The reason for this is that despite the recent revival of harshly punitive, backward-looking vengeful measures, a modern legal system is in large part a tool for guaranteeing the future by minimizing risks. The English theorist Thomas Hobbes, writing at a time when modern European states were tak-ing shape, opined that (liberal) individuals are always resistant to foregoing either income or liberty. He argued that this is precisely the reason why it is so important for "moral and civil science" (including jurisprudence) to help state authorities to anticipate and minimize future "miseries" – that is, to govern under the sign of risk:

> For all men are by nature provided of notable multiplying glasses (that is their Passions and Self-love) through which every little payment appeareth a great grievance; but are destitute of those prospective glasses (namely Moral and Civil Science) to see a farre off the miseries that hang over them, and cannot without such payment be avoided. (Hobbes 1968 [1651], 239)

The miseries that hang over humanity, however, do not always appear as risks. As numerous scholars have pointed out, future miseries can be experi-enced as "dangers" rather than as risks (Castel 1991) or, alternatively, as an unpredictable series of one-off "uncertainties" (O'Malley 2004). And even when we see the term "risk" explicitly used and consciously separated from old-fashioned dangers and uncertainties, we still need to investigate the knowledge manoeuvres being used. Clinical risk, determined by a profes-sionally trained, discretionary gaze aimed at a particular individual, is a different sort of entity from the epidemiological risk affecting subpopula-tions, to give only one example from the health context. Clinical risk and epidemiological risk have different subjects (the wise professional versus the number-cruncher) and different objects (the individual patient versus the population). Yet, the one thing they share is a reliance on expert knowledges imparted through years of higher education. In legal contexts, however, risk determination is often thought to be something that the average prudent person does, and in some cases is obligated to do, without recourse to any particular experience of life or any educationally certified knowledge. Judges in breach of contract cases are not expected to use much, if any, expert knowledge to make decisions about which risks should or could have been foreseen by the parties. And perhaps more importantly, a whole array of legal contexts goes so far as to impose a responsibility to monitor risks on every person who happens to be present, regardless of training or personal experience (Levi and Valverde 2001).

We could proceed to lay out a typology of risks, or, more accurately, of risk knowledges, using such criteria as the presence or absence of statistics, the presence or absence of specialized professional judgment, and so forth. Typologies are useful; indeed, they are necessary, if one's goal is to elaborate a static model (of law, of society, of knowledge in general, and of the relation between law and society). This is why typologies are the key tool of traditional sociological theory. Yet our goal is not to elaborate any general model but rather to develop tools for the empirical, and, we emphasize, the dynamic, study of concrete situations. For this reason, we are interested in developing not a complete typology in the Max Weber tradition but rather a simple inventory of the sorts of knowledge moves that occur in various legal contexts. Using scientific language to authorize common sense (as observed in both of the case studies outlined below) and the swapping of knowledges between legally trained personnel (the prosecutors in the Megan's Law case study and the judge in the Toronto Drug Treatment Court study) and extra-legal professionals are two of the moves that we document, but which are not unique to these situations.

A dynamic analysis needs to regard not only knowledge but also law as dynamic. Thus, to avoid the reification that is inherent in the use of the noun "law," we prefer to speak about "legal processes" and "legal complexes" (Rose and Valverde 1998). The literature on legal pluralism pointed out a long time ago that law is a problematic term insofar as it privileges state regulation and state-enforced norms, separating them from mechanisms of regulation housed in other sites and institutions. We accept this insight, but we add to it that it is not sufficient to de-centre state law in favour of studies of informal or customary law and norms. It is also necessary to develop theoretical tools that will capture the actually existing heterogeneity and dynamism of state law itself. The fact that the risk knowledges that count in contract law are very different from those that are used in environmental assessments, which are in turn very different from those found in dangerous offender hearings, is well known to practising lawyers. We think it is crucial for scholars to reflect this heterogeneity – a heterogeneity sometimes reaching total incommensurability[6] in our own, once-removed work.

Law's Relation to Extra-Legal Knowledges: Beyond Normalization and Autopoeisis

In the 1970s and 1980s, legal and criminological scholars working with a variety of tools, and advocating a variety of agendas from feminism to law and economics, argued in different ways that legal determinations were increasingly shaped by extra-legal knowledges, particularly expert knowledges from psychology and genetics to economics and management studies. Feminists talked about "the medicalization of women's deviance" and denounced the use of psychiatry in legal and correctional settings, while a range of other studies and theoretical analyses forecast a day in which the legal system would be totally open to social science and to technical and biomedical evidence. Some, reinventing the wheel of earlier American legal realism, thought that this would make law more objective and more responsive to modern conditions. Others denounced this change as a new ruse through which extra-legal experts would gain new powers by appropriating legal mechanisms. Yet whether coming to praise expertise or to denounce it, these different kinds of studies tended to agree that – as François Ewald put it in an article that became a crucial reference in subsequent discussions of law and risk – the old world of sovereign power working through juridical yes-or-no rules was giving way to a new modern world of discipline and norms:

> The normative allows us to understand how communication remains possible even within a historical moment characterized by the end of universal values. The norm is a means of producing social law, a law constituted with reference to the particular society it claims to regulate and not with respect to a set of universal principles. More precisely, when the normative order comes to constitute the modernity of societies, law can be nothing other than social.
>
> This kind of law possesses two remarkable qualities: first, it is no longer based on a model in which the law emanates from a sovereign will. In a normative order, there is no room for the sovereign. No one can pretend to be the subject that establishes the norm: norms are created by the collectivity without being willed by anyone in particular ... The norm eliminates within law the play of vertical relations of sovereignty in favour of the more horizontal relations of social welfare and social security ... A norm is a self-referential standard of measurement for a given group; it can make no pretense to bind anyone for an indefinite period, as a law can. This is not to say that norms are ephemeral, for they are enormously durable. But they are

also inconstant, almost by definition. In the eyes of the business community, this capacity for adaptation and flexible response to changing conditions makes normalization superior to laws or regulations as a management
technique. Part of the norm's value derives from the fact that it is completely time-bound. (Ewald 1991a, 155-56; see also Ewald 1991b)

There is no lack of empirical support for Ewald's thesis about the normalization of law. Ewald's own study of the emergence of international standards
through the International Organization for Standardization; criminological studies of the proliferation of forensic risk assessments; and studies of
the tremendous popularity of "normalizing" knowledge formats (for example, best practices and audits [Power 1994]) across a wide range of fields
all suggest that contemporary legal complexes have indeed become recep-
tive to extra-legal knowledges to the point of sometimes deferring to them.

The evidence about the normalization of certain areas or activities of law
does not, however, justify a general theoretical claim that law as a whole is
functioning more and more like a norm. Technical information, social science, and other extra-legal types of evidence are not becoming uniformly
more powerful across law in general. There are a large number of instances
one could cite that would contradict Ewald's normalization of law thesis.
The case studies that we present below do not support such a wholesale
claim. Neither does the analysis of the knowledge practices supporting
"sexual orientation" human rights claims in recent Canadian law (Valverde
2003c, chapters 4 and 5). And if the normalization thesis would be difficult
to prove empirically, given that there is likely to be just as much evidence
against it as for it, perhaps more relevant to present purposes is the fact that
this thesis already presupposes that law is one thing that can be characterized as becoming more X or less X, as a whole.

Taking the perspective described earlier – the concrete analysis of specific
legal processes and complexes – allows us to sideline and circumvent the
never-ending, irresolvable arguments about whether it is somehow true that
law is increasingly normalized, dominated by expert knowledges, and so
on. We find it more productive to begin not by asking questions about law,
as such, but rather by asking questions about the specific role played by
knowledges of extra-legal and legal provenance in particular "problematizations" (Rose and Valverde 1998; Castel 1994).[7] The Drug Treatment
Court studied below, for example, is certainly a forum that is, by design,
unusually open to pharmacological knowledges of drugs and their effects.
Yet only the most superficial *a priori* analysis would suggest that this means
that the *Controlled Drugs and Substances Act* (1996, c. 19) has been handed
over to extra-legal professionals. The ethnographic study below paints a
dynamic picture of the actual workings of pharmacological knowledges,

one that among other things recognizes the great effectivity of common-sense pharmacology alongside expert-produced facts and norms. And it is important to recall that in any case, like so many other specialized courts, this court is designed to process only a small subset of all drugs charges, so that even if drug experts and/or their expertise were more powerful in the Toronto court than they actually are this would not warrant more general claims about law.

The normalization of law thesis is very popular in certain, largely socio-logical, quarters, but it has made little headway within legal scholarship, narrowly defined – not surprisingly, given that François Ewald and others writing in a loosely Foucaultian vein are mainly concerned to de-centre and deprivilege law. Within faculties of law, a more influential theoretical frame-work, seeking to provide a general explanation of the relation between law and extra-legal, mainly expert, knowledges, is that developed by Niklas Luhmann and Gunter Teubner, known as "autopoeisis" (*inter alia*, Luhmann 1989; Luhmann 1990; Teubner 1989; Teubner 1997).

Autopoeisis theory has drawn our attention to the ways in which law manages to incorporate not only eyewitness evidence but also other facts, such as scientific knowledge, into its own framework. Yet these theorists emphasize that these extra-legal knowledges become transmuted and lose much of their previous identity in the process. Law thus appears to be more open to outside knowledges than it really is, insofar as paying heed to these knowledges, and even using them to adjudicate, does not at all mean that legal logics are being displaced or trumped by scientific or technical logics of the norm. Luhmann and Teubner, as is well known, conclude that law is cognitively open but is normatively closed, by which they mean that infor-mation from other sources can flow in and even be held to be determinative even as legal logics retain their quasi-regal autonomy. This view of knowl-edge flows is grounded not in empirical studies but rather in Luhmann's general theory of society. In adopting biological evolutionary models to develop a "social systems theory," Luhmann believes that there is such a thing as society (a thesis firmly rejected by Foucault and all other post-structuralist thinkers) and that society is made up of subsystems, including law, which retain and even maximize their autonomy as society becomes more differentiated through what is presented as a well-nigh inevitable or-ganic process of internal differentiation.

For the same reasons that ground our critique of the use of law as a noun, we also reject the nineteenth-century teleological belief that society is best described as an organism or an ecosystem that becomes increasingly differ-entiated through a non-conflictual, organic, apolitical process. We hold that it is possible to agree with autopoeisis theorists that law's epistemological creativity should indeed be acknowledged – in contrast to the lack of recognition of this creativity shown by Ewald and Foucault – without thereby agreeing to the claim that law is an "autonomous epistemic subject" (Teubner 1989) that thinks in specific ways that sharply differentiate it from other subsystems. As the literature on law's constitutive power has amply shown (without any help from autopoeisis theory, incidentally), it is important to highlight the specific ways in which legal mechanisms and actors can and do totally transform the "inputs," including the knowledge inputs, that they receive or appropriate.

To conclude this very brief summary of how our approach differs from two influential alternatives – the normalization thesis and autopoeisis – it is perhaps sufficient to state that our main quarrel with both perspectives is not that they are unsubstantiated but rather that they are asking an impossible to answer, overly general question about law in general and its relation to extra-legal knowledges. Recognizing the importance of documenting processes of normalization that go on in legal contexts, we nevertheless see no need to make general statements about the likely domination of all legal forums by statistics-wielding experts. Similarly, we agree with autopoeisis theorists that legal processes have a great deal of epistemological autonomy and creativity. However, we see no need to postulate an ontologically separate social subsystem known as law. Whether legal networks are or are not relatively insulated from other networks is a matter for empirical investigation, not for *a priori* pronouncements. The numerous works in sociolegal studies that document unexpected reversals, unpredictable outbursts of successful resistance, tactical alliances of strange bedfellows, and highly creative uses of legal machinery have collectively demonstrated that the building of abstract models – of law, of society, of capitalism, and so on – did not always further, and often hampered, researchers. What requires a great deal more work than constructing theoretical models is the documentation and analysis of specific networks. For the purposes of physics, a model of an oxygen molecule works as a substitute for an actual molecule, but what is interesting about the social (including the legal) world is precisely the kind of inventiveness and historicity that escapes all model building. In this sense, we find ourselves agreeing with the pragmatist approach of Stanley Fish, which encompasses the main point of autopoeisis theory but without turning the point into a general theory:

> Legal autonomy should not be understood as a state of impossibly hermetic self-sufficiency, but as a state continually achieved and re-achieved as the law takes unto itself and makes its own (and in so doing alters the "own" it is making) the materials that history and chance put in its way. (Fish 1991, 69)

Keywords in ANT: Network, Actor, Translation, Black Box
Our study of legal knowledges draws much of its theoretical strength from the burgeoning field of science studies, in which researchers have investigated the ways in which scientific facts come to be produced (as well as known and disseminated). This research tradition has developed an approach known as actor network theory (ANT). Rather than blandly suggesting that scientific facts are "socially constructed," a move that merely opposes one knowledge (sociological and cultural) to another (the natural sciences), actor network studies suspend the usual distinctions between nature and culture, facts and values, material objects and human agency, in work that investigates the contingencies of knowledge production without presupposing a nature/culture binary. The focus of each study is a particular *network*. Networks are composed of certain relations among people, objects, ideas, scientific instruments, measuring practices, information codes, biological or chemical entities, and so on. These components are the actors.

Human, physical, and discursive elements are shown to be in constant relation with each other, as alliances, interests, controversies, and contingencies are negotiated by different *actants*. In Latour's study of Louis Pasteur's laboratory, for instance, the bacillus that gave rise to the bacterial theory of infection is treated as an actor alongside Pasteur himself (Latour 1988); also in his study of the ARAMIS failed transportation system, the politics of Parisian administrative practices are treated as an actor alongside train cars and computer chips (Latour 1996). The ultimate success or failure of particular networks may in fact turn out to hinge on the abilities of the human actors or on technological factors, but neither human agency, technological determinism, nor cultural determinism is assumed *a priori*.

Let us give a brief example. Latour's recent study of the Conseil d'Etat treats the architecture of the building, the portrait of Napoleon that is the only human representation in the building, and the wooden pigeonholes in which the members of the Conseil get their files as minor, but nevertheless significant, actors (Latour 2002). This is done not to claim that internal legal problems and logics are not worth studying but rather simply to show that all networks need specific material as well as discursive actors. In the case of the pigeonholes, their physical arrangement, which is by seniority rather than alphabetical, is shown to do a certain amount of political and legal work in the network that is the Conseil. And the fact that the *conseillers* are constantly going to their seniority-ranked pigeonholes to get their raw materials creates certain patterns of interaction. The interactions among walking bodies have minor, but nevertheless not trivial, legal effects that would be eliminated or changed if they received their documents by e-mail.

Both ideas and things are shown to depend, for their success, on chains of *translation*. Translation means both transposition into a different language, key, or code and the physical movement that was the original meaning of "translation." Translations of knowledge claims made by, and through, arranging components of a network are never exact reiterations but are always – like all translations of texts – unfaithful to some extent. If an idea or a technical invention is not taken up by other actors for their own network-building purposes, it will fail for lack of translation. ANT studies thus do not focus only on successful inventions or programs. They also document the time and energy spent developing various scientific, financial, and political inventions that did not in the end manage to become useful to a sufficient number of powerful networks. Since lawyers suffer the occupational hazard of being trained to ignore outdated law or unsuccessful arguments, something that has the unintended effect of making existing law seem inevitable, this emphasis on analyzing failures as well as successes is particularly helpful. Even if one studies a successful network, the methodology of ANT stresses contingency. The complex dynamic relations among people, things, texts, myths, buildings, and so on that make up a successful network (say, a point of "settled law") can be exposed, in all of their contingency, by focusing on the translations and other moves that keep the network constantly afloat. These relations, which make up all sociolegal life, become invisible if one simply looks at the outcome.

In legal practice, lawyers are keenly aware of the often unexpectedly crucial role played by objects – exhibits, advocacy skills, the physical appearance of witnesses and lawyers who are present in courtrooms, and so on – in the eventual success or failure of legal claims. After a case is finished, lawyers often talk about whether this or that tactic or object was the crucial entity that turned the jury or the judge this or that way. And experienced lawyers often know just what effects something (say, a photographic exhibit) will have on the network. Yet this practical knowledge has received little scholarly attention. Traditional legal scholarship tends to scrutinize law as a static and disembodied entity, paying no attention to the particular, physically located arrangement of entities, words, bodies, and documents. Whereas "law in action" studies do document struggles and tactics, they focus strictly on people and not on things or texts. Borrowing a few tools and terms from ANT may help to lay the groundwork for sociolegal scholarship that goes beyond the tired dichotomy of "law in the books" versus "law in action," which usually amounts to an unnecessarily stark choice between studying texts and studying people. A judgment of the Supreme Court of Canada can be read as law in action, we would argue, if one pays close attention to the processes and objects involved in its elaboration. The law that is "merely in the books" is also "in action" – it is an actant – insofar as it is constantly recycling objects and texts from other sources, being translated into new networks in innovative ways.

Thus, what we focus on is the constant circulation of various terms, tools, legal powers, non-legal knowledges, and so forth, in particular networks. This entails empirical work – and we want to stress that studying legal documents such as intervenor briefs is also empirical work – documenting how facts, legal principles, and institutional forms take various shapes, some of which eventually become successful. This eventual success has the effect of erasing (*black-boxing*, in ANT terminology) the process by which it was produced. An example of successful black-boxing in Canadian law is the *R. v. Oakes* test. At one point, this was a carefully elaborated, innovative network, whose components had to be explained and justified by the inventor. By now, however, it has become a "black box," used by courts and lawyers with the same nonchalance with which scientists in laboratories use inventions (for example, the microscope) that were once the subject of much admiration and controversy, but which have now become taken-for-granted tools whose contingent history can be ignored.

Risk and the Constitution of Expertise in Megan's Law

In this case study, we focus on the legal adjudication of community notification statutes – commonly known as Megan's Law – in the United States.[8] Among other measures, these statutes authorize, and at times mandate, the public dissemination of the identity of convicted sex offenders found to present a moderate to high risk of recidivism. Individuals subject to notification are not only those who commit their crime subsequent to the implementation of these statutes but also may include past offenders who have already been released and whose neighbours may now be informed of both their presence and their past offences.

As is well known, sex offenders have occupied a central place in criminal justice policy throughout the twentieth century (Jenkins 1998) – a place that cultural historians and historians of sexuality link to broader concerns over acceptable sexual behaviour, changing gender expectations, and the structure of the family (Chauncey 1993; D'Emilio 1989; Freedman 1987; Jenkins 1998). This focus resulted in a wide range of governance strategies designed to respond to different versions or forms of "sexual offending" over the course of the century.

The most recent governance strategy involves a partnership between the state and civil society, through which local residents are alerted to the presence of a sex offender in their neighbourhood. It is premised on the expert identification and assessment of risk factors, while encouraging individual residents, not experts, to manage that risk in their daily lives. With community notification now instituted across the United States, this model has resulted in four broad approaches that have been implemented in different states (Bedarf 1995; Finn 1997). In some jurisdictions, a state agency determines the level of risk an offender poses and then implements a community notification plan that reflects the offender's level of risk. In others, certain types of offenders are statutorily determined to be subject to notification, with the method of notification also determined by statute and carried out by a state agency. Not all approaches, however, involve notification carried out by the state alone. In some, offenders themselves are required to do the actual notification, while elsewhere community groups and individuals must request information about whether a sex offender is living in their community, sometimes for a fee.

In the present study, we focus on the implementation of community notification in New Jersey, the site of the original Megan's Law, named after a seven-year-old New Jersey girl raped and strangled by a neighbour who was a twice-convicted sex offender. Released from a treatment centre for compulsive sex offenders, he was living in the neighbourhood – along with two other sex offenders – unbeknownst to other residents (Siegel 1995). As with past measures designed to respond to sex offending, Megan's tragic story fuelled public support for community notification laws (Hagan 1985, 33; Klein, Luxenberg, and Clearly 1996; Levi 2003).

The management of risk figures prominently in the New Jersey model, which classifies sex offenders in three tiers. Using the results of a registrant risk assessment scale (RRAS), prosecutors classify registrants depending on the degree of risk of re-offending. No offenders are in Tier 0 since all registered sex offenders are presumed to pose some risk of re-offending. Tier 1 registrants are not subject to community notification – prosecutors notify only those law enforcement agencies likely to encounter the offender. When, however, a registrant is assessed as posing a moderate risk (Tier 2), prosecutors also notify those community organizations that are eligible to receive notification and that are "likely to encounter" the offender – organizations "in a location or in close geographic proximity to a location which the offender visits or can be presumed to visit on a regular basis." This determination is in the discretion of the prosecutor's office and may be "as small or large as the facts and circumstances warrant," although the discretion is subject to judicial review. Tier 3 offenders – found to present a high risk of re-offending – are subject to full-blown community notification. The prosecutor not only notifies law enforcement and community organizations but also notifies members of the public likely to encounter the offender, subject to judicial review.[9] This generally includes residents in the offender's neighbourhood and in areas he is likely to visit (*A.A. et al.* v. *New Jersey* 2001, 280). Fifteen years after being released, a registrant may apply to terminate the obligation to register, by proving that he is not likely to pose a threat to others. As of March 2001, 7,605 individuals had registered with the New Jersey State Police, with approximately 70 registrants added monthly. Of these, nearly 60 percent have been placed in Tiers 2 and 3 (Administrative Office of the Courts 2001, 7-14).

While past efforts, especially those that defined sexual offending as psychopathy, often involved attempts to reintegrate the offender after being treated by experts, community notification works instead on identifying and classifying offenders' risk profiles. This is justified not as a measure to treat or a means of condemnation but rather as a regulatory strategy designed to manage the risks of offending (Garland 2001; Feeley and Simon 1992). It is evident in the following passages from the constitutional litigation around Megan's Law in New Jersey:

> There can be no doubt that the Legislature acted with the purpose to address a present, serious public safety problem, not to punish past offenders. It is clear that protection of the public is a legitimate, non-punitive purpose. "There is no doubt that preventing danger to the community is a legitimate *regulatory* goal ... And, as [past cases] require, community notification under Megan's law is rationally related to the legitimate, non-punitive purpose – i.e. the unpleasant consequences must come about as a relevant incident to a regulation of a present problem. (Attorney General 1995, 25)

> The Registration and Notification Laws ... do not represent the slightest departure from our State's or our country's fundamental belief that criminals, convicted and punished, have paid their debt to society and are not to be punished further. They represent only the conclusion that society has the right to know of their presence not in order to punish them but in order to protect itself. (*Doe* v. *Poritz*, N.J. Supreme Court 1995, 372)

The prediction and management of risk factors have replaced the confrontation of individual dangerousness. Whereas Robert Castel (1991, 288) influentially argued that this shift away from danger and towards risk is a move away from the individual and towards collections of expert-determined factors and correlations, Nikolas Rose (1998) goes further by demonstrating that this risk thinking opens a space for different forms of community involvement and different relations between the individual pathological person, the community, and mental health professionals. The subsequent reconfiguration of risk – this time in combination with the political and cultural imagery of "community" – has implications for governance and law well beyond the realms of psychiatry and mental health.

Whereas most of the work concerning Megan's Law and its offspring focuses on questions about the legality of community notification practices, our study is drawn from a broader project in which the tools of ANT are relied upon to investigate how conceptual tools – in this case, notoriously vague concepts of community and risk – circulate in and through legal processes and shape the adjudication and normative contestation that take place in these domains (Levi 2003). Following this approach, we have elsewhere drawn on the ways in which the constitutionality of Megan's Law, although framed by courts and commentators as resulting from doctrinal tests, turns on an interaction between the knowledges of risk and community that are authorized by courts (Levi 2000; Levi 2003). In contrast to the view that is often invoked by many risk scholars, namely that we are witnessing the convergence of law with scientific normalization, our research, in this case study and the next, demonstrates that risk functions in different ways even within the same political/legal program and that this hybridity allows for the successful legal design of community notification. This is done by designing a program in which state expertise is marshalled in risk assessment, while lay notions of risk and prudence are mobilized to shift the daily burden of monitoring offenders onto residents, thereby insulating the state from legal and political challenges (Levi 2000). This structure recodes the state role regarding risk as information management rather than as crime control (Ericson and Haggerty 1997).

In the constitutional adjudication of Megan's Law, the courts have emphasized the scientific expertise that is said to be behind the registrant risk assessment scale (RRAS) in order to argue that Megan's Law is not a tool of punishment but rather an objective measure to regulate a social problem. And yet, all the while, the actual management of sex offenders is devolved onto police officers and, to an unusual extent, to members of a public constructed as entrepreneurially involved in their own safety.

Design of Risk Assessment in Megan's Law

Reliance on external expertise on risk plays an important legal function in the design of the law. The law's constitutionality is in large measure tied to its design as a regulatory (rather than punitive) scheme, and, in turn, its regulatory design is inextricably linked with the use of expert knowledge to classify these offenders. First, actuarial risk assessments are relied on by legislatures to conclude that sex offenders, as a group, present higher risks of recidivism that require some form of management post-release (Logan 2000). Second, the RRAS relied on in assessing a particular offender's risk is said to be based on science (see, for example, Sanderson 1995; Attorney General 2000, Exhibit E; Ferguson 1998, 3-4).

Yet, even at the initial stages of design, the actuarial justice that some might think is at the heart of Megan's Law is negotiated in and through non-expert criteria. First, legislatures are making political choices to rely on selected and sometimes contested scientific evidence regarding recidivism rates (Janus 1997; Heilbrun *et al.* 1998). Legislative reliance on these statistical findings is thus as much a legal and political choice as a decision taken on the basis of science (Logan 2000), with law being used to put an end to scientific debates (Beder 1991; Engelhardt and Caplan 1987). These non-expert determinations of closure are fundamental to allowing state and federal courts to come to terms with scientific debates. Whereas science is thought to justify, in broad terms, a program of community notification, it is law that is given primacy. As the New Jersey Supreme Court puts it, "conflicting studies and interpretations, especially concerning the precise numbers, abound, but as noted above, the resolution of the controversy in this area is solely a legislative matter" (*Doe* v. *Poritz*, N.J. Supreme Court 1995, 374 n. 1; *W.P.* v. *Poritz*, N.J. District Court 1996, 1221 n. 22).

Second, the validity of the RRAS itself had not been empirically demonstrated prior to being adopted. This is particularly telling. Although it includes criteria found to be positively related to sex offender recidivism, the scale excludes criteria that, though empirically found to correlate with recidivism, are insufficiently concrete, too cumbersome, too expensive to ascertain, or too difficult to reliably gather (*In the Matter of Registrant C.A.*, N.J. Supreme Court 1996, 104). Furthermore, the scale does not provide for clinical interviews of offenders, although it was agreed that this would improve its predictive reliability. Finally, the criteria included in the scale can be overridden (the override is a well-known feature of correctional RRASs), with exemptions for the use of the scale being based on offender statements or physical conditions.

Within the legal field, then, scientific conflicts and debates are erased:

> Although the scale was not field-tested, it was subjected to intense scrutiny by experts. Empirical validation of the scale is neither feasible nor practicable. Researchers would have to release offenders and then wait for five or ten years until they have enough data ... Obviously, it was not the Legislature's intent for the Attorney General to wait ten years before assigning offenders to tier levels. (*In the Matter of Registrant C.A.*, N.J. Supreme Court 1996, 107)

The problem is not only that closure is imposed on the scale's scientific value by political concerns. The scale, offered as a rationally derived, scientifically based objective standard, explicitly incorporates *legal* determinations of offence seriousness. A panel of mental health and legal experts developed the scale jointly and included not only the usual factors that are incorporated in clinical assessments but also legal factors. The manual explaining the use of the scale states:

> If, for example, one is dealing with a compulsive exhibitionist, although there may be a high likelihood of recidivism, the offense itself is considered a nuisance offense. Hence, the offender's risk to the community would be judged low, consistent with the low legal penalties associated with such

offenses ... Conversely, with a violent offender who has a history of substantial victim harm, even a relatively low likelihood of recidivism may result in a moderate or high potential risk to the community given the seriousness of a reoffense. (Attorney General 2000, Exhibit E)

The very design of New Jersey's Megan's Law, then, provides some hint that "risk" – although often thought, in New Jersey as in other places, to be the hallmark of shifts towards actuarial justice and the normalization of law – is itself the subject of contested forms of knowledge. We reiterate that we are not suggesting that outside expertise should play a larger role. Drawing together the work of Michel Callon (1986), Latour (1987, 2002), and Pierre Bourdieu (1987), we are interested in the process of "translation" – the alchemical changes that risk and its evaluation undergo when taken from the scientific to the legal field.

In the remainder of this case study, we draw this argument out further by focusing on risk management stages that lie beyond the initial design of the assessment instrument. In so doing, we highlight the creation of an intermediary form of knowledge regarding risk that is said to be enjoyed by legal actors, generated not through any particular training but instead earned on the job, through experience. This happens at two points in the legal process: (1) the determination and review of an offender's risk profile, reviewing prosecutorial decisions based on the RRAS and evidence presented by offenders; and (2) determinations regarding the proper geographic scope of notification and the role of expert witnesses in this context.

Determining Risk: Prosecutors, Judges, and Expertise

As originally contemplated by New Jersey's attorney general, determining an individual registrant's risk of re-offending was a matter for individual prosecutors, with no official notice being given to registrants so they could challenge their assessment. What is most interesting for our purposes is that implementing the scale was left to prosecutors, not clinicians or risk assessment experts. The attorney general justified this decision by invoking "the learning, the experience, the analytical skills and the insights bred from day-to-day involvement in the work of law enforcement" (Attorney General 1995, 12-32, 36). To aid them in their risk assessment work, prosecutors were provided with guidelines issued by the attorney general. These were largely illustrative and were designed to create a bridge from the criteria in the RRAS to the fact patterns that prosecutors might encounter. With these illustrations as their guide, prosecutors were then expected to assess whether the offender was best classified as posing a low, moderate, or high risk of re-offending. The illustrations provided were to be used only as a guide for decision making, so that prosecutors were to rely on their own discretion in deploying the scale and determining the meaning of the factors by relying on all "credible evidence" and taking into account "any information available" (Attorney General 2000, Exhibit E; *In the Matter of Registrant A.I.*, N.J. Superior Court, 1997).

While mental health experts argued that prosecutor-administered risk assessments may cause increased measurement error (Freeman-Longo 1996), the New Jersey courts took a different approach. These courts were also concerned with relying on prosecutors for this work. Yet, rather than defer to scientific experts, they instead translated the risk assessment into a different, more legal, format. The courts identified a hybrid form of expertise – a translation of risk expertise from actuarial and clinical prognostications to a format that is said to be the preserve of prosecutors and judges. Calling risk assessments an "inherently sophisticated business," the New Jersey Superior Court in *Doe* v. *Poritz* initially criticized the prosecutor's guidelines as "rather soft." The court noted the extensive discretion granted to partisan prosecutors as well as the lack of opportunity for registrants to challenge the results of any assessment:

> The Court finds it somewhat disturbing that the Legislature in its wisdom did not provide prosecutor offices with any additional resources to implement thorough risk assessments. Traditionally, in civil commitments and in domestic violence cases, the question of predicting future conduct of an individual has been perceived as the province of experts ... The same idea undergirds Megan's Law. Yet the law does not provide the prosecutor offices with professional help to assist them in evaluating the risk of re-offense and they must therefore make do with existing staff, whose training as lawyers did not include assessing the potential for recidivism by sex offenders. (*Doe* v. *Poritz*, N.J. Superior Court 1995, 1351-52)

The conclusion, however, is not that prosecutors must now rely on experts. Rather, the court determined that *judges* are "particularly well suited to the delicate task of weighing and balancing the private and public concerns inherent in risk assessment, and thus the level of notification merited by a particular case" (*ibid.* at 1352).

The New Jersey Supreme Court, however, decided on appeal that prosecutors were indeed to be presumptively accepted as experts on measuring the risk of re-offence, given their experience with sex offenders and their adequate knowledge of research in this area. The court even went as far as to claim that legal personnel (prosecutors) ought to be charged with making risk assessments not only on the grounds of fairness, or of familiarity with the practicalities of the legal system, but also because legal experts have the potential to produce more accurate risk assessments.

Much of the court's reasoning stems from its scepticism about scientific expertise. Research on re-offending risks is said to be "conflicting in its conclusions." Appealing to the anti-scientific prejudices of both politicians and legal personnel, the court went as far as to give courts "substantial power, beyond that permitted or used in ordinary litigation, to allow, reject, control, and limit expert testimony" so as to avoid "long drawn-out contests between experts" (*Doe v. Poritz*, N.J. Supreme Court 1995, 384). Registrants challenging their tier designation can in limited circumstances present some expert testimony, but the court privileges the knowledge of risk gained by prosecutors in their work experience. The court admits that legal expertise may provide inaccurate risk determinations, but it suggests that this situation – in which measurable risk is haunted by the spectre of non-measurable uncertainty – is no different than the potential inaccuracy of scientific risk assessments: "[W]e realize the generality of the standard against which the court will decide the correctness of the Tier level decision, but given the unavoidable uncertainties in this entire area, we do not believe it is realistic to impose requirements of proof of some statistical differentiation of the risk of reoffense" (*ibid.*).

This displacement of scientific expertise comes to a head in the New Jersey Supreme Court's 1996 decision in *In the Matter of Registrant C.A.* Faced with the registrant's argument that the scale is insufficiently reliable, the court responded by shifting the debate away from the scale entirely, rendering risk assessment a purely legal question:

> The scale, however, is not a scientific device. It is merely a useful tool to help prosecutors and courts determine whether a registrant's risk of reoffense is low, high, or moderate. Yet, the scale is just that – a tool ... a court should not rely solely on a registrant's point total ... any classification based on the scale should not be viewed as absolute ... there is still a value judgment to be made when determining a registrant's risk of reoffense and proper classification. (*In the Matter of Registrant C.A.*, N.J. Supreme Court 1996, 108-9)

If there was any question as to what was going on here, the New Jersey Supreme Court goes on in a later decision to emphasize that risk predictions must remain within the province of legal expertise because judges can enhance not only the fairness but also the very accuracy of those determinations:

> The benefit of allowing testimony to override a tier designation is that it can assist a court in arriving at a fairer and more accurate tier determination. Although experts opine that actuarial predictions are the best indicators of recidivism, it seems incongruous, given the statute's allowance for registrants to present evidence, to afford a seemingly rehabilitated offender no opportunity to alter his tier designation. (*In the Matter of Registrant G.B.*, N.J. Supreme Court 1996, 1263)

This subordination of risk assessment to the legal logics of adversarial justice and judicial and prosecutorial discretion was turned upon itself. The New Jersey Superior Court determined that the RRAS is neither binding on a court nor on the office of the prosecutor. The prosecutor enjoys discretion in applying the RRAS – it needs "not be rigidly followed in all cases" (*In the Matter of Registrant E.I.*, N.J. Superior Court 1997, 508-9). This discretion extends to status conferences, where registrants who have objected to their assessment can seek to reach an agreement with prosecutors so that full-blown hearings are not required. Not only might agreements be reached on tier determinations, but even within a tier the registrant and prosecutor might agree to circumvent the scope of notification that might otherwise be required. For instance, the parties and the judge might agree on the number of schools within a zone that will be notified; a registrant's score on the scale might be changed; or the scope of notification may be narrowed substantially, rather than following the guidelines (see situations in *Alan A. v. Verniero*, N.J. District Court 1997, 1166-67).

Thus, while the RRAS is continually invoked as evidence that Megan's Law relies on objective, scientific knowledge, the courts have created an intermediary knowledge in which legal actors – prosecutors and judges – are said not only to be more fair but even more reliable and accurate in determining a registrant's risk of re-offence. The judicial review process, with its attendant capacity for changing the results of risk assessments, is said to protect registrants from potential abuses, while the scale itself is described as protecting registrants from arbitrary subjective decisions that may otherwise have been reached by legal and law enforcement personnel.

However, a second conclusion arises. In an example of what we elsewhere in this essay call "knowledge swapping," courts, despite privileging legal knowledge in the risk assessment process, then rely on non-legal paradigms to renegotiate legal practices. For instance, in invoking risk as part of a predictive managerial strategy, New Jersey courts have determined that risk assessments can include acts or alleged acts that have not been the subject of a conviction. Prosecutors and judges can rely on reports of events in assessing risk levels even if the registrant was acquitted or never prosecuted for this event and may do so by relying on evidence from a range of sources that the court can then effectively authorize as reliable:

> We hold that the details of a sexual offense, which is not the subject of a conviction, may be considered in the risk assessment scale calculus. The judge may rely on documentation he or she considers relevant and trustworthy in making a determination ... This may include but is not limited to, criminal complaints not the subject of a conviction but which are supported by credible evidence, victim statements, admissions by the registrant, police reports, medical, psychological or psychiatric reports, pre-

sentencing reports, and Department of Corrections discharge summaries. (*In the Matter of Registrant C.A.*, N.J. Superior Court 1995, 347-48)

In a move that closes the circle of knowledge swapping – justified by reauthorizing the very same experts who had been earlier displaced by the courts in the risk assessment process – the state Supreme Court decided that non-conviction offences need to be included in this calculus because experts generally agree that past conduct is the best predictor of future behaviour (*In the Matter of Registrant C.A.*, N.J. Supreme Court 1996, 90).

Regulating the Spread of Risk Information

The goal of the risk assessment process in New Jersey is to determine the proper scope of community notification. The identity of Tier 1 registrants is released only to certain law enforcement agencies, not to the community; Tier 2 registrants are identified to specific organizations; and Tier 3 registrants are identified to a broader range of individuals and institutions that are likely to encounter him or her. The scope of notification, then, is closely tied to the image of community that is deployed in notifying the public of a registrant's presence, bringing the concepts of risk and community together in mutually constitutive ways. In addition, New Jersey courts have eschewed relying on expertise, using instead assumptions regarding community life and social interactions, but seeking to integrate these knowledges – legal knowledges of the social – with technical tools for standardization across cases. Once a registrant has been assigned to a tier, the scope of notification is determined through a "likely to encounter" standard. Prosecutors are given little direction in this process. Notifying selected organizations is discretionary. Even inclusion on the list of registered organizations does not guarantee that notification will be forthcoming. Prosecutors are told that a decision about the scope of notification should be made "on a case by case basis."[10] One prosecutor, when pressed to give reasons for his choice of scope of notification, asserted that "those locations that were within a two-mile radius of [a registrant's] place of residence and place of employment, he would likely encounter people in that area" (*In the Matter of Registrant G.B.*, N.J. Superior Court 1996, 307).

Courts have sought to deprivilege any expert evidence as to who a registrant is likely to encounter, adopting instead the following reading of the "likely to encounter" standard: "[T]he word 'likely' shall be taken in its usual sense: to mean not 'possibly' but 'likely', not in the sense of 'probably' but rather in the sense of 'having a fair chance to encounter'" (*Doe v. Poritz*, N.J. Supreme Court 1995, 385). One prosecutor had developed a set of criteria through which the scope of notification was tailored to population density. Registrants living in urban, high-density centres were thought to be likely to encounter people within a small area with a radius of 1,000 feet. Registrants in suburban and rural areas, by contrast, were likely to encounter people over a larger area of up to two miles radius. These criteria were not based on any evidence regarding the actual density of the population in the specific area or on any studies that population density is any guide for determining how far people will habitually travel. This fact, however, did not perturb the New Jersey Superior Court:

> Common sense projects that population density and societal mobility have a mutual relationship. The more concentrated the population, the more likely an adult is to limit his or her range of contact with members of the public. In high-population density areas, it is more likely that available resources, such as food stores, places for socializing, places which provide legitimate personal service, and the like, will be found with greater concentration. (*In the Matter of Registrant E.A.*, N.J. Superior Court 1995, 1081)

This theory of community is simply invoked as common sense. The theory depends on a second proposition, which is presented without empirical support, namely that population density leads to organized economic development. This is in turn connected to a theory that is not articulated here, namely that people will travel only as far as they have to – a theory that does not take urban public transportation into account, much less cultural studies of the attractiveness of certain urban locations to people who live rather far away. This theory of community, moreover, assumes that all individuals in the state of New Jersey are abstract legal persons – they have no religious, cultural, sexual, or ethnic preferences that might move them to travel far outside the legally drawn radius of community. Community is something one can draw on a map simply on the basis of population density, taking no account of the qualitative differentiation within the population:

> We reach these conclusions despite the fact the prosecutor presented no statistical data or studies on the reasonableness of the particular distances selected ... Moreover, we are satisfied that common sense can dictate reasonableness, a concept that when applied here demonstrates the establishment of a prima facie case for the scope of notification determination to residences in the area of E.A.'s places of residence and work. (*In the Matter of Registrant E.A.*, N.J. Superior Court 1995, 1081)

The effectivity of the court's theory of community life is perhaps most apparent when the court develops a new request for prosecutors presenting evidence at these hearings:

> Recognizing the need to facilitate the judicial review process, we direct the prosecutor in the future to prepare a grid, color-coded, large-scale map of

the county to identify the low-, moderate- and high-population density areas on a municipality by municipality basis. The map can be based on census data, county planning board data, or information provided by local planning boards and law enforcement officials to assist in refining the correctness of the prosecutor's knowledge of the county. (*In the Matter of Registrant E.A.*, N.J. Superior Court 1995, 1081)

Prosecutorial common sense is thus placed within a knowledge network that includes a material technical form – the colour-coded map – without which courts will in the future be less willing to accept the arguments made by prosecutors. These maps serve to inscribe, both on actual paper and in the law, the theories of community that have been developed in these cases, including lawyers' sociological ideas about how individuals interact within neighbourhoods. Since the *In the Matter of Registrant E.A.* case, the New Jersey Supreme Court has ruled that courts need not hear evidence from the prosecutor about the actual likelihood of a registrant encountering this or that subpopulation. Instead, "epicentres of notification" are to be marked on prosecutors' maps. These centres will determine the scope of risk assessment, with "the radius of notification being dependent on the urban, suburban, or rural nature of the location" (*In the Matter of Registrant M.F.*, N.J. Supreme Court 2001, 60-64).

Case Study Conclusion: The Relationship between Law and Expertise as Constantly Negotiated

Even in a situation in which risk expertise is explicitly put at the centre of a legal program of governance, we see that the relationship between law and expertise is constantly being renegotiated and reshaped. In this process of negotiation, the parties do not confine themselves to playing the chips that they were originally assigned. As we have seen, courts and prosecutors have been given the right to actually do the risk assessment, thus displacing the usual psychologically trained personnel, but, in turn, actuarial knowledge, and even the authority of science as such, is sometimes used to justify the rationality and appropriateness of novel legal forms.

The hybridity and amazing mobility of risk knowledges allows Megan's Law to fulfill different functions. Expert knowledges on risk are used – or, in some cases, merely alluded to – as evidence that community notification can be carried out in a manner that is not punitive and in a process that is described as part of the administration of risk, not the coercion of persons. This underwrites the legal argument that Megan's Law is regulatory, not punitive. Furthermore, with community being defined only geographically and with courts theorizing that individuals interact in ways that can be predicted by abstracted characteristics of urban space, no knowledge of the person or his or her communities is required for notification to proceed.

Communities are thus constructed as homogeneous, differentiated only by the quantitative criterion of population density. The visual technique of the map reassures legal personnel that decisions are being taken on objective and standardized grounds and not on the basis of whim or prejudice. The status of the map is not something that can be contested within the network itself (as Latour and Callon would say, the map is a highly effective black box). Law thus draws on science for its authority, while displacing its logic and its experts at the same time. This study confirms what the following case study will also show, namely that the relations linking and separating law and science as well as law and other knowledges cannot be understood by means of a static model. Authorization and deauthorization are processes that are never finished. These processes and relations are unpredictable, mobile, and constantly shifting and thus require a dynamic analysis.

Knowledge Swapping: Clinical and Legal Practices in Working on the Criminal Addict

Currently, languages and rationalities of risk are often invoked to justify therapeutic correctional programming (see Hannah-Moffat 2001). Programming developed within the welfare-state context of identifying people's needs and providing therapy can be saved from the neoliberal axe, as Hannah-Moffat's studies of Correctional Service of Canada have shown, if it is successfully redefined as targeting what the Correctional Service of Canada calls criminogenic needs/risks. Some of the early work on the new penology and risk thought that the rise of risk would be the death of needs-driven services, but it has turned out that needs have risen from the ashes of the welfare state by being rearticulated with risk. Certain needs that offenders have – such as the need for substance abuse counselling – can still be met by the same old welfare-state professionals if these needs are re-described as posing a risk to public safety.

One site in which the play of knowledges of offenders' needs/risks can be observed is the Drug Treatment Court in Toronto, which has served as a model for similar special courts in Vancouver and elsewhere. Observations of courtroom dynamics over a period of several months, as well as interviews with all of the key actors in the court (judge, lawyers, therapists, court liaisons) show that risk is monitored and managed through a swapping of legal and therapeutic knowledges. Toronto's Drug Treatment Court opened in 1998 as a federally funded initiative to stop the revolving door of crime. The court accepts individuals who offer an early guilty plea on non-violent criminal charges and have a proven "addiction"[11] to an opiate (mainly heroin) or else to cocaine or crack. Those enrolled in the program must make regular court appearances (twice a week to start) as well as report to treatment sessions, undergo a regime of random drug testing, and participate in the program evaluations. The purpose of court attendance is not only for clients to report to the judge but also so that they must sit through the entire court session to learn from the experiences of others appearing in the same court. If they successfully complete the first phase of the program they "graduate" and are guaranteed a non-custodial sentence, usually with a one-year probation.

The court is organized around certain notions of the risks posed by drug use. Following broader rationalities in the criminal justice system, the court is premised on the notion that drug use increases an individual's risk of committing crimes. This individual risk in turn translates into a risk to the community (as interviews with the legal personnel have emphasized). The therapeutic response – mandated treatment – is seen as a way to manage safety risks to the community.[12] The fact that this ambitious aim places the court in the position of both delivering and evaluating treatment, which is not the usual role of courts, is openly admitted. In the words of the presiding judge, "the purpose of this court is to *cure addiction*."[13] The treatment court is composed of six key official actors: the judge, the Crown, the duty counsel, a probation officer, and two court liaisons who represent the treatment team. The presence of treatment people in a courtroom is not particularly remarkable, but what is unusual is that legal knowledges do not act as filters for other kinds of expert knowledge. Instead, the legal knowledges about offending, sanctioning, and so on are made to share space – physical and legal – with clinical (mainly psychological) knowledges about drugs, risk, and rehabilitation.

When each client reports to the judge, the report almost always starts with the judge asking whether the client has any drug use to report to the court. Clients, interestingly, are not sanctioned for drug use as long as they are honest about it. One day, a man was called up who had been on methadone maintenance for a few weeks. When the judge asked him if he had any drug use to report he admitted he had been using heroin fairly regularly for the last week. The judge thanked him for his honesty, as he always did, and then asked him why he used. The man answered that he was "craving" heroin and had not been able to overcome the cravings. The judge then resorted to his own clinical knowledge to counteract this: "[L]ook, the whole purpose of methadone is to stop you from having cravings. That's why you're on methadone, so you don't feel that need to use the heroin anymore. That's how methadone works. And it's dangerous to mix methadone and heroin." The judge combined a certain pharmacological knowledge of the properties of drugs with the standard psychological knowledge of "craving" and coping mechanisms. This mix of pharmacology and psychology is precisely what is usually dispensed in assessment and treatment programs, although in these programs it is dispensed as clinical knowledge, whereas in the courtroom the same knowledge has both a clinical and a legal function.

Another example illustrates this mobility of risk knowledges. A woman we shall call Jane had been enrolled in the court program for over six months. From various comments made in court it appeared that Jane, a heroin user, was also suffering from hepatitis. Jane was clean for a long time but then relapsed. When she arrived in court after her relapse the judge gave her an extended lecture. He offered the usual police and correctional arguments about the undesirability of having a criminal record and the benefits of going "straight" and stressed that as long as she continued to use heroin she would not overcome the risks of being caught up in criminal justice sanctions. Yet the judge also offered Jane a clinical analysis of the interaction of drug use with her particular medical condition. He said:

> Using heroin isn't going to make your other medical problems better, it's going to make them worse. The [Jane] before me today is not the same person who was in this court a few weeks ago. You look worse, tired. Your eyes are sunken in and you look haggard. I can see the change in you.

As well as engaging in this sort of routine clinical risk assessment, the judge also took up psychological knowledges. Addressing "Courtney," a man who had been having recurrent problems in the program, the judge stated:

> I have never seen any period of time when you weren't in conflict with the program. It would seem at first blush that you really don't want to change but there is some part of you that does want to change. You come to court and you go to your programs. You know you're looking at significant time if you don't do it (the program). External pressure is fine but at some point the internal pressure has to come to make you want to change.

The judge was referring to a body of knowledges of "recovery," particularly motivation-based psychology, which holds that before you can expect someone to change a set of behaviours he or she has first to be motivated to change. Programming can be developed, according to this influential school, which starts to foster those motivations by using external forces such as the sanction and reward system followed by the court. At a certain point, the theory goes, the individual will begin to internalize motivations, and programming will no longer need to rely on external incentives to get an individual to want to change.

The judge's ability to bring his own psychological knowledges into the court did not merely serve the purpose of lecturing clients. It also acted as justification for legal actions. In the court, there is a standard set of bail conditions placed on each client. Invariably, one of them is that the client abstain from the use of alcohol. This condition is worth noting, in that the court is not mandated to deal with alcoholism, and, for the most part, clients do not have serious drinking problems. Still, alcohol is one of the drugs screened for, and, while at times, the judge will overlook alcohol use, drinking to the point of drunkenness is sanctionable behaviour. Alcohol is not designated as an addictive drug, but it is included on the theory that some substances that are not themselves targeted by the court's treatment (alcohol and marijuana, primarily) lower an individual's inhibitions and thus make clients less able to cope with "triggers," thus putting people at risk of relapse.

This is clearly seen in the case of a woman we shall call Karen. She had been clean of heroin use for a number of months. One day she was called before the judge and admitted to having consumed alcohol and marijuana over the weekend. The judge was more concerned with her alcohol use than with her marijuana use, and, faced with her retort that she has never been a real drinker, he counter-argued: "[A]lcohol acts to lower your inhibitions, making you more susceptible to temptations and less able to call on all the coping strategies learned in treatment. I know you're not an alcoholic. It's not the alcohol that's the problem, it's what the alcohol does to you." The same process can be observed in another situation. "Mark" was called before the judge and reported that in the previous week he smoked crack and dope. The judge asked for an explanation, and Mark said: "I was clean for so long I guess I just got overwhelmed by it. I went drinking with some friends and one thing led to another." The judge responded: "That's why we have in the bail 'no drinking.' It's not because we want the liquor companies to suffer but because drinking alcohol often makes people relapse." Mark's bail was then revoked, which meant he was in custody for one night.

The use of clinical knowledges of risk by legal actors for legal purposes is not limited to the judge. Crowns and duty counsel also invoke these knowledges, particularly when someone is facing expulsion from the program. Reasons for expulsion include lying to the judge, breaching bail conditions, dealing drugs to those in the program, or having new charges brought against one. Clients can also be ejected if they consistently show a lack of motivation to change. While ejection is not common, more often than not the grounds for ejection that are cited relate to motivation.

In the case of "Karen," consistent heroin use was cited to discuss possible expulsion. The Crown attorney stated that her repeated use was evidence of low motivation, arguing that "she had shown poor quality and quantity of effort in her own recovery and clearly doesn't want to be here." Duty counsel argued that Karen should stay in the program and that some time in detox would address the problem of persistent use. During the exchange between the Crown and duty counsel, Karen became extremely upset and said that she was no longer interested in being part of the court's program.

At this point, counsel asked for a sidebar with her client. Upon returning, counsel explained to the judge that Karen was having a difficult time at present but that (in the duty counsel's opinion) she was still motivated and wanting to stop using drugs. Thus, counsel did not deploy legal tools to defend Karen's legal rights. Rather, she offered her own clinical assessment of Karen's psychological state to counter the assessment that was offered by the Crown. The judge agreed that Karen still had sufficient motivation and decided not to expel her.

It is important to note that the swapping of knowledges is not unidirectional. While the use of clinical and psychological knowledges by legally trained actors employing specific legal powers is the most striking feature of the court, there is also, nevertheless, a movement in the opposite direction. The treatment team, which is put in the position of making recommendations about bail, custody, and so on, often deploys legal knowledges and logics rather than clinical ones. Two examples of this process will suffice to illustrate this shift. A woman by the name of "Jess" is called up, and, when asked, she reports no drug use. The judge then looks at her file, which is in front of him, and says: "I see you missed a group last week." "That's right," says Jess, "I got the times mixed up." One of the members of the treatment team then gets up and addresses the court, saying: "Your Honour, I can confirm that Jess did miss her appointment on X day, and we are asking for two hours of community service as a sanction for this. We further want to remind her of the importance of attending groups and that it is her responsibility to be clear on the timing of appointments." This excerpt demonstrates extra-legal personnel trained in psychology and addiction studies using a typical legal rationale in asking for court-enforced punishment.

An exchange with another client is our second example of how treatment personnel sometimes participate as equal partners in the legal punishment process:

Sam is new to the program so his continued drug use has always been excused; he has typically been commended for being honest about having used.[14] Today, though, Sam admits that he missed a treatment group and a drug screen. A member of the treatment team stands up to speak. She indicates that the team is concerned about Sam missing a group, and that his case management officer has recommended that he do four hours of community service in order to make up for the group. The Crown is next to speak, arguing that Sam's continued use, coupled with his failure to attend one group session, calls into question Sam's motivation. On the basis of this judgment about motivation, the Crown asks for a revocation of Sam's bail. The defence argues that it is still early days, and that he has been honest with the court about both his use and his missed group. The judge then decides to revoke bail, agreeing with the Crown that Sam needs to show greater motivation. Sam is taken into custody and led away.[15]

We see the complete circle of knowledge swapping. The Crown argues for revocation of bail using a psychological argument – lack of motivation – rather than any claims about law breaking or public safety. On their part, the treatment team seems to take the place of the Crown, arguing for sanctions on a retributive basis (four hours of community service for having missed one group therapy session).

To conclude this case study, it is important to note that the swapping of knowledge is not simply a result of one-time social interactions between actors with different training. The swapping is built into the very structure of the court. In an interview, the judge explained that he is not himself an expert on addiction. Rather, the team structure of the court (best exemplified in the pre-court conferences, which unfortunately were not open to researchers) allows everyone in the court to use the same knowledges. The self-designated team participates in development retreats together, takes classes and workshops together, and meets together every court day to pre-discuss cases coming up that afternoon. (The court sits every Tuesday and Thursday afternoon.) The use of the term "team" is quite purposeful since it erases the institutional distinctions that would in other situations not only divide people but set them at cross-purposes.

The fact that all the regular players are able to draw on a more or less common fund of knowledges is made all the more evident when one of them is replaced by a novice. In the summer, the primary judge takes holidays and is replaced by a judge whose conduct is very different from that of his. The replacement judge asks the same pat questions of every client ("How are you doing?" "How long have you been in the program?" "Did you use drugs?") and he holds nearly all decisions over until he is able to get the opinion of the treatment team.

The swapping of knowledges documented in this essay may raise some troubling legal questions. However, for present purposes, the key finding is that it is unwise to come to conclusions about the power and influence of particular discourses and institutions interacting with, or appearing in, legal arenas without a close empirical study of how knowledges are actually deployed, for what purpose, and by which actors. A drug treatment court does not necessarily amount to "medicalizing" rather than "criminalizing" drug use, and, in turn, even when psychological and medical judgments are clearly visible, it does not mean that the effects on offenders are beneficial and therapeutic. As we have seen, clinical judgments (especially about motivation – that elusive psychic substance) can be and are used to throw people in jail. Who uses which knowledges, in what ways, and with what effects, cannot be settled *a priori*. Knowledge processes are highly dynamic and creative and are less confined by institutional and professional boundaries than the literature on medicalization and on risk suggests.

Conclusion

Contemporary legal developments often involve appeals to the preventive, future-oriented logic of risk. This is well known already from the literature on actuarial justice and from studies of environmental law, insurance, and so forth. Yet what has not yet been widely noticed is that these contemporary developments do not necessarily involve parachuting scientific or technical experts to make determinations of risk in legal contexts. Often, they not only feature legally trained personnel, mainly judges and prosecutors, but also government lawyers writing briefs, taking on the task of measuring risks, and assessing their potential impact on victims, on neighbourhoods, on public safety, and on the community.

This process cannot be described as a one-way street in which the law somehow absorbs and transforms and dominates extra-legal knowledges (as would be suggested by autopoeisis theorists). The process is much more dynamic, interactive, and, if one can use this word without appearing to downplay the very serious consequences that law has for people, playful. We have seen New Jersey courts hand over the power to measure the risk of sexual offending to prosecutors, but they justify this process by reference to the scientific authority of the knowledge facilitating the prosecutor's measuring work. We have also seen a specialized court in Toronto make the rather non-judicial claim that the court's purpose is "to cure addiction." And yet close analysis of all the actors involved in this court shows that legal and judicial rationales (such as making a decision to detain someone in custody subject to the logic of retribution rather than that of therapy) are by no means displaced by the new therapeutic ambitions. We have documented a process that we have dubbed "knowledge swapping," but we emphasize that the processes are much more complex than the word "swapping" would suggest, since the exchange is never final, and the exchange transforms the thing or the idea that is swapped.

ANT is by no means the only useful source of analytical tools for the dynamic study of the interactive processes by which knowledges and powers are constantly re-created and reinvented in legal networks. It offers much as a potential analytical resource, and we present this framework – and our case studies – not as the truth about law but rather in the spirit of analytical experimentation. If the game of law can be usefully described as a constantly re-negotiated series of networks, then this work itself is but an actor whose later fate we cannot determine, control, or judge.

Notes

1 We follow Michel Foucault, whose work, by contrast with traditional studies identifying "knowledge" with science, always stressed the plurality of knowledges and rationalities. Max Weber, of course, pioneered the research-grounded study of varieties of rationality, but his theorization generated very broad categories, such as means-end rationality. We follow the Foucault-inspired governmentality literature in focusing on more specific rationalities (see Rose 1999).

2 The "everyday life of law" literature, informed by legal pluralism, has been the key sociolegal project to draw our attention to the importance of studying how non–legally trained people use and interpret law. Although we do not place ourselves in this school, our work would not have been possible without it (for example, Greenhouse, Yngvesson, and Engel 1994; Ewick and Silbey 1998; Merry 1990).

3 "But the 'lawful aim' is the last thing that should be used to investigate the history of the genesis of law: there is, rather, no more important principle for all types of history than the following one, which it has taken such effort to acquire ... and that is, that there is a world of difference between the reason for something coming into existence in the first place and the ultimate use to which it is put, its actual application and integration into a system of goals; that anything which exists, once it has somehow come into being, can be reinterpreted in the service of new intentions, repossessed, repeatedly modified to a new use" (Nietzsche 1996, 57).

4 Latour's description of the overall modern project to replace ideology by enlightenment certainly applies to critical legal studies, whose political aims we share but whose intellectual tools we seek to replace. In this project, "it was only a matter of choosing a cause for indignation and opposing false denunciations with as much passion as possible ... To reveal the true calculations underlying the false consciousness, or the true interests underlying the false calculations" (Latour 1993, 44).

5 We have been influenced by Richard Ericson's extensive work on "information formats" and by his argument that much policing and security work is not really crime control but is more accurately described as information production and information control (Ericson, Baranek, and Chan 1991; Ericson and Haggerty 1997).

6 A fascinating study of how environmental impact assessments have tried to make incommensurable knowledges commensurable through a rational-choice model is Wendy Espeland's study of a large hydrological project in Arizona (Espeland 1998). A similar point is made from another perspective by Mary Poovey in her study of early British social reformers and their efforts to make urban space homogeneous and measurable (Poovey 1995). In general, the literature on the sociology of knowledge has only begun to be read and used by legal scholars, but we think it offers legal studies extremely fruitful resources.

7 "Rather than seeking to unify law, either jurisprudentially or genealogically, we would prefer to take an alternative route. While it might seem obvious to begin by asking 'what does law govern?,' from the perspective of government we would not start from law at all. Instead, we would start from problems or problematizations. A problematization, here, is a way in which experience is offered to thought in the form of a problem requiring attention. The analysis of problematizations is the analysis of the practices within which these problematizing experiences are formed. The intellectual premises and analytic methods of legal studies tend to presuppose that objects and problems form within the workings of law itself. But in order to analyze the ways in which problems form at the intersection of legal and extra-legal discourses, practices, and institutions, it is necessary to de-centre law from the outset" (Rose and Valverde 1998, 545).

8 "Megan's Law" is a generic term.

9 *Attorney General Guidelines for Law Enforcement for the Implementation of Sex Offender Registration and Community Notification Laws* (New Jersey, March 2000) at 13-14.

10 *Ibid.* at 25.

11 The individual's claim to addiction has to be validated, first by an initial screening process conducted by the Crown and then by a clinical assessment at the Centre for Addiction and Mental Health.

12 The Crown attorney who has worked most consistently in the court, Kofi Barnes, is particularly vocal in stressing that the court manages public safety better than traditional courts.
13 Taken from Dawn Moore's research notes.
14 The focus on honesty rather than drug use, which may seem to be influenced by judicial habits such as evaluating the truthfulness of witnesses, is justified not with legal, but with psychological, knowledges. The judge, as well as other personnel, believes that anyone who does not relapse must not have been truly addicted. Thus, continued drug use, while exposing clients to sanctions, simultaneously acts to validate their participation in the program, since only addicts, not occasional users, are allowed in.
15 This quotation is taken from Dawn Moore's research journal.

References

A.A. et al. v. *New Jersey*, 176 F. Supp. 2d 274 (Dist. Ct. N.J. 2001).
Administrative Office of the Courts, Criminal Practice Division *Report on Implementation of Megan's Law* (New Jersey, 1 June 2001).
Alan A. v. *Verniero*, 970 F. Supp. 1153 (Dist. Ct. N.J. 1997).
Attorney General. *Brief of the Attorney General of New Jersey in Doe* v. *Poritz*, No. 39,989 (filed 4 April 1995).
–. *Brief of the Attorney General of New Jersey in W.P.* v. *Verniero*, No. 96-5416 (filed 26 August 1996).
–. *Attorney General Guidelines for Law Enforcement for the Implementation of Sex Offender Registration and Community Notification Laws* (New Jersey, March 2000).
Baker, T. 2000. "Insuring Morality." Economy and Society 29(4): 559-77.
–. 2002. "Risk, Insurance and the Social Construction of Responsibility." In T. Baker and J. Simon, eds., *Embracing Risk: The Changing Culture of Insurance and Responsibility*. Chicago: University of Chicago Press.
–, and J. Simon, eds. 2002. *Embracing Risk*. Chicago: University of Chicago Press.
Beck, U. 1992. *Risk Society*. London: Sage.
Bedarf, A.R. 1995. "Examining Sex Offender Notification Laws." California Law Review 83: 885.
Beder, S. 1991. "Controversy and Closure: Sydney's Beaches in Crisis." Social Studies of Science 21: 223.
Bourdieu, P. 1987. "The Force of Law: Toward a Sociology of the Juridical Field." Hastings Law Journal 38: 805-53.
Callon, M. 1986. "Some Elements of a Sociology of Translation: Domesticating the Scallops and the Fisherman of St Brieuc Bay." In J. Law, ed., *Power, Action, and Belief: A New Sociology of Knowledge?* Boston: Routledge and Kegan Paul.
–, and J. Law. 1997. "After the Individual in Society: Lessons on Collectivity from Science, Technology, and Society." Canadian Journal of Sociology 22(2): 165-82.
Castel, R. 1991. "From Dangerousness to Risk." In G. Burchell, C. Gordon, and P. Miller, eds., *The Foucault Effect: Studies in Governmentality*. Chicago: University of Chicago Press.
–. 1994. "Problematization as a Mode of Reading History." In J. Goldstein, ed., *Foucault and the Writing of History*. Oxford: Blackwell.
Chauncey, G. 1993. "The Postwar Sex Crime Panic." In W. Graebner, ed., *True Stories from the American Past*. New York: McGraw Hill.
D'Emilio, J. 1989. "The Homosexual Menace." In K.L. Peiss, C. Simmons, and R.A. Padgug, eds., *Passion and Power: Sexuality in History*. Philadelphia: Temple University Press.
Doe v. *Poritz*, 661 A. 2d 1335 (N.J. Super. Ct. 1995).
Doe v. *Poritz*, 662 A. 2d 367 (N.J. Sup. Ct. 1995).
Engelhardt, H.T., and Al Caplan, eds. 1987. *Scientific Controversies*. Cambridge: Cambridge University Press.
Ericson, R., P. Baranek, and J. Chan. 1991. *Representing Order: Crime, Law, and Justice in the News Media*. Toronto: University of Toronto Press.
–, and A. Doyle. 2004. *Uncertain Business: Risk, Insurance, and the Limits of Knowledge*. Toronto: University of Toronto Press.
–, and K. Haggerty. 1997. *Policing the Risk Society*. Toronto: University of Toronto Press.

Espeland, W. 1998. *The Struggle for Water: Politics, Rationality and Identity in the American Southwest*. Chicago: University of Chicago Press.

Ewald, F. 1991a. "Norms, Discipline, and the Law." In R. Post, ed., *Law and the Order of Culture*. Berkeley: University of California Press.

–. 1991b. "Insurance and Risk." In G. Burchell, C. Gordon, and P. Miller, eds., *The Foucault Effect: Studies in Governmentality*. Chicago: University of Chicago Press.

Ewick, P., and S.S. Silbey. 1998. *The Common Place of Law: Stories from Everyday Life*. Chicago: University of Chicago Press.

Feeley, M., and J. Simon. 1992. "The New Penology: Notes on the Emerging Strategy of Corrections and Its Implications." *Criminology* 30: 449.

Ferguson, G. 1998. "An Investigation into the Risk Validity of the Registrant Risk Assessment Scale as a Legal Tool and Clinical Instrument" (Ph.D. dissertation, Union Institute).

Finn, P. 1997. *Sex Offender Community Notification*. Washington, DC: National Institute of Justice.

Fish, S. 1991. "Almost Pragmatism." In M. Brint and W. Weaver, eds., *Pragmatism in Law and Society*. Boulder: Westview.

Foucault, M. 1973. *The Order of Things*. New York: Vintage.

Freedman, E. 1987. "Uncontrolled Desires: The Response to the Sexual Psychopath 1920-1960." *Journal of American History* 74: 83.

Freeman-Longo, R.E. 1996. "Feel Good Legislation: Prevention or Calamity." *Child Abuse and Neglect* 20: 95.

Garland, D. 2001. *The Culture of Control: Crime and Social Order in Contemporary Society*. Chicago: University of Chicago Press.

Greenhouse, C.J., B. Yngvesson, and D.M. Engel. 1994. *Law and Community in Three American Towns*. Ithaca: Cornell University Press.

Hagan, J. 1985. *Modern Criminology: Crime, Criminal Behavior, and Its Control*. New York: McGraw Hill.

Hannah-Moffat, K. 2001. "Criminogenic Need and the Transformative Risk Subject: Hybridizations of Risk/Need in Penality" (Manuscript, Sociology Department, University of Toronto).

Heilbrun, K., *et al.* 1998. "Sexual Offending: Linking Assessment, Intervention, and Decision Making." *Psychology, Public Policy, and Law* 4: 138.

Hobbes, T. 1968 (1651). *Leviathan*. Harmondsworth: Penguin.

In the Matter of Registrant A.I., 696 A. 2d 77 (N.J. Super. Ct. 1997).

In the Matter of Registrant C.A., 285 N.J. Super. Ct. 343 (1995).

In the Matter of Registrant C.A., 146 N.J. 71 (Sup. Ct. 1996).

In the Matter of Registrant E.A., 667 A. 2d 1077 (N.J. Super. Ct. 1995).

In the Matter of Registrant E.I., 693 A. 2d 505 (N.J. Sup. Ct. 1997).

In the Matter of Registrant G.B., 669 A. 2d 303 (N.J. Super. Ct. 1996).

In the Matter of Registrant G.B., 685 A. 2d 1252 (N.J. Sup. Ct. 1996).

In the Matter of Registrant M.F., 169 N.J. 45 (Sup. Ct. 2001).

Janus, E.S. 1997. "The Use of Social Science and Medicine in Sex Offender Commitment." *New England Journal of Criminal and Civil Confinement* 23: 347.

Jasanoff, S. 1995. *Science at the Bar: Law, Science and Technology in America*. Cambridge, MA: Harvard University Press.

Jenkins, P. 1998. *Moral Panic: Changing Concepts of the Child Molester in Modern America*. New Haven: Yale University Press.

Kelling, G., and J.Q. Wilson. 1982. "Broken Windows" *Atlantic Monthly*. February.

Klein, J., J. Luxenburg, and S. Cleary. 1996. *The Fire Next Door: Megan's Law and the Impact of Media Images on the Formation of Social Policy*. Society for the Study of Social Problems.

Latour, B. 1987. *Science in Action*. Cambridge MA: Harvard University Press.

–. 1988. *The Pasteurization of France*, translated by A. Sheridan and J. Law. Cambridge, MA: Harvard University Press.

–. 1993. *We Have Never Been Modern*. Cambridge, MA: Harvard University Press.

–. 1996. *Aramis, or, the Love of Technology*, translated by C. Porter. Cambridge, MA: Harvard University Press.

–. 2002. *La fabrique du droit: une ethnographie du Conseil d'Etat*. Paris: La Decouverte.

Levi, R. 2000. "The Mutuality of Risk and Community: The Adjudication of Community Notification Statutes." Economy and Society 29(4): 578-601.

–. 2003. "The Constitution of Community in Legal Sites: A Study of Law, Crime, and Its Control" (S.J.D. dissertation, Faculty of Law, University of Toronto).

–, and M. Valverde. 2001. "Knowledge on Tap: Police Science and Common Knowledge in the Legal Regulation of Drunkenness." Law and Social Inquiry 26(4): 819-46.

Logan, W.A. 2000. "A Study in 'Actuarial Justice': Sex Offender Classification Practice and Procedure." 3 Buffalo Criminal Law Review 593.

Luhmann, N. 1989. "Law as a Social System." Northwestern Law Review 83: 136-50.

–. 1990. *Essays on Self-Reference*. New York: Columbia University Press.

Merry, S. 1990. *Getting Justice and Getting Even: Legal Consciousness among Working Class Americans*. Chicago: University of Chicago Press.

Moore, D., and M. Valverde. 2000. "Maidens at Risk: Date Rape Drugs and the Formation of Hybrid Risk Knowledges." Economy and Society 29(4): 514-31.

Nietzsche, F. 1996. *On the Genealogy of Morality*, translated by D. Smith. Oxford: Oxford University Press.

O'Malley, P. 2000. "Uncertain Subjects: Risks, Liberalism, and Contract." Economy and Society 29(4): 520-31.

–. 2004. *Risk, Uncertainty, and Government*. London: Cavendish.

Poovey, M. 1995. *Making a Social Body: British Cultural Formation, 1830-1864*. Chicago: University of Chicago Press.

Power, M. 1994. "The Audit Society." In A. Hopwood and P. Miller, eds., *Accounting as a Social and Institutional Practice*. Cambridge: Cambridge University Press.

R. v. Oakes, [1986] 1 S.C.R. 103.

Rose, N. 1998. "Governing Risky Individuals: The Role of Psychiatry in New Regimes of Control." Psychiatry, Psychology and Law 5: 177.

–. 1999. *Powers of Freedom: Reframing Political Thought*. Cambridge: Cambridge University Press.

–, and M. Valverde. 1998. "Governed by Law?" Social and Legal Studies 7(4): 541-52.

Ruppert, E. 2002. "The Moral Economy of Cities: Security, Consumption, Aesthetics" (Ph.D. dissertation, Sociology Department, York University).

Sanderson, B. 1995. "Battles Loom over Sex Crimes Score Card: Point System Part of Megan's Law." Record, 16 September 1995, A1.

Siegel, R. 1995. "Megan's Alleged Killer Appears before Judge: Mercer Prosecutor Can Stay on Case." Record, 10 June 1995, A3.

Simon, J. 2002. "Taking Risks: Extreme Sports and the Embrace of Risk in Advanced Liberal Societies." In T. Baker and J. Simon, eds., *Embracing Risk*. Chicago: University of Chicago Press.

Teubner, G. 1989. "How the Law Thinks: Toward a Constructivist Epistemology of Law." Law and Society Review 23(5): 727-58.

–. 1997. "The King's Many Bodies: The Self-Destruction of Law's Hierarchy." Law and Society Review 31(4): 763-87.

Valverde, M. 1999. "Justice and Gender in Deconstruction" (review-essay of Derrida's *The Politics of Friendship*). Economy and Society 28(2): 300-11.

–. 2003a. "Police Science, British Style: Pub Licensing and Knowledges of Urban Disorder." Economy and Society 32(2): 234-52.

–. 2003b. "Pragmatic and Non-Pragmatic Knowledge Practices in American Law." Forthcoming in Political and Legal Anthropology Review.

–. 2003c. *Law's Dream of a Common Knowledge*. Princeton: Princeton University Press.

W.P. v. Poritz, 931 F. Supp. 1199 (Dist. Ct. N.J. 1996).

5
Evidentiary Principles with Respect to Judicial Review of Constitutionality: A Risk Management Perspective
Danielle Pinard

> In the premodern world, the division between fact and theory, among other things, had class overtones ... "lower strata collected facts while higher ups advanced principles ... contact between the two types of knowledge was discouraged by custom."[1]
> – Sheldon Krimsky, citing Philipp Frank, *Philosophy of Science*

To a certain extent, the legal realm still seems to be relatively premodern in this respect. A hierarchical distinction appears to be drawn between the nobility associated with addressing the great questions of law and the humble nature of using petty evidentiary techniques to establish facts. This hierarchy is misleading. Significant and frequently subtle judicial power is exercised under cover of the so-called passive establishment of facts. The idea of risk has given rise, in recent years, to a wide and impressive range of intellectual output. In economics, in political science, and in environment and public health, questions are being asked about risk and appropriate methods for its assessment and management.[2] With the exception of insurance issues, or the dangerousness of individuals within a criminal context, the legal realm seems to have been slower to integrate the concept of risk as a conceptual tool. However, it is making up for lost time. As proof of this transformation, important publications, such as a journal dedicated exclusively to the management of risk through law,[3] have recently made an appearance. The very emergence of this fascination with the concept of risk is in itself a phenomenon worthy of interest.

The role of the concept of risk in the legal realm, although not entirely foreign to this general context, still presents some special features. In this text, we will try to use this idea of risk as a tool for analyzing the interaction of factual and normative issues at play in constitutional challenges with respect to the violation of rights and freedoms. After some reflection on the concept of risk and its usefulness in matters of tests of constitutionality

(Part 1), we will present illustrations of the judicial handling of risks and, therefore, of factual uncertainty (Part 2).

Part 1: The Concept of Risk and Tests of Constitutionality

Concept of Risk

A simple definition of risk will be used in this document, namely the possibility of experiencing a harmful, dangerous, or otherwise undesirable event.[4] This definition emphasizes two essential components of the concept of risk: the factual element, or uncertainty with respect to the event's occurrence, and the normative element, or its undesirable nature. The first requires statistical and mathematical analyses in order to establish correlations and causal relationships – it is the world of objectivity and empirical observation, the realm of scientific experts. The second, the normative aspect, is less certain, less clear. It is the social, political world, the world of value judgments with respect to desirability, undesirability, reasonableness, beneficial effects, and prejudice.

It seems that the literature with respect to risks mainly addresses the factual component – the so-called objective aspect of the issue. In no way the result of chance, this interest is a reflection of the significant ideological utility of this literature, which obscures the social and political in favour of the empirical, scientific, and objective.[5] Debates on the social utility or the political expediency of a project therefore give way to expert debates on complex scientific systems of analysis, debates in which, by definition, lay opinions lose all relevance.[6] However, political choices cannot be reduced to empirical considerations, for at least three reasons. First, there is confusion with respect to type. Social or political issues and questions of values are not limited to the consideration of empirical data. A complete analysis of the relevant factual data does not exhaust the issue of a project's relevance. The issue of choice, decision, or preference cannot be avoided.[7] Second, scientists cannot guarantee the certainty or objectivity that we expect from them. On the one hand, scientists quite often do not have an answer to the question at hand. Those outside the world of science commonly have a naïve and legendary view[8] that science can provide us with all the factual information required to unequivocally justify social choices. However, we are told that it is too late for such a naïve point of view. Once of the opinion that it was omniscient, science now is aware of the things it does not know.[9] On the other hand, scientists can only rarely provide the "neutrality" or "objectivity" attributed to them by this naïve view. Beyond the laboratory and statistical models, scientific knowledge is developed under social conditions of production, which, duly considered, should mitigate all expectations of absolute objectivity.[10]

Finally, beyond the double limitations inherent in the world of science (its inability to answer normative questions or even to fully answer the factual questions that are at the heart of these normative questions), recourse to science alone cannot satisfy the inherent requirements of the process related to any social or political decision. In a society with claims to democracy, the process by which norms are developed becomes crucially important. Especially in the context of risk management, the rationality of the decision implies a process that makes the democratic legitimacy of the decision maker a relevant issue – an issue through which those who are expected to assume the risk must have the opportunity to be heard.[11] Regardless of its relative ineffectiveness, this attempt to obscure the discussion of social choices with scientific debates on empirical issues obviously serves the interests of those who control the means of knowledge production and those whose normative position, alone, is not convincing.[12]

Tests of Constitutionality
What is the relevance or utility of this concept of risk in the context of judicial tests of constitutionality based on alleged violations of rights and freedoms? In order to attempt a response to this question, we must recall an aspect of the historical development of tests of constitutionality, namely, the movement from a conceptual and abstract approach to a concrete and factual one. For a long time, Canadian courts have handled the constitutional questions presented before them as pure questions of law,[13] requiring an analysis of legislative and constitutional texts, interpretation, reasoning, and, if necessary, the study of the preparatory work.[14] Concerns with respect to any factual aspect have emerged only slowly and progressively. Generally, the 1976 *Anti-Inflation Act* reference,[15] with its discussion of Canada's economic situation, is considered pivotal in this respect. Shortly thereafter, the 1982 adoption of the *Canadian Charter of Rights and Freedoms*[16] confirmed and increased this judicial requirement to demonstrate the empirical basis of laws in order to confirm their constitutional validity. The constitutionalization of rights and freedoms has, in effect, stimulated a debate on the legitimacy of the courts' implementation of this constitutionalization process. There has been particular concern regarding the enormous power inherent in judges' determination of the compliance of democratically adopted laws with rather vaguely labelled rights, such as "freedom of expression" or even "security of the person."

No doubt aware of the existence of this debate, and probably itself troubled by the enormous responsibility foisted upon it when the *Charter* was enshrined in the Constitution, the Supreme Court of Canada quickly developed burdens of proof to be used as parameters for the debate. These burdens of proof included the responsibility of the party invoking a violation of rights or freedoms to demonstrate that it is so and the responsibility of the party alleging, if applicable, that there are reasonable limits within the meaning of the first section of the *Charter*[17] to prove the facts required to establish this claim.[18] The defence of the reasonable nature of a limit on rights and freedoms requires, according to the court, proof of the importance of the objective of the prejudicial measure and of the proportionality of the intended objective in relation to the means used to accomplish the objective. This proportionality will itself be established by demonstrating a rational connection between objective and means, by showing that there are no less-prejudicial means, and by demonstrating a balance between the prejudicial effects and the advantages of the means that would be favourable to the latter.[19] Moreover, the court specified that evidence is generally necessary "to prove the constituent elements" of such an analysis.[20] The court thereby prescribed an essentially empirical constitutional jurisprudence, enjoining Parliament to use explicitly factual foundations for its legislative choices that are likely to infringe upon rights and freedoms.

Paradoxically, this search for facts, which some may see as an indicator of judicial activism,[21] could give rise to jurisprudence that presents itself as passive. Using this evidence, the court may decide that the reasonable nature of the infringement has or has not been demonstrated. It may thus distance itself from the decision or even refuse to take responsibility for it since the court does not *decide* that a limit is or is not reasonable, as applicable, but rather *observes* that it is or is not reasonable in light of the evidence presented.[22] In addition to constructing this semblance of exteriority and detachment, recourse to a language of facts to be established, of evidence, and of onus also creates an illusion of certainty.[23] The assessment of the reasonable nature of limits imposed on rights and freedoms is presented, not as a subjective weighing of the social values at issue but rather as an objective exercise in the assessment of empirical data, correlations, and causal relationships established by scientific studies.[24] This recourse to factual language creates an illusion of neutrality – judges' values have no role to play in this weighing of objective data. Furthermore, the test of reasonable limits, as outlined by the Supreme Court of Canada, seems to be based on two premises: laws can be systematically conceived as a means of ensuring the achievement of concrete ends and parliaments act only in a context of absolute factual certainty. In actual fact, the various steps outlined in *R. v. Oakes* assume a problem whose existence and causes are well documented as well as the development of solutions whose effectiveness are also demonstrable by existing and available empirical data. In addition, these steps seem to take for granted that lawmakers intervene only in circumstances of certitude, with respect to both the identification of a problem and its sources and the effectiveness of the chosen solution.

Yet the utility of legislative action sometimes lies more in the realm of the symbolic than in the realm of concrete, utilitarian effectiveness. Prohibiting advertising of a dangerous product can only be intended to affirm a social consensus about the harmful nature of the product. The *Criminal Code*[25] certainly has, at least in part, a purely symbolic purpose, namely the expression of the fundamental values of Canadian society. Furthermore, legislative action is not systematically based on undeniable factual knowledge. In fact, legislative measures that will be challenged in the name of a violation of rights and freedoms are very often marked by uncertainty. On the one hand, all laws are not necessarily based in fact. Some may even be anchored in urban legend.[26] On the other hand, scientists are not omniscient. Lawmakers do not necessarily know everything that scientists know. And the institutional restrictions of the judicial forum, as well as the rules of evidence, mean that the court may not necessarily know everything that lawmakers know. Unconditional social assistance for individuals under thirty years of age *may* be less of an incentive to return to the job market than conditional assistance.[27] Possession of child pornography *may* be dangerous to children.[28] Tobacco advertising *may* increase tobacco use.[29] Marijuana *may* be harmful to the user or to society in general.[30] These are situations of risk, which give rise to the possibility that events, deemed to be harmful or dangerous, may occur. The "free," unregulated world gives rise to certain risks. Legislative regulation of these risks reorganizes their distribution. Judicial review of the constitutionality of this legislative regulation recasts this distribution.

Legislators have intervened in these contexts of risk. They have made choices and redistributed the cost of uncertainty by potentially interfering with the rights of some individuals in the name of protecting the rights of others, which are adjudged superior. These are the choices expressed by the adopted laws, the constitutionality of which will then be challenged in the name of the violation of rights and freedoms. A judicial review assesses this legislative distribution of risks in light of new parameters – constitutionally protected rights and freedoms.

An analysis of the justices' discourse reveals, among other things, a desperate effort to convince us that this is merely an objective evaluation of the facts. It is alleged that the facts dictate the decision. Yet the uncertainty inherent in social facts complicates this attempt to obscure the real decision-making power or choice being exercised. Since the available knowledge is relatively uncertain and it cannot inform the development of the complete factual reasoning that is solid and infallible, various accommodations are thus made to facilitate intervention in the legislative management of risks while maintaining the pretence of it being rooted in factual terrain. Some of the accommodations were evaluated in 2000, including respect for legislative manoeuvring room in the context of scientific uncertainty, the acceptance of a simple rational foundation, and recourse to common sense.[31] The second part of this chapter is devoted to an analysis of the fact-management strategies developed by the Supreme Court of Canada during recent tests of constitutionality that took place in a context of uncertainty.

Part 2: Some Applications

This part of the essay will address judgments with respect to contesting social assistance programs, the criminalization of the possession of child pornography, the prohibition of tobacco-product advertising, and the prohibition of marijuana possession. We shall concentrate on the judicial treatment of facts and ignore any consideration of the applicable law. We shall see how the justices of the Supreme Court of Canada, wishing to legitimize their opinions with objective justifications, have resorted to makeshift measures in order to compensate for the gaps in factual reasoning that occur within a context of risk and, therefore, uncertainty.

Social Assistance

For several years, Quebec's social assistance program has had provisions that recipients under thirty years of age receive only a fraction of the basic benefit payment amount, unless they participate in internship or professional development programs. In December 2002, the Supreme Court of Canada released a judgment in *Gosselin* v. *Québec (Attorney General),*[32] confirming that the scheme complies with the equality rights protected under section 15 of the *Charter.* Because the court had concluded that there was no violation of rights and freedoms, it was not necessary for it to discuss the possibility that an infringement on a right or freedom may be of a reasonable nature.[33] Four dissenting judges concluded that the scheme in question was unconstitutional.[34]

The risk identified by legislators may be understood in the following way. In difficult economic times, most notably marked by a significant unemployment rate, there is a risk that people under thirty who receive social assistance and who are not compelled in some manner to acquire useful ways of joining the labour market will become dependent upon social assistance over the long term. Knowledge with respect to this question of social fact is fragmented. The legislative intervention takes place in a context of uncertainty. The legislator imposes the cost of this uncertainty upon social assistance recipients under the age of thirty: they assume the costs associated with the risk. They will be put in an immediate situation of extreme difficulty in the hope of better days that are merely possible. This legislative distribution of risk was challenged as a violation of constitutionally protected equality rights under section 15 of the *Charter.* The Supreme Court of Canada confirmed the distribution of risk established by the legislator.

In this essay, we will look at the way the court manages the factual uncertainty inherent in questions of relevant social fact. The strategies used include the selection of the location for the debate, an emphasis on the scheme's philosophy, deference to the trial judge, and confusion of the normative and the factual. The judgment also demonstrates the considerable importance conferred upon the evidence, a refusal to interpret fact, an acceptance of the legislator's factual hypotheses, an application of the principle of *stare decisis* to issues of fact, and, finally, the use of various conceptual tools in order to complete factual reasoning.

Determining the Location of the Debate over Risk: Establishing a Violation of a Right as Such, Rather Than Assessing the Reasonable Nature of a Potential Infringement
Some time ago, the Supreme Court of Canada established the distribution of onus, which is now the parameter for all debates on the compatibility of a law with the *Charter*. The party invoking the violation of rights and freedoms must demonstrate the violation, and the party alleging the reasonableness of a potential infringement must present the relevant facts in support of this claim. However, the distinction between the respective content of each of the steps (establishing the violation of a right and consideration of reasonable limits that may be imposed by the state) is not dictated by a natural and pre-existing order. Judges, who are legitimate interpreters of the Constitution, will decide, as need be, what must be proven in order to establish a violation and what must be established in order to demonstrate the reasonable nature of an infringement. This is a normative decision and a fundamental determination with respect to risk management – the party responsible for proving a fact will assume the cost of scientific uncertainty with respect to that fact.

In *Gosselin*, the court believed it could not conclude that there had been a violation of equality rights since the elements required to reach such a conclusion had not been demonstrated. The majority judgment therefore did not address the issue of the reasonable limits permitted by section 1. This judgment was devoted entirely to an analysis of the alleged violation of section 15. The victim of this alleged violation bore the onus of establishing its constituent parts. The court confirmed comments that have been consistent since *Law* v. *Canada (Minister of Employment and Immigration)*,[35] namely that a violation of equality rights cannot be established unless the victim demonstrates, among other things, an infringement of his or her essential human dignity. It believed that the victim had not, in this case, succeeded in demonstrating this infringement.

It should be noted, however, that this responsibility is an enormous burden on the victim, who apparently in this case had to inform the court not only of her own situation but also of the overall impact of the legislative measure being challenged. The court wrote:

But even if we are prepared to accept that some young people must have been pushed well below the poverty line, we do not know how many, or for how long.[36]

One should remember that Justice Frank Iacobucci had written in *Law*, this time on behalf of a unanimous court, that although social science research "may be of great assistance to a court in determining whether a claimant has demonstrated that the legislation in question is discriminatory,"[37] it is not required[38] and that there were no requirements, under section 15, "that the claimant prove any matters which cannot reasonably be expected to be within his or her knowledge."[39] He added:

A court may often, where appropriate, determine on the basis of judicial notice and logical reasoning alone whether the impugned legislation infringes s. 15(1).[40]

However, as Ms. Gosselin learned to her detriment, the lack of social science research, in combination with the judicial refusal to compensate for this absence using judicial knowledge or logical reasoning, would result in her case being lost. Can it really be said, then, that evidence is not mandatory?

The fact that all discussion of the social measure being challenged took place within an analysis of a violation of rights, in which the victim assumed the burden of proof, illustrates the weight of this burden. Thus, it was written that

[t]he record in this case does not establish lack of correlation in purpose or effect between the ground of age and the needs and circumstances of welfare recipients under 30 in Quebec.[41]

It should be recalled that *Law* had established that the connection between grounds for the legislative distinction and the real needs of a group of individuals constituted a relevant contextual factor for the purposes of establishing the discriminatory nature of the distinction. *Gosselin* emphasizes the fact that the victim's burden also encompasses the evidence of these elements and that this victim could be required to establish the "absence of a connection," which is difficult to prove since it probably relies on social science research about the socio-economic status of youth under thirty years of age in Quebec, about which the state is more likely to be better informed than the plaintiff. Moreover, in this respect, Justice Michel Bastarache wrote a reminder, in a dissenting opinion, of the superior resources available to the government and the fact that the latter is better able to "adduce proof of the importance and purpose of the program."[42]

The fact that the analysis of the social measure under challenge took place exclusively within the framework of the violation of a right, for which the victim bore the burden of proof, facilitates in many ways the task of the state, which has only, in principle, to intervene to justify limits under section 1. Thus, under section 15, the legislative hypotheses are deemed to be "reasonably grounded in everyday experience and common sense,"[43] whereas it is far from certain that these are acceptable justifications within the framework of the analysis of the reasonableness of the limits on rights and freedoms.[44] Realistic recognition of the factual uncertainty under which many laws take shape has already led the Supreme Court of Canada to mitigate certain criteria. Faced with the fact that it is impossible to meet the rigorous evidentiary requirements in *Oakes*, the court occasionally developed adjustments that allow the state to justify the measures in a context of factual uncertainty.[45] Transferring the discussion of social facts that are subject to such factual uncertainty to the phase of establishing whether or not there is a violation is, for this purpose, a much more drastic and effective process. Only on rare occasions can a victim meet the evidentiary requirements thus imposed. In addition, the state need only rely on the victim's ignorance in order to validate the law's constitutionality. The state has nothing to justify since it is now the violation that has become almost impossible to prove. In real terms, Ms. Gosselin assumed the cost of the uncertainty with respect to the concrete social effects of the challenged initiative on social assistance recipients who were under thirty years of age.

Emphasis on "Scheme Philosophy"
In *Gosselin*, the legislator's laudable intentions appear within the analysis of the violation of equality rights. This argument would have seemed pertinent in the context of an analysis of the justification of facts under the *Charter*'s first section. In addition, this factor requires no proof and is used by the court to counter arguments of deleterious effects invoked by the victim in this case. Another strategy used to bypass the difficulties of evidence that are inherent in situations of factual uncertainty is to subtly and consciously confuse the purpose and the effects of a legislative initiative, such that good intentions end up putting a positive spin on the analysis of effects that are themselves uncertain. A majority of the court emphasized that "the new scheme was based on the philosophy"[46] of integrating youth into the labour market. This subtle assimilation of an admirable goal into salutary effects is most notable in the treatment of certain contextual elements. The contextual factor consisting in the connection between the grounds and the group's actual situation, outlined in *Law*, concerned "the relationship between the grounds upon which the claim is based and the nature of the differential treatment."[47] In the context of a constitutional challenge to rights and freedoms based on effects rather than on intentions, in

which the idea of material equality and the existence of discrimination caused by deleterious effects have been acknowledged, this factor can be understood as essentially concerned with the effects imposed by the initiative under challenge. Yet the element of connection is assessed in *Gosselin* in light of the admirable legislative goal and not in reference to the concretely and immediately imposed treatment. Thus, it was written:

> The *purpose* of the challenged distinction, far from being stereotypical or arbitrary, corresponded to the actual needs and circumstances of individuals under 30.[48]

In opposition to an argument related to the immediate and disastrous impact of the program imposed on individuals under thirty years of age, the court presents the importance of long-term effects, which it nonetheless seems to address more from the point of view of intention rather than concrete achievement:[49]

> The argument is that it imposed short-term pain. But the government thought that in the long run the program would benefit recipients under 30 by encouraging them to get training and find employment.[50]

In the same way, the goal, which appears noble since it is in keeping with the values that underlie equality (such as self-determination, personal autonomy, and responsibility for one's own destiny), seems to be knowingly confused with the achievement of positive effects:

> Assessing the severity of the consequences also requires us to consider the positive impact of the legislation on welfare recipients under 30. The evidence shows that the regime set up under the *Social Aid Act sought to promote* the self-sufficiency and autonomy of young welfare recipients through their integration into the productive work force.[51]

Moreover, the "thrust" of the scheme is made to prevail over its short-term "negative impact."[52]

Dissenting justices insist on the importance of concrete effects and decry the recourse to legislative goals within the framework of establishing a violation of equality rights.[53] Bastarache J. writes:

> Groups that are the subject of an inferior deferential treatment based on an enumerated or analogous ground are not treated with dignity just because the government claims that the detrimental provisions are for their own good.[54]

The consideration of legislative intentions within the context of establishing whether rights have been violated and the subtle confusion, in this respect, between the intention and its achievement are methods capable of ensuring judicial confirmation of the legislative distribution of risk.

Demonstrating Extreme Deference with Respect to the Factual Conclusions of the Trial Judge
Confirmation of the risk management carried out by the legislator is also accomplished in *Gosselin* by unusual deference on the part of the Supreme Court of Canada with respect to the conclusions developed by the trial judge – in this case, Justice Paul Reeves of the Superior Court of Quebec. Never, it seems, have the conclusions of fact made by a trial judge been respected to this degree. Justice Reeves, we are to understand, had confirmed the constitutional validity of the legislative scheme.[55] The majority of the Supreme Court of Canada, in fact, have insisted many times over on the limits to the debate imposed by the factual conclusions of the trial judge, specifically those relative to the absence of evidence of "actual adverse effect"[56] on recipients under thirty years of age. "With respect," writes Justice Beverley McLachlin for the majority, "I am of the view that it is not open to this Court to revisit the trial judge's conclusion absent demonstrated error."[57]

This deference therefore has a bearing on the essential factual conclusion, thus precluding any conclusion of the violation of equality rights. Yet, in the context of factual uncertainty with respect to social fact, the court has not accustomed us to such restraint. In actuality, it is now accepted that general social facts that are relevant in a constitutional context do not lend themselves well to rigid application of the traditional rules and principles of evidentiary law and that deference with respect to the conclusions in the trial must be viewed as being relative when it comes to evaluating general social effects.[58] However, recourse to such deference may be useful as justification for a decision not to intervene. In addition, it creates an illusion of non-responsibility. The Supreme Court of Canada did not make the decision to confirm the scheme's validity. Rather, it had no choice since it was constrained by the conclusions of fact established by the trial judge.

Confusing the Normative and the Factual
The Supreme Court of Canada placed the concept of dignity at the centre of the determination as to whether there has been a violation of constitutionally protected equality rights.[59] According to the court, the purpose of section 15 is to protect essential human dignity, and an allegation of a violation of equality rights, in order to succeed, must absolutely demonstrate an infringement on this dignity. The *Law* decision states:

It may be said that the purpose of s. 15(1) is to prevent the violation of essential human dignity and freedom through the imposition of disadvantage, stereotyping, or political or social prejudice, and to promote a society in which all persons enjoy equal recognition at law as human beings or as members of Canadian society, equally capable and equally deserving of concern, respect and consideration.[60]

...

Human dignity means that an individual or group feels self-respect and self-worth. It is concerned with physical and psychological integrity and empowerment.[61]

The nature of a violation of this dignity is, however, ambiguous – is it a question of empirically observable fact, subject to the burdens of proof, or is it a normative evaluation, in other words, a value judgment that is made logically through reasoning?

In these terms, the majority of the court emphasized, in *Gosselin*, the factual aspect of the concept of dignity and the burden of proof that governs its establishment:

We agree that a claimant bears the burden under s. 15(1) of showing on a civil standard of proof that a challenged distinction is discriminatory, in the sense that it harms her dignity and fails to respect her as a full and equal member of society.[62]

...

The complainant argues that the lesser amount harmed under-30s and denied their essential human dignity by marginalizing them and preventing them from participating fully in society. But again, there is no evidence to support this claim.[63]

This insistence on the factual aspect of the issue and, therefore, on the need for evidence allows the court to reject the victim's allegation that human dignity has been violated.

However, the court makes other comments that lead us to think that it is ready to make a decision on this normative question of dignity outside of any factual context:

The government's longer-term purpose was to provide young welfare recipients with precisely the kind of remedial education and skills training they lacked and needed in order eventually to integrate into the work force and become self-sufficient ... This was not a denial of young people's dignity; it was an affirmation of their potential.[64]

...

I do not believe that making payments conditional in this way violated the dignity or human worth of persons under 30 years of age. The condition was not imposed as a result of negative stereotypes.[65]

...

In my view, the interest promoted by the differential treatment at issue in this case is intimately and inextricably linked to the essential human dignity that animates the equality guarantee set out at s. 15(1) of the *Canadian Charter*.[66]

Ironically, this approach allows the court to confirm the scheme's compatibility with personal dignity, without relying on evidence by invoking the goals of the scheme. A conclusion that there had been a violation of human dignity was therefore refused for lack of evidence, whereas the compatibility of the scheme with this dignity was affirmed, apparently as an issue of principles and values. The ambiguity of the concept of dignity makes it very useful.[67] Basing their decision on the same factual information, the dissenting justices easily concluded that there was a violation of physical and psychological integrity sufficient to determine that there had been a violation of personal dignity.[68]

Basing the Decision on Evidence
The Supreme Court of Canada had also justified its confirmation of the legislator's management of this risk by affirming that "the evidence fails to support Ms. Gosselin's claim on any of the asserted grounds."[69] The majority's decision goes on to say: "We must decide this case on the evidence before us, not on hypotheticals, or on what we think the evidence ought to show."[70]

The risk management carried out by the lawmakers is therefore confirmed for a formal and objective reason: the party did not appropriately discharge the burden of proof incumbent on it. The court witnesses this "fact"; makes no judgment; and has no involvement with it. And, yet, it is certainly a truism in law to affirm that all decisions must be based on evidence. Reference to proof – to conclusions that are dictated by evidence – may sometimes be a rhetorical procedure that operates both to justify the decision and to disqualify any lay opinions on the issue. The justification means that we are given the impression that the conclusion somehow creates itself autonomously and that it is the result of the evidence itself. The judge is simply an observer and no longer an actor. Yet we know full well that evidence "decides" nothing – a Solomon is required.[71]

Disqualification occurs by exclusion – we were not there nor did we read or hear the evidence – yet it seems that the evidence "reveals" something. There can be no criticism of "observation" since the view of the "ignorant" layperson is disqualified. As a rule, individuals reading a Supreme Court of Canada decision are informed only by the information found therein. They do not have direct and independent access to the evidence presented nor have they attended the hearing or often read the decisions of the lower courts. Yet decisions refer, here and there, to certain data and facts, the source of which is most often absent. Subscription to a decision that claims to be essentially based on a lack of evidence therefore becomes an act of faith – we were not there, we do not know, we did not see, we must believe. However, the absoluteness inherent in this act of faith is better accommodated by a decision made by one judge alone, containing only one opinion. A multitude of opinions is likely to sow doubt. In fact, the various opinions found in *Gosselin* support healthy scepticism by putting the majority opinion into perspective and thereby also testing our faith.

Refusing to Interpret the Facts
The absence of an interpretation of facts before the court also supports the refusal of the majority to intervene in the legislative management of the uncertain situation of young social assistance recipients. The factual uncertainty related to the recipients, both with respect to the causes of their situation and their current living conditions and with respect to the methods for integrating them into the labour market, is certainly at the heart of the case. Nonetheless, some of the raw data, included in the following list, seem to have been present before the court:

- In 1987, the poverty line for a single person living in a metropolitan area was $914 per month.[72]
- The basic allocation payable to individuals thirty years of age and over represents only 55 percent of the poverty line for a single person.[73]
- In 1987, recipients under thirty years of age who did not participate in any program were entitled to $170 per month and those over thirty received $466.[74]
- Thirty thousand internships and school placements were available for more than 75,000 social assistance recipients under the age of thirty.[75]
- In 1982, 14.4 percent of the population was unemployed.[76]
- In 1982, 23 percent of "youth" were unemployed.[77]
- The percentage of recipients under thirty years of age who succeeded in raising their benefits to the regular rate was 11.2 percent, according to Justice of Appeal Michel Robert, citing apparently an economist's 1988 report.[78]
- Only about one-third of eligible welfare recipients participated in the programs.[79]

The majority's decision recalls: "There is no evidence on why only one-third of eligible welfare recipients participated in the programs."[80] They make note of the fact that they were not presented with "evidence on the actual income of under-30s who did not participate,"[81] commenting that "aid received" is not necessarily equivalent to "total income."[82] They believe that "the record here simply does not support the contention of adverse effect on younger welfare recipients,"[83] and they refuse to "infer from the apparent lack of widespread participation in programs that some recipients under 30 must at some time have been reduced to utter poverty."[84] The majority of the court therefore refused to give any interpretation to the facts before it. However, the dissenting justices did not hesitate to interpret these "raw" facts, explaining that the low rate of participation is a sign that the program "simply did not work"[85] and that "[i]n these conditions, the physical and psychological security of young adults was severely compromised during the period at issue."[86]

Accepting the Legislator's Unverified Factual Hypotheses
Another judicial strategy, which makes it possible to confirm the legislative intervention developed in the risk context, involves accepting, as such, the unverified factual hypotheses that have been used as a basis for the legislator's actions. This is a kind of validation of the facts outlined by lawmakers in the context of factual uncertainty. The majority of the court seems, in fact, to consider the government's position justified, since the government developed "social assistance measures *that might help* welfare recipients ... achieve long-term autonomy."[87] They believe that these measures are founded "in reality and common sense,"[88] that they are supported by "logic and common sense,"[89] and that they are "reasonably grounded in everyday experience and common sense."[90] The majority write that the "legislator is entitled to proceed on informed general assumptions."[91] Lawmakers are therefore left with a considerable margin of manoeuvrability.

This approach lies in obvious contrast to the position of the dissenting justices. Bastarache J., for example, specifically decries the absence of research into the living conditions of people under the age of thirty[92] as well as the unfounded assumption that "all persons under 30 received assistance from their family"[93] and "the unverifiable presumption that people under 30 had better chances of employment and lower need."[94] He develops, under these terms, what he feels to be "[t]he only logical inference for the differential treatment"[95] imposed by the legislator:

Younger welfare recipients will not respond as positively to training opportunities and must be coerced by punitive measures.[96]

Bastarache J. also believes that in this case the file does not establish this assumption, which he believes is the foundation for this legislative scheme, according to which "there would be less incentive to enter the workforce or to participate in the programs if the full benefit was provided unconditionally."[97] In addition, he condemns the government's use of an unverified assumption about the certain attraction full social assistance premiums will have for people under thirty years of age.[98]

Justice Louis LeBel seems even more vehement in his condemnation of this "stereotyped view," according to which

> a majority of young social assistance recipients choose to freeload off society permanently and have no desire to get out of that comfortable situation. There is no basis for that vision of young social assistance recipients as "parasites."[99]

He adds that nothing makes it possible to assume that participation in the program would be lower without the financial incentive.[100] It is tempting to affirm that the justices have accepted only the legislator's factual assumptions that are in harmony with their own world view. It is this connection, or lack of connection, that results in the validation of some assumptions based on common sense or their rejection as not being supported by the evidence. Yet, it remains that the judicial acceptance of unverified factual assumptions is an effective means of validating risk management carried out by the legislator.

Recognizing the Precedential Value of the Factual Conclusions Drawn in Previous Judgments
The most convincing judicial validations of the legislator's management of risk will use accepted and recognized legal techniques – thus, the recourse to *stare decisis*. Although this technique is traditionally reserved for issues of law, it seems to have been slowly and progressively extended to certain judicial conclusions regarding social facts.[101] In *Gosselin*, the refusal of the majority of the court to consider individuals under thirty years of age as a socially disadvantaged group takes its support, in part, from the words of Iacobucci J., who wrote in *Law*:

> Relatively speaking, adults under the age of 45 have not been consistently and routinely subjected to the sorts of discrimination faced by some of Canada's discrete and insular minorities ... It seems to me that the increasing difficulty with which one can find and maintain employment as one grows older is a matter of which a court may appropriately take judicial notice.[102]

The technique used is an interesting one, in that it validates factual assumptions not by their connection to the real or by their confirmation by empirical data but rather by their previous affirmation by a superior court. This argument is authoritative – a fact exists because a court has already affirmed that it exists.

In the same way, the precedent in *Law* is invoked as a basis for the claim that "[t]he legislator is entitled to proceed on informed general assumptions without running afoul of s. 15."[103] It is once again interesting to compare this approach, which was preferred by the majority, to the one used by the dissenting justices to support the opposing conclusions of fact. It is sufficient to recall the conclusion of Justice Claire L'Heureux-Dubé, dissenting, who, relying on the evidence, concludes that young adults were incontestably victims of a pre-existing disadvantage:

> [I]f 23 percent of young adults were unemployed by comparison with 14 percent of the general active population, and if an unprecedented number of young people were entering the job market at a time when federal social assistance programs were faltering, I fail to see how young adults did not suffer from a pre-existing disadvantage.[104]

Similarly, by relying on the data presented in evidence, Bastarache J. qualified the conclusion that young people suffer no special economic disadvantages as an "old assumption" and "stereotypical."[105]

Using Various Conceptual Tools to Complete Factual Reasoning
Legislative intervention in the context of risk is conducted, by definition, in situations of factual uncertainty. None of the parties to the constitutional challenge can therefore bring decisive and complete factual evidence to support their claims. A flawless factual justification must therefore use devices. The majority opinion in *Gosselin* illustrates this only too well. Factual affirmations are supported as being general matters[106] based on "our understanding of society,"[107] on their foundation in reality,[108] on legislative perception,[109] or even on logic.[110] Everyday experience[111] and supposedly obvious statements[112] are apparently also sources of information. Judicial notice also constitutes a source of information, but its use is unpredictable. The majority believes it is impossible to take judicial notice of the fact that young adults may constitute a vulnerable group,[113] but it could take judicial notice of the "increased difficulty older people may encounter in finding employment."[114] Justice Louise Arbour, in a dissenting opinion, stated that it would have been possible to take judicial notice of the fact that "the modern welfare state has developed in response to an obvious failure on the part of the free market economy to provide these basic needs for everyone."[115]

As we have seen, recourse to common sense also justifies certain factual affirmations. Thus, the majority justices believe that considering youth to be vulnerable is contrary to common sense.[116] They hold that common sense supported the incentive mechanism provided by the program.[117] Presumptions of fact are also used. The majority justices agreed to surmise "that the lower amount caused under-30s greater *financial anxiety* in the short term,"[118] whereas L'Heureux-Dubé J. stated, in her dissenting opinion, that "there should be a strong presumption that a legislative scheme which causes individuals to suffer severe threats to their physical and psychological integrity as a result of their possessing a characteristic which cannot be changed does not adequately take into account the needs, capacity or circumstances of the individual or group in question."[119]

Child Pornography

The possession of pornographic material involving children may be harmful to them. This is an issue on which everyone has rather fixed ideas. Yet empirical knowledge on the issue is still incomplete. So it is also a subject of scientific uncertainty as well as one of risk. The federal Parliament criminalized the possession of child pornography, thereby imposing the cost of this uncertainty upon those who possess it. The constitutionality of this legislative provision was challenged in the name of freedom of expression protected by the *Charter*.[120] The majority of the Supreme Court of Canada ruled, in *R. v. Sharpe*,[121] on the validity of this criminalization of child pornography, with the exception of two specific cases that they believed were not a reasonable limit on the freedom of expression.[122] They therefore essentially confirmed lawmakers' distribution of risk. This case is one of the rare instances in which the court makes explicit use of a vocabulary of risk. From the outset, the majority stated that, in fact, once correctly interpreted, the disputed provisions were not intended to prohibit "all material that might harm children"[123] but only that which "poses a reasoned risk of harm to children."[124]

We will examine various arrangements of a factual nature made by the court in order to validate the distribution of risk determined by the legislator in a context of uncertainty, but without reconsidering the test for the assessment of reasonableness of the limits to the rights and freedoms established in *Oakes* – a test based on a postulate of certainty. The judgment documents the decision to affirm facts and the idea of hypothetical scenarios, the relaxing of certain evidentiary requirements, the simplification of the object of proof, and the application of the principle of *stare decisis* to factual issues. Unlike *Gosselin*, which was entirely devoted to determining whether a right had been violated – the onus of which fell upon the victim – *Sharpe* assesses the reasonable nature of the limitation on freedom of expression, which was conceded.[125] Therefore, it is the state that assumes the burden of proof in this case, and it is the state that will benefit from the arrangements that the court has made. However, before we address the strategies used by the court to manage the facts, some comments are required with respect to the inevitable manifestation of the return of the repressed – that is, the world of values.

Return of the Repressed: Recourse to a Consideration of "Values"
Considerations of value are at the heart of all risk management. Very often, it is the seriousness attributed to the occurrence of an event that is decisive in a decision. Yet value judgments inevitably appear subjective, relative, and are less likely to garner support. The illusion of certainty that facts can create thus explains, in large part, their use in decisions with respect to situations of risk. A decision said to be based on facts will seem to be more legitimate. However, we are very often witness to a "return of the repressed." It is all very well to justify the decision as much as possible with convincing empirical data, yet a situation of risk, by definition, cannot be entirely understood from this perspective. The treatment of child pornography is a paradigm of a risk that is not reducible to the purely factual. The values underlying the issue cannot be silenced. Thus, the very first portion of the *Sharpe* decision is devoted to a discussion of the related values (such a discussion is no longer a common occurrence in analyses of the reasonableness of restrictions on rights and freedoms, which are mainly based on factual data). The importance of freedom of expression, its relationship to personal development, and the equal significance of protecting children against any type of exploitation are all addressed. It is essentially a consideration of these values that will in reality justify both the validation of the constitutionality of the criminal prohibition and the creation of the two exceptional situations.
It is indeed concluded that,

[i]n the vast majority of the law's applications, the costs it imposes on freedom of expression are outweighed by the risk of harm to children.[126]

Also, because it believed the two exceptional situations to be so important to freedom of expression that they should not be forbidden, it excluded them from criminal prohibition. The clear impression is given that, above and beyond all the steps of any test and beyond all the available factual data, the simple consideration of values, in reality, forms the basis for the decision on the distribution of risk. With respect to the issue of child pornography, it would seem that the illusion of certainty based on facts is ineffective. The dissenting opinion confirms this impression – the explicit use of values seems even more clear and vehement. First and foremost, the opinion imperiously states that

[t]he very existence of child pornography ... is inherently harmful to children and to society.[127]

The possession of child pornography has no social value.[128] In addition, the relative importance of the freedom of expression is minimized by the declaration that it is the "most base aspect" of personal development, namely that of "pure physical arousal."[129] The dissenting justices fully affirmed the legislator's "social policy," which was "set having regard to moral values."[130] It is therefore difficult to see how any kind of empirical evidence could have influenced such an essentially moral decision.

Affirming Facts: Developing Hypothetical Scenarios
Considerations pertaining to the realm of value judgments therefore seem to be the basis for confirming the constitutional validity of the risk management expressed by criminalizing the possession of child pornography. The development of the two exceptions that are said to be unconstitutionally prohibited also seems not to be based on evidence. In fact, if a majority of the court believes that possession of self-created expressive material, or private recordings of legal sexual activity, is constitutionally protected, it seems that this is by virtue of a simple assertion of facts or by virtue of imagined scenarios and not on the basis of factual conclusions inferred from the evidence. Without making direct connections to the evidence, a majority of the court declared that these activities created "little or no risk of harm to children."[131] They added:

> Further, the risk of harm arising from the private creation and possession of such materials, while not eliminated altogether, is low.[132]

The court qualified its statement when it asserted that these are "materials that arguably pose little or no risk."[133] This is no longer the sphere of fact but rather of supposition. In addition, the court explicitly recognized that the exceptions it deemed appropriate to protect constitute hypothetical applications[134] – a hypothetical scenario that has not yet arisen.[135] We therefore find, in the context of a social risk that is insufficiently documented from an empirical perspective, a judgment based, in part, on a balancing of values and, in part, on affirmed and imagined facts.

Relaxing Evidentiary Requirements in Order to Establish the Reasonable Nature of a Restriction: Openness to Other Sources of Information
The rigidity of the test developed in *Oakes* and the impossibility of meeting its evidentiary requirements when challenging a legislative scheme developed in a context of risk and therefore factual uncertainty have already been emphasized. In continuing a movement that was already under way,[136]

Sharpe relaxes the evidentiary requirements for demonstrating the reason-ableness of restrictions on rights and freedoms under section 1 of the *Char-ter*. Thus, it is not necessary to have "scientific proof based on concrete evidence."[137] It was agreed that human behaviour does not necessarily lend itself to a purely and precisely scientific assessment. In *Sharpe*, the majority wrote:

> The lack of unanimity in scientific opinion is not fatal. Complex human behaviour may not lend itself to precise scientific demonstration, and the courts cannot hold Parliament to a higher standard of proof than the sub-ject matter admits of.[138]

Moreover, it is not required that the "evidence" presented covers the field entirely – other elements of the factual realm will be taken into account in the judicial reasoning dealing with the relevant social facts. The majority recalled that this demonstration of the reasonable nature of the restrictions will be "through evidence supplemented by common sense and inferential reasoning"[139] and by "experience."[140] The evidence constitutes the means of information traditionally preferred in the legal world. We are relatively fa-miliar with its ins and outs. Inferential reasoning goes a bit like this:

> Children are used and abused in the making of much of the child pornogra-phy ... Production of child pornography is fuelled by the market for it, and the market in turn is fuelled by those who seek to possess it. Criminalizing possession may reduce the market for child pornography and the abuse of children it often involves.[141]

"Common sense" is itself a vague notion. Although it may be unavoidable and a systematic part of all reasoning, it is far from objective, timeless, or universal. Giving it formal authority by raising it explicitly to the ranks of admissible, useful sources of information used to establish the reasonable nature of restrictions on rights and freedoms seems at best useless and, at worst, dangerous. Will it in future be authorized as a legitimate source for totally erroneous factual statements? Relaxing the evidentiary requirements affects not only the means but also the object of proof, that which is to be proven.

Developing a New Object of Proof: Acceptance of the Mere Demonstration of "Risk"
In addition to requiring a certain openness with respect to sources of ac-ceptable information for risk management in the context of tests of consti-tutionality, the factual uncertainty inherent in situations of risk gives rise to the development of a new object of proof. Instead of requiring proof of a

fact's existence, it is sufficient to provide evidence of a rational basis for the legislative assessment of this fact.

Establishing the Adequacy of the Purpose   Thus, to establish the importance of the purpose of the measure violating rights and freedoms, proof of actual damage caused by the possession of child pornography is not required. The existence of a "reasoned apprehension of harm" is satisfactory. Addressing the existence of a risk, therefore, rather than the existence of proven harm could be considered a goal of a nature sufficiently urgent and real as to justify an infringement on rights and freedoms. The court in this case ruled that the objective "to criminalize possession of child pornography that poses a reasoned risk of harm to children" is sufficiently urgent and real to justify a restriction on freedom of expression.[142]

Establishing the Rational Connection   Similarly, with respect to the rationality of the connection between the intended goal and the means for achieving it, it is enough for there to be a reasoned apprehension of harm caused to children by the possession of child pornography.[143] Proof of a sure connection, established by scientific evidence, is not required.[144] In this case, it will also be sufficient to demonstrate a possible connection and therefore a risk.[145]

Recognizing the Precedential Value of Factual Conclusions Drawn in Previous Judgments
As in *Gosselin*, some of the factual propositions used in *Sharpe* rely on the principle of *stare decisis*, the scope of which is enlarged to encompass factual conclusions. A majority of the court justified the fact that they are satisfied with a reasoned demonstration of prejudice by relying, tersely, on the precedent set in *R. v. Butler*.[146] Similarly, the dissenting justices also relied on *Butler* to affirm that "some forms of pornography create attitudinal harm."[147] It should be noted that the use of *stare decisis* to justify the existence of a factual conclusion is rooted in fiction. A factual proposition is no more true and no more realistic simply because it has already been accepted by a court. However, it is more acceptable within the realm of law for jurists. While this acceptability is not insignificant, it does not make it fact.

Tobacco Advertising
Tobacco advertising may increase tobacco use. There is a risk. Parliament has prohibited such advertising and, as a result, has imposed the cost of the uncertainty in this area on the manufacturers of the products. Manufacturers of tobacco products have challenged the constitutionality of this legislative intervention in the name of their constitutionally protected freedom

of expression. In the first decision in the second generation of challenges,[148] the Superior Court of Quebec in December 2002 confirmed this legislative distribution of risk, declaring it to be a reasonable restriction of freedom of expression.[149] In this case, risk management, with its inherent uncertainty, also involved tempering the criteria for justification in *Oakes*, which are based on a claim of certainty. After noting an inexorable manifestation of value judgments, this section will address (1) the confirmation of uncertain evidentiary principles; (2) the recognition of the precedential value of factual conclusions; and (3) the development of a new object of proof. Remarks will then be made with respect to (4) the use of logical reasoning; (5) the use of common sense; and (6) the explicit importance attributed to the evidence presented.

Return of the Repressed (Again): Consideration of "Values"
In this first instance decision, where the judge heard considerable factual evidence, one has once again the impression that a consideration of values plays a central role. At the start, the judge in fact outlined the fundamental values at conflict in the debate: "[F]reedom of expression versus the protection of public health."[150] He writes:

> In the case at hand, two fundamental rights are pitted against each other: freedom of expression and the right to public and individual health. Here, we are faced with two areas of the law where great care must be taken to avoid oversimplification and to "strike a balance between the claims of legitimate but competing social values."[151]

These values constitute one of the first considerations in the contextual analysis to which the lower court judge proceeded.[152] And at the end of a very long decision, which presents and analyzes in detail the significant factual evidence adduced, the lasting impression is one essentially founded on a consideration of values:

> In light of the discussion above and the evidence on record, it is clear that the Act's objective is so important to the government's comprehensive strategy for curbing smoking that the benefits of the Act outweigh the negative effects on the tobacco companies.[153]

A reasonable person may have the clear impression that the ultimate decision would have been the same, regardless of the factual information presented to the court and notwithstanding the context provided at the beginning of the quote.

Confirmation of Uncertain Evidentiary Principles, Which Are Applicable to Facts That Are Also Uncertain

The absence of general rules or clear principles governing the admissibility of extrinsic evidence in the constitutional context guarantees the justices considerable manoeuvring room with respect to the treatment of situations of risk. The statements of the court on this issue, statements that have also been the subject of a separate judgment, demonstrate a great deal of relativity. Thus, for example, the decision states that extrinsic evidence is "often essential,"[154] that "consensus is rarely reached"[155] when assessing evidence of social facts, and that "any document relevant to the questions at hand can be accepted, provided it is not inherently unreliable or contrary to public order."[156] Moreover, it is stated that these comments apply only in "cases that lend themselves to the use of extrinsic evidence."[157] The court therefore seems to have a power that is quite discretionary with respect to the admissibility and the assessment of evidence of social facts relevant to situations of risk – a power whose exercise is extremely difficult to control.

Developing a New Object of Proof: Acceptance of the Mere Demonstration of Risk

J.T.I. Macdonald v. *Attorney General of Canada* seems to assume that the object of proof – in the type of constitutional case that essentially deals with the issue of justification – is the rational basis for the impugned law.[158] This claim is quite removed from the claim of certainty that initially prevailed in the elaboration of the *Oakes* test. To accept a demonstration of the rational basis for the impugned law is in some way to accept a demonstration of the existence of a situation of risk.

Recognizing the Precedential Value of Factual Conclusions Drawn in Previous Judgments

In 1995, the Supreme Court of Canada had already ruled on the unconstitutionality of the criminalization of advertising with respect to tobacco products.[159] In *J.T.I.*, the lower court judge drew from the Supreme Court of Canada decision conclusions of fact that, in his opinion, enjoyed precedential value.[160] Once again, we find the same use of *stare decisis* in the context of the judicial management of risk situations. Expanding the scope of the principle of *stare decisis* to issues of social fact facilitates the judicial treatment of issues of risk, insofar as it allows for the validation of factual affirmations, not by their connection to reality but rather by the authority of judicial pronouncements. Thus, the establishment of a rational connection between prohibiting advertising and protecting young people from incentives to smoke will be greatly facilitated by this use of precedent. The fact is believed to have already been established:

In *RJR-MacDonald,* the Supreme Court recognized the existence of a rational connection between the objective of the T.P.C.A. *[Tobacco Products Control Act]* and the ban on advertising.[161]

Using Logical Reasoning: Accepting a Logical Connection That Has Not Been Empirically Demonstrated
The Superior Court judge also drew from *RJR-MacDonald Inc.* v. *Canada (Attorney General)* support for the position that, failing scientific certainty about an empirical connection, the existence of a simple logical connection between the intended goal and the means employed to achieve it would be sufficient.[162]

Recourse to Common Sense
Beyond evidence, the Superior Court also used common sense as an element when reasoning with respect to facts:

> The tobacco companies spend millions of dollars each year on their advertising campaigns. Common sense dictates that these sophisticated marketing campaigns, which use the services of top advertising professionals and whose impact on consumers is regularly monitored, have a decisive effect on the collective imagination, encouraging young people to start smoking and others to continue smoking.[163]

The judge concluded his decision with the following statement:

> The evidence at trial compels the Court to exercise the degree of deference that common sense would dictate.[164]

Not only does common sense complete the evidence, it also justifies the approach to judicial review, which in this case is restraint.

Basing the Decision on Evidence
The *J.T.I.* decision was made by a lower court, which is, in principle, where the evidence was heard. It is not surprising, therefore, that we see greater effort than in *Gosselin* to demonstrate that the decision is fully derived from the evidence heard, if not, in fact, dictated by it. We are therefore told that "the hearing generated nearly 10,000 pages of stenographic notes, and 988 exhibits totalling hundreds of thousands of pages were entered into the record."[165] The court attached to the decision 435 paragraphs of summaries of the testimony heard, stating that they were part of the decision and commenting on them for more than 100 paragraphs.[166] The effect of justification and disqualification discussed earlier therefore play a major role. Such

a well-documented decision must be objective, and lay people certainly do not have the knowledge required to challenge it. Disqualification could play a role in this case with respect to a court of appeal that would not wish to intervene. The findings of the lower court judge are in fact sufficiently connected to the evidence as to limit the appeal judge's manoeuvring room.

Marijuana Possession

Marijuana use may cause harm to users or to society as a whole. Faced with this risk, the legislator prohibited marijuana possession, thereby imposing the cost of the uncertainty in this matter on those who use or may wish to use it. The constitutionality of this prohibition was challenged. On 13 December 2002, the Supreme Court of Canada heard this case and adjourned it until the spring of 2003.[167] In doing so, the court used an unusual strategy. It did not make a decision but rather waited for the parliamentarians to debate the issue and produce some factual data. The chief justice of Canada, in a brief decision delivered orally, referred to a statement from the minister of justice in which the minister announced his intention to submit a bill partially decriminalizing marijuana possession. In the belief that the parliamentary initiative would lead to analyses, reviews, and debates that could be helpful to the case, the court decided to postpone hearing the appeal before it. This decision is extremely significant in the context of interaction between the governmental, parliamentary, and court proceedings with respect to situations of risk.

Since decision making in a context of relative scientific uncertainty requires minimal factual clarification, the person making the decision must become informed. In this regard, the respective institutional abilities of political and judiciary parties each have relative advantages and disadvantages. The institutional ability of the courts to establish and assess relevant social facts has been discussed. According to some, only legislators are qualified to play this role. It is undeniable that, at first glance, legislators benefit from a much greater ability to gather data than the courts. Their institutional superiority in this respect can be seen in their resources of time and money. Legislators can commission studies and expert research. Committee and parliamentary commissions may hold public hearings, thus receiving the information required to develop informed policies. The traditional legal rules of evidence, in the adversarial system, are a considerable hindrance to the judiciary's access to facts. First, courts, in principle, receive only the factual information presented to them by the parties. Financial limitations on the parties may, on occasion, unduly restrict the debate and deprive the court of important evidence. In addition, certain rules of exclusion mean that all of the available information is not necessarily considered. However, it is not certain that all the legislative resources for the assessment of social facts are used effectively prior to developing policy.

First of all, parliaments have no constitutional obligation in this respect, at least *a priori*. Legislative action is legitimized by its democratic basis and not by its scientific rigour or objectivity.

All things considered, the political choices made by parliaments are not necessarily those that would be dictated by a rational and cool-headed analysis of the specific factual context. One might even wonder whether such an analysis could "dictate" anything at all in the world of political choices and decisions. Thus, it may be very likely that a provincial legislature would limit the amount that candidates may spend during an electoral campaign in the name of equality and democracy, without having conducted any previous empirical research on the actual effects of the amount of the expenditures on electoral behaviour. In addition, one might think that these data collection mechanisms are sometimes used for political, rather than for scientific, purposes. It does not take a cynic to see that participation and consultation have often served to legitimize unilateral decisions. Finally, this idea of rational legislative action, based on an objective assessment of all the relevant facts, is often rendered illusory by the political vulnerability (or rather "responsibility"?) of parliaments. More than once, a draft policy has been jettisoned, not for a lack of awareness of the context but rather for a lack of support in some communities.

It may therefore be that, in the absence of its concrete and effective use, legislators' far greater capacity for analysis does not place them in an actual position of superiority with respect to the courts. In any event, the courts are required to adjudicate. If they are correctly queried about the constitutionality of an act, regardless of the complexity of the social facts about which they will inevitably have to make a decision, they must respond. The Supreme Court of Canada, in *Malmo-Levine* v. *R.*, took an entirely unusual position.[168] The justices did not refuse to make a decision, but they did delay the decision. Knowing that parliamentarians would soon examine the issue of the social facts of interest to them in the case, the court awaited their findings. Advocates of the metaphor of a dialogue between Parliament and the courts in the context of judicial reviews of constitutionality[169] may see an application of this metaphor, namely a type of discussion between institutions, this time with respect to fact-gathering. For the purposes of this essay, *Malmo-Levine* illustrates an innovative judicial strategy in risk management: waiting for a legislative assessment of the facts.

Conclusion

Judicial review of constitutionality is marked by the exercise of considerable judicial power. As a result of the prejudice mentioned at the very beginning of this chapter, it has long been held in the jurists' world that only the principles and rules of law discussed in jurisprudence merit any sort of attention. However, the handling of facts by judges has perhaps become their true position of power in constitutional matters. This position is obscured yet powerful. It is obscured because there is rarely direct access to the source of information from which judges draw what are presented as the "conclusions of fact" and it is powerful since relying on the facts justifies essentially debatable judicial decisions by presenting them as simple factual observation. "There is insufficient evidence" is a statement that is very difficult to contest. The judicial discourse with respect to facts merits close scrutiny. Conceptualizing tests of constitutionality as risk management exercises enables better discernment of their factual aspects. This process clarifies the strategies generated by the courts to develop the factual reasoning that is essential to their conclusions of law. Jurists in the field of constitutional law relinquish their narrow field of expertise when they desert issues of law for issues of fact. Yet they have a great adventure ahead. And we cannot shortchange this exercise.

Notes

1   Sheldon Krimsky, "The Role of Theory in Risk Studies" in S. Krimsky and D. Golding, eds., *Social Theories of Risk* (Westport, CT: Praeger, 1992) at 1, 4-5, citing Philipp Frank, *Philosophy of Science: The Link between Science and Philosophy* (Englewood Cliffs, NJ: Prentice-Hall, 1957) at 25.

2   "Both as a figure of speech and as an instrument of political momentum, risk has assumed an unusual prominence on the American scene." Edward J. Burger, ed., *Risk* (Ann Arbor: University of Michigan Press, 1993) at introduction, vii. In Europe, the 1995 publication of *Que sais-je*, which was dedicated to the sociology of risk (les Presses Universitaires de France), illustrates the popularity of the subject. David Le Breton, *La sociologie du risque* (Paris: Presses Universitaires de France, 1995). Finally, for a more modern illustration of the interest in literature on risk, see the *Journal on Risk and Uncertainty*, Kluwer, <http://www.kluweronline.com/issn/0895-5646/contents>.

3   *Law, Probability and Risk*, Oxford University Press. The first issue appeared in July 2002.

4   Danielle Pinard, "Incertitude et risques: la preuve en matière constitutionnelle" in H. Dumont and J. Bloom, eds., *Science, Truth and Justice* (Montréal: Les Éditions Thémis, 2001) at 65-95 (there is an English version as well, "Uncertainty and Risks: Evidence in Constitutional Law," 97-125 at 67).

5   "This numerology, or 'quantitative risk analysis,' which gives the appearance of increased accuracy, has been correctly described by some of its critics as a 'refuge in objectivity.'" Burger, *supra* note 2 at xii. Further, "whether their authors realize it or not, technical risk definitions do require framing commitments to models of the social realities, in which risks are generated, defined, and experienced." Brian Wynne, "Risk and Social Learning: Reification to Engagement," in Krimsky, *supra* note 1 at 275, 292.

6   Mary Douglas believes that substituting the term "risk" for "danger" is not a neutral change. She writes: "The language of danger, now turned into the language of risk, often makes a spurious claim to be scientific. But the matter is not just linguistic style. The possibility of a scientifically objective decision about exposure to danger is part of the new complex of ideas." Mary Douglas, *Risk and Blame: Essays in Cultural Theory* (London and New York: Routledge, 1992) at 14.

7   For similar views, see Danièle Loshak, "Droit, normalité et normalisation," in Centre universitaire de recherches administratives et politiques de Picardie, Jacques Chevallier *et al., Le droit en procès* (Paris: Presses universitaires de France, 1983) at 51, who writes: "En réalité, et il ne faut pas s'y tromper, la prétention à l'objectivité et à la scientificité est ici largement mystificatrice, comme toujours lorsqu'on les invoque dans des domaines qui ont trait au gouvernement des hommes. Derrière des calculs prétendûment objectifs se

dissimulent des systèmes d'évaluation qui restent fondamentalement normatifs et n'échappent pas à l'emprise des valeurs dominantes" (at 75). She adds: "Il est illusoire, même en recourant aux pédagogues, aux médecins, aux psychiatres, aux psychologues, même avec le renfort de toutes les sciences du 'psy' et bientôt de la sociologie, de vouloir trancher scientifiquement des questions qui, quoi qu'on fasse, demeurent à haute teneur idéologique" (at 76).

8　See, for example, George W. Conk, "Legend vs. Pragmatism" in Cynthia H. Cwik and John L. North, (dir.), *Scientific Evidence Review*, Monograph no. 3 (Chicago: American Bar Association, Section of Science and Technology, 1997).

9　In this regard, see Douglas, *supra* note 6 at 48: "Even if it [probability analysis] were still representing a form of scientific analysis, it arrives just at the moment in which it cannot deliver what politics most want of it. Politics requires from science its authority – certainty ... Superbia is gone; the mood is modest, cautious, insisting on vast areas of uncertainty." In 1983, she wrote: "For anyone disposed to worry about the unknown, science has actually expanded the universe about which we cannot speak with confidence," referring specifically to "the double-edged thrust of science, generating new ignorance with new knowledge." Mary Douglas and Aaron Wildavsky, *Risk and Culture: An Essay on the Selection of Technological and Environmental Dangers* (Berkeley: University of California Press, 1983) at 49. Finally, see Georges M. Von Furstenberg, *Acting under Uncertainty: Multidisciplinary Conceptions* (Boston: Kluwer Academic Publisher, Theory and Decision Library, 1990) at xi ("[R]esearch creates uncertainty ... an addition to knowledge is won at the expense of an addition to ignorance.").

10　"Bad science is easier than good. Faster and cheaper." Peter W. Huber," "Pathological Science in Court," in Burger, *supra* note 2 at 99, 115.

11　See, for example, K.S. Shrader-Frechette, *Risk and Rationality: Philosophical Foundations for Populist Reforms* (Berkeley: University of California Press, 1991) at 135, which discusses, with respect to decision making in contexts of uncertainty, the epistemological rationality of "purely scientific" decisions and the ethical, cultural, and procedural rationality of social decisions.

12　"Risk is assumed to have an intrinsic, objective natural meaning that everyone should share, rather than a meaning that has been created and imposed by particular dominant social institutions with their own interests and anxieties, and that systematically conceals certain issues and questions from public attention." Wynne, *supra* note 5 at 284.

13　See Danielle Pinard, "La rationalité législative, une question de possibilités ou de probabilités? Commentaire à l'occasion de l'affaire du tabac" (1994) 39 McGill L.J. 405.

14　It might also be asked whether such a jurisprudential approach, which essentially focuses on issues of law and principle, is not the only one constitutionally permitted. Could it not, in fact, be argued that the jurisprudential requirement to demonstrate empirical support for a law, for the purposes of confirming its validity, is itself unconstitutional? Is this not a prohibited interference of judicial power in parliamentary operations?

15　*Re: Anti-Inflation Act*, [1976] 2 S.C.R. 373.

16　*Canadian Charter of Rights and Freedoms*, Part I of the *Constitution Act 1982*, being Schedule B to the *Canada Act 1982* (U.K.), 1982, c. 11 [hereinafter *Charter*].

17　This first section of the *Charter* states: "The *Canadian Charter of Rights and Freedoms* guarantees the rights and freedoms set out in it subject only to such reasonable limits prescribed by law as can be demonstrably justified in a free and democratic society."

18　The Supreme Court of Canada detailed this distribution of onus in *R. v. Oakes*, [1986] 1 S.C.R. 103 [hereinafter *Oakes*].

19　This test was outlined for the first time in *Oakes, ibid.*

20　*Oakes, ibid.* at 138, n. 18.

21　Rogovin refers to a jurisprudential trend that requires constitutional justification of a sequence as a kind of judicial activism. See Wendy M. Rogovin, "The Politics of Facts: The Illusion of Certainty" (1995) 46 Hastings L.J. 1723, 1726.

22　Laurence Tribe thus critiques some jurisprudence designed in cost/benefit terms, which also gives the impression of inexorability: "That leads to the sixth deadly sin committed by those who take this cost-benefit perspective: abdicating responsibility for choice. That, I think, is the great appeal of all fundamental faiths, including faith in technical expertise and in methods like cost-benefit analysis. They enable each of us to don a mantle that says, 'I didn't do it.' They create an illusion, a comforting illusion, of inexorability." Laurence H. Tribe, "Seven Deadly Sins of Straining the Constitution through a Pseudo-Scientific Sieve" (1984) 36 Hastings L.J. 155, 168. Danièle Loshak refers to a discussion of the relationship between the normative and normality, to "L'irruption de la science dans le droit et [à] la réduction corrélative de la règle juridique à la pure objectivité du constat." Loshak, *supra* note 7 at 74.

23   The expression "illusion of certainty" comes from Oliver Wendell Holmes Jr, in "Privilege, Malice and Intent" (1894) 8 Harvard L. Rev. 1 at 7, cited in Rogovin, *supra* note 21 at 1723. Laurence Tribe gave a sound explanation of concerns about the dangers resulting from this illusion of certainty: "The general danger illustrated by both of these decisions is a danger well put by Justice Brennan in his dissent in *Leon*. He speaks there of the 'narcotic effect,' the 'illusion of technical precision and ineluctability,' which comes when we allow ourselves to talk like little scientists about the costs and benefits of these various rules. It is well put by Justice Marshall in his dissent in the *Quarles* case (*New York* v. *Quarles*) when he speaks of the 'pseudo-scientific precision' of cost-benefit rhetoric in this realm." Tribe, *supra* note 22 at 158.

24   In the context of American law, it was written in 1995: "The ideological call for facts is cloaked in the apolitical, apparently objective nature of the facts and so it mystifies the decision-making process." Rogovin, *supra* note 21 at 1727. Danièle Loshak refers to "valeurs camouflées sous l'objectivité du constat scientifique" and writes: "le droit, lorsqu'il s'appuie sur un tel constat, ne peut qu'en tirer un surcroît de légitimité." Loshak, *supra* note 7 at 75.

25   *Criminal Code*, R.S.C. 1985, c. C-46.

26   Rogovin, *supra* note 21 at 1742: "It is possible to enact a piece of legislation without reference to or reliance upon scientific facts. Such a law might be rooted in urban myth or popular desires."

27   See discussion of *Gosselin* v. *Québec (Attorney General)*, 2002 S.C.C. 84 [hereinafter *Gosselin*] later in this chapter.

28   See discussion of *R.* v. *Sharpe*, [2001] 1 S.C.R. 45 [hereinafter *Sharpe*] later in this chapter.

29   See discussion of *J.T.I. Macdonald Corporation* v. *Attorney General of Canada*, [2003] R.J.Q. 181 (C.S.) [hereinafter *J.T.I.*] later in this chapter.

30   See interlocutory decision in *Malmo-Levine* v. *R.*, Supreme Court of Canada, 13 December 2002 [hereinafter *Malmo-Levine*].

31   See Pinard, *supra* note 4.

32   *Gosselin, supra* note 27.

33   Chief Justice Beverley McLachlin wrote the majority opinion for the court, with Justices Charles Gonthier, Frank Iacobucci, John Major, and William Binnie concurring.

34   Justices Claire L'Heureux-Dubé, Michel Bastarache, Louise Arbour, and Louis LeBel wrote four different dissenting opinions.

35   *Law* v. *Canada (Minister of Employment and Immigration)*, [1999] 1 R.C.S. 497 [hereinafter *Law*].

36   *Gosselin, supra* note 27 at para. 64. This approach must be compared with the dissenting opinion of Bastarache J., who wrote, in paragraph 249, that the victim only had to demonstrate the harm to which she herself had been subjected.

37   *Law, supra* note 35 at para. 77.

38   *Ibid.*

39   *Ibid.* at para. 80.

40   *Ibid.* at para. 77.

41   *Gosselin, supra* note 27 at para. 58.

42   *Ibid.* at para. 259.

43   *Ibid.* at para. 56.

44   On this issue of the legislator's assumptions, see "Accepting the Legislator's Unverified Factual Hypotheses," later in this chapter.

45   See Pinard, *supra* note 4.

46   *Gosselin, supra* note 27 at para. 7.

47 *Law, supra* note 35 at para. 69.

48 *Gosselin, supra* note 27 at para. 38 [my emphasis].

49 In addition, the court emphasizes in these terms its uncertainty with respect to the concrete achievement of the intention: "We do not know whether it did so; the fact that the scheme was subsequently revamped may suggest the contrary" (para. 53). Bastarache J., dissenting, was satisfied with a simple rational basis for the legislative wish to improve the well-being of young people, but as part of the first section.

50 *Gosselin, supra* note 27 at para. 53.

51 *Ibid.* at para. 65 [my emphasis].

52 *Ibid.* at para. 66.

53 For example, L'Heureux-Dubé J. writes: "Blurring the division between the rights provisions and s. 1 of the *Charter*, by incorporating the perspective of the legislature in a s. 15 analysis, is at odds with the Court's approach to equality and surely does not serve the purposes of s. 15." *Ibid.* at para. 104. See also, in the same sense, Bastarache J.: "Indeed, giving too much weight here to what the government says was its objective in designing the scheme would amount to accepting a s. 1 justification before it is required" (at para. 244).

54 *Ibid.* at para. 250.

55 *Gosselin v. A.G. of Quebec*, [1992] R.J.Q. 1647 (C.S.).

56 *Gosselin, supra* note 27 at para. 46.

57 *Ibid.* at para. 50. See also para. 54 and 64.

58 See, for example, *RJR-MacDonald Inc. v. Canada (Attorney General)*, [1995] 3 S.C.R. 199 [hereinafter *R.J.R.*], in particular, the opinion of Justice Gerard La Forest in para. 79 ff and that of McLachlin J., in para. 140 ff.

59 On this issue, see *Law, supra* note 35.

60 *Ibid.* at para. 51.

61 *Ibid.* at para. 53.

62 *Gosselin, supra* note 27 at para. 18.

63 *Ibid.* at para. 64.

64 *Ibid.* at para. 42.

65 *Ibid.* at para. 52.

66 *Ibid.* at para. 65.

67 The usefulness of such ambiguity echoes that of the distinction between issues of law and issues of fact, of which has been written: "No two terms of legal science have rendered better service than 'law' and 'fact.' They are basic assumptions; irreducible minimums and the most comprehensive maximums at the same instant. They readily accommodate themselves to any meaning we desire to give them ... What judge has not found refuge in them? The man who could succeed in defining them would be a public enemy." L. Green, *Judge and Jury*, 270 (Kansas City: Vernon Law Book Co. 1930), in Henry P. Monahan, "Constitutional Fact Review," (1985) 85 Columbia L. Rev. 229, 233, note 25. On the same issue, see also Danielle Pinard, "Le droit et le fait dans l'application des standards et la clause limitative de la *Charte canadienne des droits et libertés*" (1989) 30 Les Cahiers de Droit 137.

68 See, as an example, *Gosselin, supra* note 27 at para. 130, 132, 134, and 258.

69 *Ibid.* at para. 5.

70 *Ibid.* at para. 66.

71 "There has to be a Solomon to judge; the evidence does not provide the judgment by itself." Mary Douglas, "Risk as a Forensic Resource," in Burger, *supra* note 2 at 12.

72 *Ibid.* at para. 7.

73 *Ibid.*

74 *Ibid.*

75 *Ibid.*

76 *Ibid.*

77 *Ibid.*

78 *Ibid.* at para. 51.

79 *Ibid.*

80 *Ibid.*

81   *Ibid.*
82   *Ibid.*
83   *Ibid.* at para. 54.
84   *Ibid.* at para. 71.
85   *Ibid.* at para. 371.
86   *Ibid.*
87   *Ibid.* at para. 44 [my emphasis].
88   *Ibid.*
89   *Ibid.*
90   *Ibid.* at para. 56.
91   *Ibid.*
92   "In fact, no effort was made to establish what living conditions were 'for persons under 30.'" *Ibid.* at para. 247.
93   *Ibid.*
94   *Ibid.* at para. 248.
95   *Ibid.* at para. 250.
96   *Ibid.*
97   *Ibid.* at para. 272.
98   "Witnesses for the respondent repeatedly referred to the 'attraction effect' [translation] that would result from increasing the benefits of people under 30, but they failed to adduce any evidence of studies or previous experience to justify the hypothesis." *Ibid.* at para. 272.
99   *Ibid.* at para. 407.
100   *Ibid.* at para. 410.
101   See, for example, *R. v. Williams*, [1998] 1 S.C.R. 1128 at para. 54, with respect to judicial statements on the existence of racial prejudice in a community.
102   *Law, supra* note 35 at para. 95 and 101.
103   *Gosselin, supra* note 27 at para. 56. See also paragraph 73 for the analogies developed by the court between *Law* and *Gosselin*.
104   *Gosselin, supra* note 27 at para. 137.
105   "Thus, the stereotypical view upon which the distinction was based, that the young social welfare recipients suffer no special economic disadvantages, was not grounded in fact; it was based on old assumptions regarding the employability of young people." *Ibid.* at para. 235.
106   "Both as a general matter, and based on the evidence and our understanding of society, young adults as a class simply do not seem especially vulnerable or undervalued. There is no reason to believe that individuals between ages 18 and 30 in Quebec are or were particularly susceptible to negative preconceptions. No evidence was adduced to this effect, and I am unable to take judicial notice of such a counter-intuitive proposition. Indeed, the *opposite* conclusion seems more plausible, particularly as the programs participation component of the social assistance scheme was premised on a view of the greater long-term employability of under-30s, as compared to their older counterparts." *Ibid.* at para. 33.
107   *Ibid.*
108   "[O]ne cannot argue based on this record that the legislature's purpose lacked sufficient foundation in reality and common sense to fall within the bounds of permissible discretion in establishing and fine-tuning a complex social assistance scheme. Logic and common sense support the legislature's decision to structure its social assistance programs to give young people, who have a greater potential for long-term insertion into the work force than older people, the incentive to participate in programs specifically designed to provide them with training and experience." *Ibid.* at para. 44.
109   *Ibid.* at para. 33.
110   *Ibid.* at para. 44.
111   *Ibid.* at para. 56.
112   *Ibid.* at para. 51 ("clearly 'aid received' is not necessarily equivalent to 'total income.'").
113   *Ibid.* at para. 33.
114   *Ibid.* at para. 60.

115 *Ibid.* at para. 383.
116 *Ibid.* at para. 33.
117 *Ibid.* at para. 44 and 56.
118 *Ibid.* at para. 64 [my emphasis].
119 *Ibid.* at para. 135.
120 For a brief consideration of the court of appeal decision, see Pinard, *supra* note 4.
121 *Sharpe, supra* note 28.
122 These are self-created expressive material and private recordings of lawful sexual activity. See *Sharpe, supra* note 28 at para. 115.
123 *Ibid.* at para. 34.
124 *Ibid.*
125 *Ibid.* at para. 5.
126 *Ibid.* at para. 103.
127 *Ibid.* at para. 158.
128 *Ibid.* at para. 186.
129 *Ibid.* at para. 185.
130 *Ibid.* at para. 191.
131 *Ibid.* at para. 75. See also para. 99 and 100.
132 *Ibid.* at para. 75.
133 *Ibid.* at para. 105.
134 *Ibid.* at para. 111.
135 *Ibid.* at para. 112.
136 See Pinard, *supra* note 4, for a discussion of some of the flexibilities developed by case law.
137 *Sharpe, supra* note 28 at para. 85. See also the dissenting opinion at para. 167.
138 *Ibid.* at para. 89. See, in the same sense, the dissenting opinion at para. 167.
139 *Ibid.* at para. 78.
140 *Ibid.* at para. 94.
141 *Ibid.* at para. 92.
142 *Ibid.* at para. 82.
143 *Ibid.* at para. 85. See also, in the same sense, the dissenting opinion at para. 198.
144 *Ibid.*
145 "Possession of child pornography increases the risk of child abuse." *Ibid.* at para. 94. See also para. 88.
146 *R. v. Butler,* [1992] 1 S.C.R. 452.
147 *Sharpe, supra* note 28 at para. 161.
148 Concluding the first generation of challenges in 1995, the Supreme Court of Canada declared the unconstitutionality of the previous prohibition of tobacco-product advertising in *R.J.R., supra* note 58.
149 *J.T.I., supra* note 29.
150 *Ibid.* at para. 7.
151 *Ibid.* at para. 63.
152 *Ibid.* at para. 217.
153 *Ibid.* at para. 285.
154 *Ibid.* at para. 62.
155 *Ibid.*
156 *Ibid.*
157 *Ibid.*
158 *Ibid.*
159 *R.J.R., supra* note 58.
160 "The Court is bound by the conclusions of law and some of the conclusions of fact drawn by the Supreme Court in the first case unless different evidence is introduced." *J.T.I., supra* note 29 at para. 105.
161 *Ibid.* at para. 261. See also para. 272.
162 *Ibid.* at para. 24.
163 *Ibid.* at para. 273. See also para. 519.
164 *Ibid.* at para. 538.

165 *Ibid.* at para. 101.
166 *Ibid.* at para. 112-216 of the judgment.
167 Some comments must be made. First of all, there are in fact three cases: *Malmo-Levine* v. *R.*; *Caine* v. *R.*; and *Clay* v. *R.*, Supreme Court of Canada, 13 December 2002 (known in collection as *Malmo-Levine*, *supra* note 30). The court decided to adjourn these cases until the spring of 2003. The court continued the hearings on 6 May 2003. "Ten months have passed since Mr. Cauchon [minister of justice] revealed his intention to punish Canadians caught smoking the prohibited weed with a simple fine. The draft is still on the drawing table, and there is no hint of any kind of debate in Parliament" [translation]. Brian Myles, "La Cour Suprême ira-t-elle plus vite que le Parliament?" [Will the Supreme Court Move Faster than Parliament?"] *Le Devoir*, 6 May 2003 at A3. In August 2003, the verdicts in these cases were under consideration by the Supreme Court of Canada. Finally, Bill C-38, *An Act to Amend the Contraventions Act and the Controlled Drugs and Substances Act*, was submitted for first reading on 27 May 2003.
168 *Malmo-Levine*, *supra* note 30.
169 For recent legal discussions of the dialogue metaphor, see especially *Bell ExpressVu Limited Partnership* v. *Rex*, 2002 S.C.C. 42; *R.* v. *Hall*, 2002 S.C.C. 64; and *Sauvé* v. *Canada (Chief Electoral Officer)*, 2002 S.C.C. 68.

Bibliography

Books and Articles

Burger, Edward J., ed., *Risk* (Ann Arbor: University of Michigan Press, 1993).

Conk, George W. *Legend versus Pragmatism: Scientific Evidence Review*, Monograph no. 3. Cynthia H. Cwik and John L. North, eds. (Chicago: American Bar Association Section on Science and Technology, 1997).

Douglas, Mary. *Risk and Blame: Essays in Cultural Theory* (London: Routledge, 1992).

–. "Risk as a Forensic Resource." In Edward J. Burger, ed., *Risk* (Ann Arbor: University of Michigan Press, 1993).

–, and Aaron Wildavsky. *Risk and Culture: An Essay on the Selection of Technological and Environmental Dangers* (Berkeley: University of California Press, 1983).

Frank, Philipp. *Philosophy of Science: The Link between Science and Philosophy* (Englewood Cliffs, NJ: Prentice Hall, 1957).

Holmes, Oliver Wendell, Jr. "Privilege, Malice and Intent" (1984) 1 Harvard Law Review 8.

Huber, Peter W. "Pathological Science in Court." In Edward J. Burger, ed., *Risk* (Ann Arbor: University of Michigan Press, 1993).

Journal of Risk and Uncertainty. Kluwer. <http://www.kluweronline.com/issn/0895-5646/contents>.

Krimsky, Sheldon. "The Role of Theory in Risk Studies." In S. Krimsky and D. Golding, eds., *Social Theories of Risk* (Westport, CT: Praeger Publishers, 1992).

Law, Probability and Risk (journal). Oxford University Press.

Le Breton, David. *La sociologie du risque* (Paris: Presses Universitaires de France, 1995).

Loshak, Danièle. "Droit, normalité et normalisation." In Jacques Chevallier *et al.*, eds., *Le droit en process* (Paris: Presses universitaires de France, 1983).

Monahan, Henry P. "Constitutional Fact Review" (1985) 85 Columbia Law Review 229.

Pinard, Danielle. "Le droit et le fait dans l'application des standards et la clause limitative de la *Charte canadienne des droits et libertés*" (1989) 30 Les Cahiers de Droit 137.

–. "La rationalité législative, une question de possibilités ou de probabilités? Commentaire à l'occasion de l'affaire du tabac" (1994) 39 McGill Law Journal 405.

–. "Uncertainty and Risks: Evidence in Constitutional Law." In H. Dumont and J. Bloom, eds., *Science, Truth and Justice* (Montréal: Les Éditions Thémis, 2001).

Rogovin, Wendy M. "The Politics of Facts: The Illusion of Certainty" (1995) 46 Hastings Law Journal 1723.

Shrader-Frechette, K.S. *Risk and Rationality: Philosophical Foundations for Populist Reforms* (Berkeley: University of California Press, 1991).

Tribe, Laurence H. "Seven Deadly Sins of Straining the Constitution through a Pseudo-Scientific Sieve" (1984) 36 Hastings Law Journal 155.

Von Furstenberg, George M. *Acting under Uncertainty: Multidisciplinary Conceptions* (Boston: Theory and Decision Library, Kluwer Academic Publisher, 1990).

Wynne, Brian. "Risk and Social Learning: Reification to Engagement." In S. Krimsky and D. Golding, eds., *Social Theories of Risk* (Westport, CT: Praeger Publishers, 1992).

Jurisprudence

Bell ExpressVu Limited Partnership v. *Rex*, [2002] 2 S.C.R. 559, 2002 S.C.C. 42.

Gosselin c. *P.G. Québec*, [1992] R.J.Q. 1647 (C.S.).

Gosselin v. *Quebec (Attorney General)*, 2002 S.C.C. 84.

J.T.I. Macdonald Corporation c. *P.G. Canada*, [2003] R.J.Q. 181 (C.S.).

Law v. *Canada (Minister of Employment and Immigration)*, [1999] 1 S.C.R. 497.

Malmo-Levine v. *R.*, *Caine* v. *R.*, and *Clay* v. *R.*, Supreme Court of Canada, 13 December 2002.

R. v. *Butler*, [1992] 1 S.C.R. 452.

R. v. *Hall*, [2002] S.C.R. 309.

R. v. *Oakes*, [1986] 1 S.C.R. 103.

R. v. *Sharpe*, [2001] 1 S.C.R. 45, 2001 S.C.C. 2.

R. v. *Williams*, [1998] 1 S.C.R. 1128.

Reference re Anti-Inflation Act, [1976] 2 S.C.R. 373.

RJR-MacDonald Inc. v. *Canada (Attorney General)*, [1995] 3 S.C.R. 199.

Sauvé v. *Canada (Chief Electoral Officer)*, [2002] 3 S.C.R. 519, 2002 S.C.C. 68.

6
Integrating Values in Risk Analysis of Biomedical Research: The Case for Regulatory and Law Reform

Duff R. Waring and Trudo Lemmens

Human participants in biomedical research are vulnerable if only because the promotion of their well-being is not the main goal of the research and because their participation may expose them to significant risks. In addition, those who participate as patients are dependent on physician/investigators not only for information about the research and its risks but also for the clinical attention they receive in the process. In our view, sufficient formal legal mechanisms to counterbalance the vulnerability of research participants and to protect their rights and well-being are currently not available. Since extra-legal guidelines provide the main focus of their protection, one could even argue that the law currently contributes to the vulnerability of participants by neglect.[1] There is currently no comprehensive legislation to regulate all research with humans, even though various governmental agencies seem to realize that there is a need to improve protection. The federal government, for example, stated in the 2002 Throne Speech that it intended to "work with the provinces to implement a national system for the governance of research involving humans."[2]

This chapter focuses on the role of law in dealing with one particular aspect of the protection of research participants: the evaluation and appreciation of risk in biomedical research. This question is obviously relevant to governments and governmental agencies responsible for research-related issues, but it is also vital to members of research ethics boards (REBs),[3] whose mandate is to protect the rights and well-being of research participants. It is their responsibility to ensure that risk to participants is minimized and proportionate to the potential benefit of the research.[4] REB review currently constitutes the major institutional mechanism evaluating research protocols, which contain the physician/investigators' perceptions of risk. After reviewing, among other things, the risks and the potential benefits of the proposed research, REBs recommend whether physician/investigators can go ahead with the study and start recruiting participants. One way that the law might contribute to the administration of risk is to offer a principled approach to the review structure that purports to assess it. Our suggested approach involves a review process that can balance the interests of those proposing the risk in formal research protocols (and subsequently producing the risk in ongoing research) by empowering the critical and protective interests of those who might assume it.[5] We contend that this process requires fundamental changes at the regulatory and REB levels. We will argue for a different kind of engagement between REB members. Our new approach could also involve a legal mandate for the involvement and decisional authority of risk-cautious participant advocates in research review.

Conrad Brunk, Lawrence Haworth, and Brenda Lee have analyzed risk assessment as an inherently value-laden, political exercise in regulatory science.[6] Following this approach, we argue that this exercise may afford questionable estimates when applied to some types of biomedical research. Given current developments in genomics and molecular biology,[7] regulatory science might be especially fallible in assessing the risks of gene transfer and stem cell research. In this chapter, we classify two general types of risk that have been highlighted by this research as it is, or will likely be, carried out in the existing research environment: risks to persons and risks to social values.[8] We then consider three different forms of risk that we believe the law should address. These are risks of physical or psychological harm to participants; risks to the objectivity and scientific integrity of research that are posed by conflicts of interest; and, briefly, risks to other social values, for example, public trust in the ethical conduct of research. These are very different areas of risk, but we think there is merit in addressing them jointly. Conflicts of interests, for example, may have a conscious or unconscious impact on the way researchers represent risks or on other behaviour of research staff during the recruitment process or during the research itself. In areas where there are problems with the understanding and transmission of risk information to participants, there is greater concern about the impact of conflicts of interest and more reason to develop a fully independent review of risks.

We sketch some principles and guidelines for institutional reforms that could inspire the further development of a regulatory or legislative model for the oversight of research involving humans. Our suggestions should help at a later stage to develop a more detailed model that would better manage the three risks noted earlier. It should also allow for the scrutiny of the methodology and the presentation of risk assessments. This scrutiny might occur locally in an REB system in which physician investigators and participant advocates negotiate the politics of risk assessment. It might occur at the provincial or federal level under the aegis of independent provincial or national agencies. Or it may be that a combination of local, provincial, and federal review will be the best solution. While several national committees and agencies currently address issues related to the governance of research in Canada, we believe that there is room for a fully independent national agency that receives paramount authority in this area. However, before sketching the contours of such a review system, we turn first to a critical evaluation of regulatory science.

Value Frameworks, Regulatory Science, and the Politics of Risk Assessment

It is now generally accepted that no medical research involving humans should proceed without proper review by an independent REB. Local REBs are mandated by various ethics guidelines and regulatory documents to review research protocols proposed by researchers and to decide whether these protocols receive their *imprimatur*.[9] During the review process, REBs examine a variety of issues. For example, although REBs often give most of their attention to informed consent, they are also expected to look at the value and validity of research protocols, the fairness of the selection criteria, potential privacy concerns, and, last but not least, the balance between the risks and potential benefits.[10]

Risk assessments are fundamental to the ethical review of biomedical research. According to existing research ethics guidelines, such as the Canadian federal funding agencies' *Tri-Council Policy Statement*,[11] REB members must ensure that the risks involved in proposed research do not outweigh the potential benefits. The Medical Research Council of Canada, the Natural Sciences and Engineering Research Council of Canada, and the Social Sciences and Humanities Research Council (Tri-Council) embrace a proportionate approach to ethics review, by which greater levels of risk require increasing levels of scrutiny. What levels of risk are considered acceptable depends on the nature of the research. A different evaluation is required depending on whether research is designed to test new interventions aimed at treating an illness or whether it is focused on gaining knowledge without expectation of therapeutic benefit for trial participants.[12] In the first case, the trial should proceed only on the REB's conclusion that there is no *prima facie* expectation that people participating in the research will be worse off in terms of the risk/benefit balance than those receiving standard treatment. The *Tri-Council Policy Statement*'s emphasis on the concept of "minimal risk" also indicates the importance of risk assessment. Risks are considered minimal if they are within the range of risks that would be experienced by research participants undergoing standard treatment. In other words, minimal risk is a range that can include "considerable" risk from the experimental treatment if the participant faces the same level of risk from standard care.[13]

Research can also be designed to answer scientific questions by means that offer no therapeutic benefit to trial participants. In this case, the trial should proceed only on the REB's conclusion that harms have been minimized and are "proportionate to the benefits that might be expected from the knowledge gained by the study."[14] In both cases, research protocols must specify the potential harms to the participants. They sometimes provide quantitative estimates of the chances that participants might sustain these harms in the trial.

Risk analysis has been presented in different ways. Three phases are often noted: risk identification, risk assessment, and risk management.[15] *Risk identification* involves determining whether a defined hazard is present and whether it is of sufficient magnitude to merit concern. A problem will be defined, the purposes of a risk analysis formulated, and the available information gathered and scrutinized. These screening assessments can be "quite crude" depending on the quality and quantity of available information and the state of the science that informs the analysis.[16] Qualitative analysis can play an important role in "characterizing the fundamental assumptions of the analysis and the state of the science supporting them."[17] The *risk assessment* phase determines qualitative or quantitative estimates of the incidence and magnitude of a hazardous, adverse event on a given population. The *risk management* phase draws upon these estimates to develop policy options that aim to prevent, minimize, or mitigate the risks and evaluate their "health, economic, social, and political implications."[18] Various subspecialties of risk studies have been developed that provide specific assistance to risk analysis. Risk perception studies, for example, examine how people perceive the risks and benefits as well as their preferences for various risk/benefit trade-offs.[19] Risk communication studies examine the effectiveness of different formats for interpreting risk analysis results to the public.[20]

Brunk and colleagues, who have written on environmental risk debates, present the classical model of risk analysis as a two-stage process that moves from risk assessment, or estimation, to risk evaluation. The *risk assessment* stage is said to involve a purely factual estimation of the level of an identified hazard that measures the magnitude of the potential harm multiplied by the probability of its occurrence. This stage is often alleged to be a value-free assessment of the objective risk. The magnitude of the harm sustained in the event that a hazard occurs, as well as the probability of its occurrence, are usually presented as issues of fact and mathematics.[21] The second stage involves *risk evaluation* – that is, a normative determination of the risk's acceptability. Also known as risk management, this phase is not value-free. It involves the setting of safety and compensation standards and the allocation of management costs. These decisions reflect value judgments about norms of acceptability. While risk management proceeds from the estimate made at the first stage, it is influenced by public notions of subjective risk or risk perception. In the classical model, the rationality of these public judgments is assumed to depend on how closely they reflect the assessors' objective estimates of both the magnitude of harm and the probability of its occurrence. Lower estimations should inform higher levels of risk acceptability and vice versa. Differences between the assessors and the public on risk acceptability have been presented as conflicts between those rational experts who understand the objective risks and those irrational lay people who do not.[22] If values exert an unavoidable and significant influence on risk estimations, then the two-stage distinction is suspect.

Some argue that the line between risk assessment and risk management should be drawn less strictly.[23] Even assuming the best of intentions, the assessors' assumptions and beliefs may have normative implications that will make it difficult, if not impossible, to uncouple the quantitative task of risk assessment from the value judgments involved in determinations of safety.[24] Risk assessments may thus have as much or more to do with the values that influence our definitions of harms and benefits as they do with the quantitative methods by which the occurrence of harms is estimated.

There are at least four reasons why risk assessments, including those presented to REBs, should be scrutinized more closely. First, risk assessment is a regulatory or mandated science that seldom produces conclusions with the confidence levels employed by laboratory science. Brunk and his colleagues describe a significant gap between theoretical, or laboratory, research and the need to make defensible regulatory or management decisions. The laboratory scientist is trained to wait until all the necessary data are in and all the variables are sufficiently controlled. Only then can reliable conclusions be drawn. Risk assessors may not have this luxury. Their estimates often undergird a decision to proceed with, or curtail, some potentially risky plan of action "before the data concerning that risk are complete."[25] Their conclusions will not attain the high confidence levels employed by laboratory science. This process attempts to protect the general public from products and activities that pose unacceptably high levels of risk. Agencies that administer this process must decide among the conflicting interests of the parties to a risk debate. These parties can be more or less risk cautious. Regulatory decision making can protect the interests and values of some parties and curtail those of others.[26]

Second, numerous studies have shown that the parties to a risk debate can assess the same data with widely divergent results. William Freudenburg notes that calibration errors, or mistakes in estimating probabilities, present "serious problems" for scientifically trained assessors. He claims that "the most serious problems occur in the absence of reasonably definitive data, but [that] the general tendency in risk assessment is for even reasonably definitive data to be in unreasonably short supply."[27] These problems have been especially relevant to environmental issues, such as the ocean dumping of pollutants, "that are characterized by sparse scientific data useful for making policy."[28] These problems can be less relevant if extensive toxicological and epidemiological data on environmental health risks are available. There may, however, be gaps or inconsistencies in the data.[29]

Freudenburg's observations can be applied to assessing the general risks of harm from participating in biomedical research. This task raises issues relevant to both stages of the classical model of risk analysis. These issues concern, first, the methodology by which these risks are estimated and, second, the normative determination of risk acceptability. For instance, while clinical trial staff communicate drug-specific information to potential volunteers, they provide little or no data on the general risks of research participation. Statistical information on the general risks of drug trials might address the following questions: How many participants experience a serious reaction to a study drug? How many participants die annually during a clinical trial? Yet, according to *CenterWatch*, a monthly industry-sponsored publication that monitors US clinical trials, "this information is simply not available."[30]

CenterWatch made a provisional attempt to gather some of this information. It collected data from 130 randomly selected new drug applications that received Food and Drug Administration (FDA) approval between 1987 and 2001. These trials represented just under one-third of all new drugs approved by the FDA during this period.[31] Although the data consist of averages that do not "convey the high level of variability between clinical studies,"[32] the *CenterWatch* findings "suggest that death is a rare occurrence during clinical trials while adverse events occur routinely."[33] On average, *CenterWatch* concluded, one out of every thirty participants per new drug application will have a serious adverse event (for example, one that is "life threatening, permanently disabling or that result[s] in hospitalization").[34] In reviewing reports from the pharmaceutical industry to the FDA, *CenterWatch* concluded that one out of ten thousand participants "has died as a result of study drug effects while participating in clinical research studies."[35] While we are in no position to verify these figures, we agree that the provision of accurate information on general research risks should play a crucial role in the recruitment of clinical trial participants. The estimated one-in-thirty odds of experiencing a serious adverse event from taking a study drug might give some potential trial participants pause.[36] It seems crucial for the protection of research participants, therefore, to create the greatest possible transparency with respect to adverse events and research findings resulting from previous studies. Too often, negative trials and trials deemed uninteresting by research sponsors remain unpublished and unreported.[37]

However, even if negative trials were published and reported, the task of estimating these general risks would be challenging given the high level of variability between studies. The methodology of risk assessment would have to account for the numerous variables that impact on general research risk – for example, the type of intervention, the trial duration, the severity of the target illness, and the differences in the researchers' subjective definitions of adverse events. We can also question the extent to which such general averages relate to any one participant's relative risk – that is, the risk to an individual from a specific intervention of a particular dose and at a particular time:[38] "The risks that members of a group may run as individuals are not the same for each. For instance, one subject may be in better physical condition; another may suffer from heart disease that would make the experience even more dangerous for him."[39] In terms of infrastructure, providing estimates of general risk would require a central repository to receive data from all relevant trials as well as a comprehensive reporting scheme that researchers, REBs, research participants, and regulators could utilize.

Brunk and colleagues talk about risk assessment in the context of environmental harms. Their point is that the absence of a sufficient body of accumulated data makes risk assessment an attenuated science.[40] Stem cell and gene transfer research on humans also proceeds in the face of much uncertainty about long-term risks or benefits to humans. We argue that some of the insights of Brunk *et al.* and others also apply to this area. Who among us can say reliably that stem cell interventions pose minimal risk to research participants? Notwithstanding encouraging reports about the potential clinical applications of stem cell research in cardiology, a recent article in *Nature* warned in its introduction that "we should be wary of prematurely pushing laboratory research into clinical practice."[41] The risks posed to gene transfer research participants vary with the techniques used to transfer genetic material into the body.[42] While a risk assessment could plausibly aim to quantify the risk of malignancy, we may currently lack the established database to estimate this hazard with anything approaching the confidence level used by laboratory science. This uncertainty is the gap that risk assessment confronts in the context of this research. And it is this gap that has sustained the characterization of gene transfer research as "high risk."[43]

The third reason for scrutinizing risk assessments is that safety standard issues such as the protection of human research participants are "transscientific," that is, they oscillate between facts and values. Roger Kasperson avers an "oft-forgotten truism of risk analysis – that damage to people and what they value is the product of environmental or technological threat, human vulnerability to such threats, and values."[44] All three terms, and, in particular, the latter two, "are socially and economically dependent."[45] This fact might limit the extent to which risk analysis is a science for specialists as opposed to a normative exercise to which properly trained laypersons could contribute. The assessment process can reveal implicit normative choices at work in the uncertainty gap "between the ideal of laboratory science and the reality of risk estimation in the regulatory situation."[46] The challenge to the classical model of risk analysis is that values also exert an unavoidable influence on first-stage estimations. Kristen Shrader-Frechette argues that the quantitative risk assessment of hazardous substances is laden with value judgments in the face of uncertainty: "Assessors must make value judgments about which data to collect; how to simplify myriad facts into a workable model; how to extrapolate because of unknowns" and how to choose the statistical tests, sample sizes, and any other criteria that will be used.[47]

Several other inherently normative questions are relevant to the first-stage estimation of the risks of gene transfer research. For example, is it fair to expect that researchers will always take every effective precaution to minimize the risks of contamination during vector preparation? In order to measure these risks, we need to determine an applicable safety standard. How much significance should we give to the risk of human error? What institutional or individual factors should be seen as increasing this risk and by how much? How much care should we expect researchers to take when preparing the viral vectors to ensure that they are incapable of virus reproduction?[48] How do we define magnitudes of harm? What constitutes a serious adverse event? These are not factual questions. The process of answering them is prescriptive, not descriptive. Values are influential in this case because we have to define what we are trying to estimate. Available facts can help us to identify issues, but these issues can be resolved only by invoking values related, for example, to the acceptable levels of risk. The risk assessor's value framework thus contributes to the framing of the risk assessment. Since scientific data do not interpret themselves in the estimation of risk, the assessors have no choice "but to employ an interpretive point of view."[49]

Most risk analyses use numbers. A harm's probability of occurrence might be rendered statistically. The magnitude of harm might be measured by estimating the expected number of deaths in the relevant population and by assigning some value to these statistical lives. It could also be measured by estimating the incremental risk of death to an average person in this population and attaching some value to this risk. Either way, the "magnitude" of a harm is still a value-laden notion – it produces an expected value, which can be compared against other costs and benefits. For example, once we assess the magnitude of a harm, we might use that information to decide that it is worth $X to society to save a statistical life. The social value of a human life is a controversial issue in assessing the magnitude of risk.[50] Magnitude also relates to the seriousness or severity of harms, which may refer to notions of pain, discomfort, suffering, disability, perceived injustice, or the debasement of values.[51] Unlike death, these aspects "come in different qualities and degrees" and are thus even more difficult to measure and evaluate.[52] Therefore, merely reviewing the methodology by which the numbers are generated is insufficient. To understand a risk assessment, we need to understand the values in terms of which the risk is framed – that is, defined and presented. This focus on the qualitative dimensions of risk assessment is also relevant to somatic gene transfer and stem cell protocols since we currently have little in the way of quantitative data on the general risks of participating in this research. Without such data, the promise of benefits to be gained can be seen as a decisive reason for taking risks.[53]

In practice, risk assessment is often dominated by human judgment in the face of uncertainty.[54] The uncertainty inherent in many forms of research adds to the complexity of the risk assessment process. This is clearly the case in the context of genetic research. Indeed, the presentations of risk in some somatic gene transfer protocols admit to pervasive uncertainty about the potential harms.[55] There is, we suggest, still much uncertainty about molecular behaviour that complicates risk assessments of gene transfer and stem cell research. As Akshay Anand and Sunil K. Arora point out, "[c]linical genetics is still in its infancy."[56] According to Evelyn Fox Keller, we have not found that gene location explains gene function. The structural gene is the indispensable raw material in the dynamic process of stable genetic development. Yet this process now involves many other variables, including regulatory sequences found elsewhere on the genome, the products of other structural and functional genes, and the signalling network of the living cell. Keller would argue that we are just beginning to understand the complexity of this process.[57]

In even the clearest examples of single gene disorders, much remains to be learned about the processes by which a defective gene is linked to the onset of disease. The limits of current understanding are "far more conspicuous" in conditions that involve the participation of many genes (for example, heart disease or stroke). Keller posits a "therapeutic gap" between proficient genetic screening and medical benefits from gene transfer interventions. In terms of laboratory science, the data are far from collected.[58] As of 2001, attempts to treat single-gene diseases comprised an eighth of the world roster of about 500 approved clinical protocols for gene therapy research. Transient gene expression research, which targets coronary-artery disease and various types of cancer, accounted for most of the remainder.[59] This research involves growth-factor genes or genes that might stimulate the immune system. They are transferred into the body through viral vectors for short periods of activity. This might cause new blood vessels to grow around blocked coronary arteries or help to shrink tumours. In short, transient gene expression is a developing hypothesis. Theoretically, the infusion of growth-factor genes should be sufficient to start the process. According to specialists, while these approaches to vascular diseases and tumour immunotherapy are promising, "they are still in their infancy."[60]

By January 2004, there were 918 approved clinical trial protocols for gene transfer research. Only 15 (1.6 percent) were Phase III trials, which focus on efficacy and therapeutic value in a larger sample of patients. Most (589 or 64.2 percent) were Phase I trials designed to assess safety. There were 120 (13.1 percent) Phase II trials designed to assess efficacy and 185 (20.2 percent) combined Phase I/II trials. There were 9 (1 percent) combined Phase II/III trials.[61] Thus, most of this research cannot be claimed to have potential therapeutic benefit to participants. We suggest that risk assessment of gene transfer research still takes place in an environment where reasonably definitive data are, in Freudenburg's words, in unreasonably short supply.[62] Simply put, assessing the risks of gene transfer and stem cell research is not on par with estimating the risks of lung cancer from smoking, of mesothelioma from asbestos, or of HIV/AIDS from unprotected sex. Indeed, epidemiologic studies can identify factors that increase a person's risk for many chronic diseases.[63] Yet, while access to genomic sequences will increasingly shape risk assessment in the coming decades, "genomic researchers are not necessarily focused on risk assessment problems."[64]

There is a fourth reason for the law to be concerned with the scrutiny of risk assessments. Those individuals who propose research in which the harm could be sustained may be less cautious about risk than those who might be harmed. Some of those who assume the research risks may be more inclined to err on the side of protection than those who propose them. Brunk and his colleagues remind us that "risk" is a Janus-faced term. A serious risk of harm with a low probability of occurrence can be seen as a good gamble in a scientific attempt to realize great potential benefit. One might even characterize the greater risk as the loss of opportunity to realize potential benefit if the study does not proceed. Yet this risk can also be seen as something to avoid despite potential benefit. These risk perceptions depend on whether one is inclined to risk taking or to risk caution. They can also reflect different values about the importance of certain biomedical technologies or the range of benefits that should be realized in the health-care system. This can politicize risk debates in terms of the agendas the different parties bring to the table. We are sceptical of the notion that risk debates arise between those whose judgments are determined by objective analysis of the risks and those whose judgments are determined by irrationally subjective risk perceptions.[65] We argue that they are, in fact, debates "among different value frameworks, different ways of thinking about moral values, different conceptions of society, and different attitudes toward technology and towards risk-taking itself."[66]

Concerns about risk assessment in somatic gene transfer research were raised in the mid-1990s. European critics noted in 1994 that inflated publicity about "gene therapy trials" risked misleading the public. They called for a full public review of ongoing trials in 1994 to provide a "realistic assessment of the risks and state of the technology currently available."[67] In a report to the US National Institutes of Health (NIH) in 1995, an expert review panel concluded that many physician/investigators and their sponsors were "overselling" the technology and promoting the idea that "gene therapies" were further developed than they were. Despite anecdotal claims of successful therapy and NIH approval of more than 100 human studies, the review panel found that clinical efficacy had not been reliably demonstrated. Contrary to public perception, somatic gene transfer research was still in a very early stage. The panel found that little was really known about the vectors used to transfer genes into target cells. Many of the studies reviewed were found to have a weak design that yielded scant data. The panel also expressed concern that misleading publicity could give research participants erroneous ideas about what was feasible. It warned that turning a "blind eye to the hype could lead to serious consequences."[68] Even so, there was very little public or academic discourse about the risks of somatic gene transfer research before the first known death in a US gene transfer study in 1999.[69] Jesse Gelsinger, an eighteen-year-old man with a mild disorder of nitrogen metabolism known as ornithine transcarbamylase deficiency, participated in a gene transfer study at the University of Pennsylvania in which an adenovirus was being tested as a means of transmitting a gene to correct the disorder. He died from an immune reaction four days after the adenovirus was injected into his liver. His was the first death attributed directly to gene transfer research. It resulted in worldwide publicity, a suspension of all "gene therapy" trials at the University of Pennsylvania, and a senate subcommittee investigation.[70]

Three Particular Risks in Biomedical Research

We classify two very different types of risk from gene transfer and stem cell research: risks to persons and risks to social values. We consider three risks in particular that we feel the law should address. These are risks of physical and psychological harm to participants, risks to the objectivity and integrity of science that are posed by conflicts of interest, and risks to other social values, for example, the sanctity of life and public trust in science. Although the risks are not exclusive to gene transfer and stem cell research, the combination of these risks in these forms of new biomedical research merits our attention. Gene transfer and stem cell research are used for our purposes as paradigm cases of new forms of research.

The risks discussed in this essay can also overlap. Risks to participants are often unrelated to conflicts of interest, and conflicts of interest will not necessarily create a situation in which participants are more likely to be exposed to the risk of physical harm. Yet such conflicts seem to have contributed to tragic consequences for research participants,[71] and they may also compromise professional conduct regardless of participant harm. They also can affect the social value of public trust in the conduct of research. Strong correlations have been observed between trust and the public acceptance of estimated risks and benefits, especially those pertaining to new technologies about which the public lacks "scientific" knowledge.[72] Uninformed trust can make research participants vulnerable to biased risk assessments of gene transfer and stem cell research. We can cite other examples in which such values could be threatened regardless of conflict of interest. For instance, the creation of embryos for stem cell research can affect widely shared assumptions about the sanctity, or the special value, of human life.[73] While we include all of these forms of risk in our discussion, we realize that some risks to social values may not be suitable for REB scrutiny but should be the subject of wider public debates.

Risks of Physical Harm to Research Participants

Recent events have led to growing concerns about the physical risks of, and risk reporting systems for, gene transfer research. Following the death of Jesse Gelsinger, the NIH was quickly informed of 652 previously unreported serious adverse events that occurred during gene transfer trials, of which six were deaths.[74] This new information led to congressional hearings on the oversight of patient safety.[75] The first Canadian "gene therapy" trial was conducted in 1993, and at least thirty other trials have been approved since that time. The first known death of a Canadian gene therapy research participant occurred in 1997. James Dent was diagnosed with a malignant brain tumour and enrolled in a gene transfer study. He was injected with a virus that carried genes to his tumour. He died a few days later. According to the Canadian Broadcasting Corporation (CBC), a Health Canada report found that the second stage of the trial in which James Dent was enrolled contributed to his death. The consent form that he signed contained no information about the "serious adverse brain events" that afflicted seventeen out of thirty patients in a similar trial. Allegedly, James Dent was unaware of this information, despite the fact that it was known both to US regulators and to Novartis, the company that sponsored his trial. There were other omissions. It was never reported to Health Canada that a US patient died in Indiana only days before in the same multi-centre trial. Nor was this first death reported, as required, to the US NIH, which posts such information on its website. According to the CBC, Novartis later acknowledged that it was its responsibility to report the Indiana death to Health Canada within seven days. The company has since terminated all research on the "gene therapy product" that was tested on James Dent.[76] In December 2002, twenty-seven of the more than 200 ongoing US gene transfer trials were suspended after French researchers reported that the vectors used in some of their trials were apparently associated with cancer in two young participants. The

US trials were allowed to resume on March 2003, although the FDA refused to approve two suspended US trials similar to the French research that led to the cancer cases.[77]

We still face significant challenges in determining the physical risks of somatic gene transfer research. We can characterize four of the most important risks: (1) contamination during vector preparation; (2) immune responses that interfere with treatment efficacy; (3) malignancy, that is, if vectors disrupt host tumour-suppressor genes or activate oncogenes; and (4) viral recombination.[78] However, vector toxicity levels for animals may diverge from those of humans and immunological predispositions to vectors may vary between individuals. There are also concerns about the reliability of transferring preclinical data from the animal model to therapeutic application in humans.[79] In short, while we can characterize these physical harms, we may not yet be able to reliably assess their probability of occurrence. "A reliable assessment of the risk of cancer," for instance, "will require long-term follow up of large numbers of patients."[80]

A long-term monitoring system would have to retrieve, on an annual basis, information covering the causes of any deaths, the appearance of new cancers, any unusual abnormalities or illnesses, and the birth of any children to participants after the trial. Surprisingly, the United Kingdom's Gene Therapy Advisory Committee found in 2000 that there was no formal long-term monitoring system for gene transfer research participants anywhere in the world. Although the need for such follow-up was recognized early on, the comprehensive retrieval of required data has not proceeded apace with the growth of gene transfer research.[81] Indeed, the national databases by which the general risks of this research might be estimated are still being developed.[82]

In the context of stem cell research, two recent Canadian developments are worth mentioning. The first initiative came from the Canadian Institutes for Health Research, which has convened a Stem Cell Oversight Committee to review government-funded stem cell research. This committee will, however, have no authority to monitor private-sector stem cell research.[83] A more rigorous regulatory structure was introduced with the new legislation on assisted human reproduction. Bill C-6, *An Act Respecting Assisted Human Reproduction and Related Research*,[84] requires the establishment of a Canadian Assisted Human Reproduction Agency. It will oversee and control research activities related to assisted human reproduction and enforce various statutory prohibitions (for example, a prohibition on reproductive and therapeutic human cloning).[85]

Members of the risk analysis community have argued that new genomic data may require an assessment framework that has yet to be appropriately developed.[86] We see no reliable basis for stating that, as of 2004, the hypothetical benefits of gene transfer or stem cell research outweigh the risks about which we are just beginning to learn.[87] Indeed, we may be running risks of physical harm that we have yet to discern.[88] Consider the current state of stem cell research. It is very difficult to remove implanted stem cells from the body should something go wrong. There is still speculation about how implanted stem cells, especially embryonic ones, might proliferate in the human body. Embryonic stem cells are undifferentiated and pluripotent – that is, they have an unlimited capacity to divide. Hence, there is the concern that they might form teratomas or cancerous growths.[89] For instance, a recent study by Lars M. Bjorklund and colleagues involved the transplantation of mouse embryonic stem cells into the brains of twenty-five adult mice. Five of these mice died and were found in a post-mortem analysis to have teratoma-like tumours at the implantation site.[90]

Writing for the NIH in 2000, Ron McKay noted that "we may gain a deeper understanding of the process of cell replacement" by studying stem cells.[91] Furthermore, this research hypothesizes huge potential benefits to human health, ranging from generating new neurons for treating patients with Parkinson's disease to learning about the molecular processes that cause tumours. However, McKay also noted that we have much to learn about the processes by which stem cells replicate and differentiate. We know "little about how stem cells can differentiate across boundaries [for example, how blood cells might differentiate into brain cells] and how we could divert them into the pathway of choice."[92] He also reminded us that we do not know "where unexpected benefits may suddenly emerge."[93]

Fair enough, but we suggest that McKay's last statement is also applicable to unexpected risks. If so, the risk assessment of stem cell research may face problems similar to those encountered in the risk assessment of novel environmental health hazards. Scientific knowledge usually refers to "known processes and their influence on known state-variables. Within this domain of reproducibility and control, uncertainty can be explicitly stated and reduced by reproducible experiments under controlled conditions."[94] Thus, our lack of knowledge about stem cells might be characterized by the "interaction between unknown processes and/or unknown state-variables."[95] This might pose a "fundamental obstacle to credible risk assessment" at this early stage of stem cell research.[96] Government regulators, scientists, and REB members should approach risk assessments of this research with caution. We see a need for the ongoing collation and independent appraisal of risk assessment data that is beyond the capacity of local REBs.

Risks Posed by Conflicts of Interest: Impact on the Conduct and Outcome of Research

Conflicts of interest (COIs) are traditionally not discussed in the same context as the issue of risk assessment. We believe that the potential impact of COIs ought to be considered by regulatory agencies and REBs as risk factors in medical research. The impact of COI on behaviour is hard to quantify and can be estimated only on the basis of comparisons with retrospective studies. Like the determination of risk to human health or the natural environment posed by the introduction of new biomedical technology or chemical agents, the influence of COI is seldom established clearly in individual cases. It is measured in terms of the likelihood of occurrence. "Guesstimates" of influence of COIs are determined through studies indicating patterns of behaviour. Like risk to the environment or to health, the impact of COI is determined through statistical measurements.

The Committee on Assessing the System for Protecting Human Research Subjects of the US Institute of Medicine points to the link between COI and risk assessment. Although it suggests that REBs should not bear the primary responsibility for assessing COI, they should, according to the committee, be concerned about how "bias or overly optimistic promises of potential benefits are clouding risk assessments." The committee therefore believes that REBs should assess how "financial conflicts of interest have the potential to affect participant safety, and, if necessary, how participants should be informed of any resulting risk."[97]

The subject of COI in medical research has received an extraordinary amount of attention in the professional literature of the last decade.[98] New articles appear weekly in leading medical journals discussing the increasing commercial interests in medical research. Their authors note the potential impact of these interests on the conduct of investigators, on research participants, and on the objectivity and integrity of the scientific enterprise. Commercial interests are not the only interests that create conflicts for investigators. Inherent in any form of medical research involving patients is a tension between the clinical duties of health-care professionals and their research interests.[99] Many – if not most – of the historical instances of research misconduct have taken place in the context of government-funded research and were unrelated to significant financial interests. They have resulted mainly from an inherent drive by researchers to proceed with research without proper regard to the rights and well-being of research subjects.[100] Indeed, the desire for fame, the need for academic publications, or, perhaps, simply a strong enthusiasm for what researchers believe will be a scientific breakthrough have often been the main causes of inappropriate research behaviour. The review of research protocols by a committee without a direct interest in the research was introduced as a counterbalance to this potential for an overzealous commitment to science. The system of REBs is thus in itself a recognition of the inherent conflict involved in medical research.

The sheer number of recent publications on the growth of financial conflicts of interest suggests that they merit special attention. Official reports and guidelines that have recently been developed by various agencies, including the US Office of Human Research Protection[101] and the Association of the American Medical Colleges,[102] explicitly recognize that financial conflicts of interest are an increasing cause for concern in medical research. As Denis F. Thompson points out in a frequently cited article in the *New England Journal of Medicine*, many of the other conflicts of interests are unavoidable and are an inherent part of conducting research.[103] They require a balanced review, but they cannot completely be avoided. Financial conflicts, in his view, deserve special attention for two reasons: first, because many of them can be avoided; and, second, because money is a strong motivator and a driving force behind many human actions.

We agree with Thompson that financial conflicts merit special attention, given the growing private-sector investment in medical research. Medical research, more than ever before, is part of a highly profitable pharmaceutical and biotechnology industry. Research undertaken outside of academic health centres and universities has systematically increased and is now more prevalent than academic research.[104] Private-sector funding is currently the driving force behind much of the clinical research taking place in industrialized countries. Moreover, academic institutions have significantly augmented their collaboration with industry. Academic research is increasingly aimed at the development of commercial drugs or medical devices, often in partnership with industry sponsors. A growing part of the income generated by universities comes from patents on research inventions. Governmental funding agencies are increasingly making funding for research conditional on matching funding from the private commercial sector.[105]

Genome Canada is an example of an agency that is a major funder of health research, yet one that has as its main mandate the economic development of genomics and biotechnology. Genome Canada and several other agencies involved in the funding of health research require that every dollar allocated for research purposes be matched by private contributions. These agencies emphasize the importance of creating patents and intellectual property through the research they fund. Research accomplishments, which are crucial determinants for future funding opportunities, are measured with those outcomes in mind – the idea being that economic development of the health-technology sector goes hand in hand with medical progress and that both economic development and health care will benefit from such stimulation. The Canadian Stem Cell Network, a research network funded through the Canadian Centres for Excellence, follows the same approach. It is planning the establishment of a commercial stem cell company, in collaboration with the various universities and hospitals involved in the network, and is promoting interaction with industry.[106] The creation of patents and the promotion of Canadian-based biotechnology companies are important outcome measures of this network.

What are the concerns? They can be divided into two main categories. First, the concern for the impact of financial interests on the recruitment of participants and on the conduct of researchers during the trial is directly relevant to the protection of research participants. A second major concern, which deals more with the long-term impact of COIs, has to do with the integrity of the scientific process and the independence of medical science. A detailed discussion of how financial interests may impact on patient recruitment and on the conduct of researchers exceeds the scope of this essay. It suffices to refer to some of the issues discussed in the literature. The significant financial interests in clinical drug trials, for example, have had an influence on recruitment practices. An increasing number of drug trials are being undertaken, with the result that there is growing competition for research subjects between contract research organizations (CROs), pharmaceutical companies, academic institutions, and private physicians. Payments to research subjects[107] and financial rewards to clinicians, health-care workers, and research coordinators to promote fast recruitment[108] may undermine crucial aspects of what should be voluntary informed consent. Patients increasingly participate in research because of the financial rewards or to obtain access to new therapies, often ignoring the potential risks involved in the study. The sometimes staggering amounts of money offered to reward fast recruiters in industry trials[109] are sufficient to make us worried about violations of informed-consent procedures and even about the potential bending of inclusion criteria to enter people into a clinical trial.[110]

Financial conflicts in the recruitment process are obviously related to other structural and even more significant COIs. Patients, clinical investigators, and others involved in the research are offered money because of the financial interests in the development of drugs, medical devices, or therapies. Lawsuits launched by the Securities and Exchange Commission in the United States, as well as recent empirical studies, indicate, for example, that insider trading exists in clinical research.[111] While this fact does not necessarily mean that research subjects are directly threatened by such behaviour, it does indicate that people who are involved in research may act according to their financial interests and that some of them are even tempted to engage in illegal behaviour.

The death of Jesse Gelsinger in a gene therapy trial in 1999 is an indication of what can happen when financial interests are significant.[112] Although it is hard to prove that the commencement of the trial and the inclusion of Jesse Gelsinger were directly related to the financial interests of the investigator, the amounts of money involved, the shortcomings of the informed-consent process, and other related issues clearly suggest a link. The principal investigator of the gene therapy trial, who was the director of the Institute for Human Gene Therapy at the University of Pennsylvania, owned 30 percent of the stock of the sponsoring company. This company was the major funder of the research institute, in which it had invested US$20 million. Moreover, the sponsorship contract between the institute and the company was up for renewal, and significant results in research would clearly have provided an incentive for further funding. In this context, it is hard not to make a connection between the financial interests involved and the fact that research risks were either depreciated or not disclosed. Various commentators have pointed out that researchers with strong financial interests in recruiting participants for a clinical trial may oversell the trial to their patients by depreciating the risks or exaggerating the potential benefits.[113]

Financial interests in drug trials may influence investigators' choice of research design. Placebo-controlled trials, for example, require fewer research subjects than active control trials to obtain statistically significant results. Placebo trials are therefore cheaper and can be conducted faster, which may serve the interests of investigators since the increase in research activities has made it much harder to find sufficient numbers of trial participants. These trials, however, also expose subjects to the risks of being deprived of treatment. This factor is problematic, in particular, when we are dealing with serious medical conditions.

The impact of COIs on the protection of research participants is just one of the concerns expressed in the literature. Concerns about the potential impact of the commercial interests of investigators on the scientific process and on the outcome of research have received even more attention. The various ways in which commercial interests shape research have been identified.[114] Several studies have shown a correlation between the sources of funding and the research outcome, which suggests that either researchers are pre-selected on the basis of their favourable views towards sponsors' products or the source of funding influences more directly the results of research.[115]

Research sponsored by industry is much more likely than independent research to conclude that drugs of the kind produced by sponsors are efficacious. Commercial interests may affect the study outcome in different ways. The selection of the study population and the choice of statistical method will influence the research outcome and may thus be used to manipulate the results. Studies can be designed in such a way that they will more likely result in a positive outcome, benefiting drug approval and post-approval marketing. Increasingly, studies are either undertaken by the commercial sponsors or are under their control. Research coordinated through CROs often involves many community-based physicians, who are less likely to be interested or trained in analyzing the appropriateness of the methodology and the results. In addition, some commentators have noted how sponsoring companies sometimes control the writing process by using a so-called ghostwriter and then subsequently approach academic investigators to present the study results as their own.[116]

Various controversies – for example, the well-known controversy involving Dr. Olivieri and her dispute with the pharmaceutical company Apotex, the Hospital for Sick Children, and the University of Toronto – have shown that sponsors may try to hinder the publication of negative results and that the financial interests of research institutions may influence, or appear to influence, support for researchers.[117] Interestingly, one study also indicates that even when no explicit publication restriction exists, many researchers who receive gifts from those who sponsor their research still think that they have to obtain permission from the sponsor before publishing the results of a study.[118] The impact of these developments should not be underestimated. Given the growing emphasis on evidence-based medicine, the outcome of research will influence clinical practice. Drug agencies, clinicians, and the public depend on research results to determine whether particular drugs are safe and efficacious. If medical research is compromised by COI, then trust in medicine as a social endeavour is at risk.

Risks to Social Values
The risks posed by COI to the conduct and outcome of research brings us to another type of risk: the risk to social values. In our estimation, this involves more than the risks to social values from, for example, the sources of stem cell research (for example, embryos) or the uses to which genetics might be put (for example, eugenics). COIs also risk compromising the social value of public trust in the ethical conduct of research. Social values can be characterized as "the importance to members of the group of experiencing their public lives and social interactions in certain ways ... [V]alues about how the society's risks are structured and distributed ... are social values, not individual feelings."[119] They pertain to notions of how persons are treated; how society is to be structured in terms of the risks that its members will jointly face; how public policies promote the sense of solidarity citizens feel towards each other; or how these policies reflect the shared values that give society its identity. Distributive issues of risks, costs, and benefits as well as the value of human life are examples of social values.[120] These values can reflect concerns about justice – for example, if risks are deliberately confined to an uninformed and vulnerable group whose members are abused in the acquisition of scientific knowledge. Jeremy Frailberg and Michael Trebilcock capture the role of this idea of social values in an insightful way, noting "the instinctive aversion most people have to placing certain groups under high risks for the benefit of other groups ... even when one is a member of the group that benefits. This aversion is heightened when those at risk are among society's already disadvantaged."[121] In this way, the Tuskegee syphilis study and the Cold War radiation experiments violated social values as well as the unwitting participants.[122]

Ethical research is premised on achieving scientifically and socially important aims. Public trust is thus crucial to the conduct of ethical research. Students must trust supervisors; principal investigators must trust subordinates; and colleagues need to trust each other. Researchers need to trust journals, granting agencies, and research institutions. Research participants and other citizens need to trust researchers.[123] Given the billions of dollars invested annually in North American research and development, it can be argued that "the erosion of public confidence in science that may occur" if society does not deal effectively with COI could be "damaging and corrosive to democracy."[124]

We noted earlier that strong correlations have been observed between social trust and the public acceptance of the estimated risks and benefits of new technologies about which the public may lack "scientific" knowledge. Indeed, research indicates that the lay public relies on social trust in risk/benefit judgments when personal knowledge about hazards is lacking.[125] "Biotechnology and especially its implications for the 'new' human genetics raise major concerns about risk and trust in regulatory regimes."[126] Some critics argue that there has been a loss of trust in biotechnology because of inherent weaknesses in its conventional regulatory agencies.[127] Brian Salter and Mavis Jones argue that human genetics, especially its controversial domains of stem cell and gene transfer research, cannot be regulated solely through an expert discourse on technical safety. At the political level, the regulation of risk must address dynamics of value and belief and incorporate value assessments into the assessments of technical safety.[128]

"Our policies for reducing risks," writes Douglas MacLean, "must remain sensitive to our social values." Furthermore, these values can determine that different principles can guide policies in different contexts of risk.[129] We suggest that these analyses highlight the need for law reform in the governance of biomedical research. We want to know that things we value deeply – for example, the welfare of research participants and the integrity and reliability of scientific investigation – are being protected by the institutions that we have created to be the trustees of these values. Consequently, REBs are easily seen as "public institutions, which the public expects in part to give voice to the ideals of a society that cares deeply about the lives and the health of its citizens."[130]

Principles for Law Reform

What are the general ideas, or principles, that might guide aspects of law reform in biomedical research with human participants? We cannot present an exhaustive list of these guiding principles, but we intend to present ones that we hope will incite a conceptual as well as policy-oriented debate. We will propose our own ideas about the legal infrastructure that might reflect these principles in the next section.

After noting the limitations and value-laden nature of regulatory science, and the importance of maintaining trust in risk-assessment agencies, Paul Slovik sees the need for a new approach – one that focuses upon more public participation in both risk assessment and risk decision making. This approach would aim at making the decision process more democratic, improving the relevance and quality of technical analysis, and increasing the legitimacy and public acceptance of the resulting decisions.[131] Numerous models for public participation in regulatory science have been proposed.[132] The need for a similar approach to research review has been a recurring theme in bioethics since at least 1975, when the philosopher Robert Veatch alleged a basic disjunction in REB structure. Veatch saw REBs as anomalous committees that fell between two different regulatory models: the model of professional review and the model of the citizens' jury. The membership of REBs consisted predominantly of scientific experts, with some spots reserved for lay people who were supposed to function as community representatives. Veatch felt that this predominance could shift the framing of risk towards the researchers' value framework. It might even lead to a shift towards greater risk taking. He was not convinced that community members could prevent this predominant shift in favour of the researchers' interests.[133] These interests could include the ones noted earlier in this essay, such as the desire for professional renown, the need to acquire funding and publish academic papers, and a strong enthusiasm for scientific development. This enthusiasm implies a particular sensitivity to benefits that are achievable only if the research proceeds, and it creates a mind-set that favours the launching of the research project.[134] In the risk environment of increasingly commercialized science, researchers' interests can also reflect a shift in values towards profit and economic growth.[135]

Paul McNeill claimed in 1993 that "the schism described by Veatch is still apparent in [REBs] all over the world."[136] We argue that McNeill's claim is no less relevant today. Since REBs will be evaluating protocols and risk assessments that are formulated by those who endorse the research, we suggest a principled approach to review that could balance the interests of those proposing the risks by empowering the risk-cautious interests of those who might assume them. This balance could "be found in a process that allows the holders of various points of view to have an equal opportunity for expression and control."[137] There should be as many participant representatives on REBs as representatives of science.[138] This approach will require a different kind of engagement between REB members by which risks and values are negotiated.[139] It should involve a legislated mandate for REB structure and membership, including the participation and decisional authority of participant representatives or advocates from relevant consumer health groups. These members should be informed of the research issues from the perspective of the participants that they would represent. Ideally, they would be accountable to an appropriate community group that can represent the interests of the research participants. Like McNeill, we argue that community group affiliation is required to give participant representatives "some ground and support for their views."[140] To avoid bias towards the researchers' values, participant representatives should have no past or present affiliation with the research institution.[141] Indeed, we would take this precaution a step further by mandating that the community groups they represent must also not be affiliated with, or funded by, private-sector corporations that conduct or fund research. While the representatives' fundamental concern would be to protect research participants from harm, they would also address concerns about methodology, participant selection, access to research results, privacy, and "the manner of arriving at conclusions and the conclusions themselves."[142] We argue that these representatives should be legally mandated to reflect a risk-cautious value framework in deciding whether the study should be approved.

A risk-cautious value framework would favour a review of risk assessments by those with no financial or competing interest in the research. It would appreciate the potential importance of biomedical research without assuming that proposed investigations are *prima facie* benign and worth a decision to run considerable risks in order to realize benefits that might otherwise be lost.[143] It would raise questions that would reflect a predominant concern for risks to participants and the objectivity of science. For instance, REB members should inquire carefully about whether the research participants have been informed of the latest reported adverse events in similar trials. Not only should they review the informed-consent documents presented to them, but they should also monitor how consent is really obtained and what information has been given. Jesse Gelsinger and James Dent were not adequately informed of the risks involved in their studies.[144] REB members should also inquire about whether the investigators have done a thorough review of the relevant literature in formulating their risk assessment of the drug being studied. This was not the case in the 1999 asthma study at Johns Hopkins University in which Ellen Roche died after inhaling hexamethonium. Numerous available studies documenting the pulmonary toxicity of hexamethonium were overlooked before the protocol was submitted to the REB. Neither the researchers nor the REB assessed this literature. A better assessment of the literature by the REB could probably have prevented the death of this healthy woman.[145]

We have acknowledged that different parties to a risk debate can bring different risk perspectives to the table. Differences of opinion also exist in the patient and patient advocacy populations. There are various examples of research participant advocacy that have not reflected a risk-cautious protective approach. The work of HIV/AIDS activists to hasten the development and availability of new anti-retroviral drugs is a seminal case in point.

Indeed, much of this advocacy has expressed an enthusiasm for "the bright side" of research and a willingness to assume risk that many scientific investigators did not share. Rebecca Dresser observes that this attitude is "sharply evident in advocacy efforts to expand patients' access to clinical trials and unproven interventions."[146] These advocates have tended to avoid REBs that examine the risks faced by research participants. They have regarded ethics review as a paternalistic distraction from the main goal of promoting benefits to patients. Nor have they complained when researchers or journalists have "put an overly positive spin on the significance of study findings."[147] Not surprisingly, drug companies and other businesses have sought public alliance with such groups. This outcome has made some advocates susceptible to the same COI that has beset researchers.[148] These precedents might lead one to think that participant advocacy is synonymous with the uncritical promotion of research. We have three reasons for thinking otherwise.

First, we note that it is simply mistaken to conflate participant advocacy with this overly positive approach to research. There are numerous models of advocacy that can be used to promote different mandates: "Advocacy programs, in addition to including many diverse activities, vary according to their objectives, modes of operation, and relationships with the institution or group of institutions within which they function."[149] Advocacy can thus be concerned with challenging existing practices. The point is to specify a mandate. We suggest that participant representatives on REBs should have a specific mandate to advocate a risk-cautious perspective. Their primary focus would be the protection of research participants. Scrutinizing risk assessments by those who endorse the proposed research would be a crucial responsibility for which they should receive sufficient education and training. This mandate would reflect what has historically been the "main reason" for including "community members" on REBs, namely to represent a concern for the protection of research participants that is free of any bias towards research interests.[150] Like Paul McNeill, we argue that this mandate should be "explicit." Without such a mandate, participant representatives lack a clear role. Without appropriate training, they may lack "recognised expertise" and be disempowered in their relationships with institutional and professional REB members.[151]

Second, the precedents noted earlier do not tell the whole story. According to Dresser, perspectives on research participant advocacy are currently changing. Some HIV/AIDS activists have qualified their early enthusiasm for expanded access. They have come to question the benefits of the FDA's accelerated approval program and now argue that "patients would be better off if the agency applied more rigorous standards in deciding when new drugs may be marketed for clinical use."[152] It has become increasingly clear to such advocates that experimental drugs can be ineffective or dangerous.

Further, there is a growing awareness that an exclusive emphasis on expanded access could hinder attempts to discern which new drugs are safe and effective. Dresser notes other examples. Certain women's health advocates now protest the widespread availability of high-dose chemotherapy and bone marrow transplantation for breast cancer, for which they once advocated. This change came with the release of trial data showing no benefit from these interventions. These advocates now argue that women "would be better served if constraints were placed on their access" to these "burdensome and questionably effective" procedures.[153]

Third, there are indeed research participant advocacy groups whose mandates reflect a risk-cautious, protective approach. For instance, the Alliance for Human Research Protection is a US network of lay and professional people with a mandate to advance ethical research practices; to ensure that the human rights, dignity, and welfare of research participants is protected; and to "minimize the risks associated with such endeavors."[154] This group argues that the "explosion" of biomedical research over the past decade has not been accompanied by "an effective system of oversight or enforcement" to protect research participants. COI in commercially funded research and the incomplete disclosure of risks are two systemic problems that this group aims to address.[155] Citizens for Responsible Care and Research is another US group of lay people and professionals that is dedicated to the protection of vulnerable research participants, especially "the mentally incapacitated, children, seniors, the homeless and the poor." This group has been instrumental "in bringing documented evidence of abuse in human subject research to public attention."[156] These groups may become more influential as public awareness of research risks is heightened. We feel that they serve as timely models for a risk-cautious mandate in research review.

Obviously, we do not want to suggest that lay members of REBs necessarily have to take the same often strongly critical stand of some of these advocacy groups or to have the same approach towards research. We simply believe that because of the protective function of REBs, it is important to have an REB membership that has no direct and strong interest in seeing specific forms of research immediately proceed. People who have for several years been involved in advocacy to promote funding for stem cell research on Parkinson's and who are themselves affected by the disease, or who have close family members affected by it, can be more biased and enthusiastic about experimental clinical trials than the researchers. In our view, a legislative basis for REBs would also symbolically reflect the importance of their administrative function. They are regarded *de facto* as crucial players by funding agencies and drug regulators. They are also given an increasing role in other statutory regimes, such as those introduced by certain provincial privacy statutes.[157] And yet, REBs do not fulfill basic standards that are imposed by administrative law on regulatory and judicial bodies.[158]

The risks posed by COI to medical research should be dealt with at various levels. As pointed out, REBs have been developed to deal with the general COI embedded in research. Their role in assessing financial COIs, however, is more complex. REBs have the mandate to protect human research participants and to assess the informed-consent procedure. They also have to determine whether there are particular factors that would increase the risk to participants. This should include an assessment of the likelihood that investigators will act inappropriately, for example, by misinforming participants about the risks and potential benefits. In the current climate of pervasive COIs, REBs must not avoid questioning the impact of financial interests.[159] They certainly have to decide whether those interests require additional safeguards, such as independent monitoring of the consent process or increased monitoring of who is included in the trials. However, they generally lack both the expertise and the means to obtain all the relevant information about financial conflicts.[160] It thus seems problematic that Health Canada's Therapeutic Products Directorate relies currently on REBs as *the* authority to deal with COIs. This reliance is highlighted by a regulatory impact analysis statement, which accompanies new regulations on clinical trials.[161]

In recognition of how financial interests may impact on the rights and well-being of participants, various agencies and commentators have recommended the establishment of independent COI Committees in research institutions.[162] Clinical investigators and other research personnel should have an obligation to divulge any financial relationships between themselves and potential research sponsors. This should include information on consulting relationships, remunerated lectures, membership on advisory boards, and any stock in a company that could benefit from their research. These committees should also have the mandate to review institutional COI that could impact on research. REBs should be informed by the COI Committee of all relevant financial interests.

While we believe that this oversight would be an important first step in dealing with the immediate impact of COI on participant safety, it seems an insufficient means of dealing with the broader impact of COI on the integrity of science. The review by COI Committees would work only in academic institutional settings. Since much research is undertaken outside these institutions, only a small portion of research activities would be affected. We have noted that Canadian REBs are currently affected by both financial and institutional COI. We see a COI when REBs decide upon the ethical acceptability of research protocols "when the institution in which they are based stands to gain from research it conducts."[163] It is therefore untenable to rely on REBs within these institutions to deal with such conflicts. Moreover, many research protocols are being reviewed by private REBs located in for-profit CROs or pharmaceutical companies. These REBs are also affected by fundamental COIs.[164] If REBs ought to play any reliable role in the area of COI, then it seems to us that they should be fundamentally reformed to guarantee their administrative independence.[165] We will make some suggestions later in this essay about the establishment of a governmental agency for the protection of research participants. REBs should report to such an agency and be disconnected from their institutional conflicts and the commercial interests of research sponsors.

However, we believe that a more fundamental solution is required to deal with the impact of financial interests on the integrity of the scientific enterprise. Other commentators have already noted that the pressures created by the staggering increase in clinical research and the lack of control over drug development can be dealt with only by a national drug review and testing agency.[166] Such an agency would determine on the basis of preliminary data which trial could go ahead and would coordinate the clinical research using a clinical trial design that it would develop internally, in consultation with the producer of the compound. This type of national agency would relieve the pressure that currently leads to inappropriate competition for research participants and lower standards of protection. It would also allow for a more independent assessment of drug development, which is crucial to safeguard public confidence in evidence-based medicine.

Other measures could be integrated in the existing system. Indicating an increased awareness within professional organizations of these issues, the Association of American Medical Colleges made some interesting recommendations in two reports on COIs.[167] One of them is particularly relevant to our discussion. The association recommends that institutions introduce a rebuttable presumption that an individual who holds a significant financial interest in a study may not participate in its conduct. This recommendation is a recognition of the evidence discussed earlier, which indicates that financial interests risk undermining the integrity of research and may affect the behaviour of researchers. The association also recommends that it may be inappropriate to have research conducted in institutions that have a significant financial interest in the research outcome.

There are two problems with recommendations of this sort. First, they are mere guidelines issued by an organization that has no impact outside academic institutions. Second, they open the door for various exceptions by introducing the qualifier "rebuttable." Considering the extreme variability by which North American institutions embrace the commercialization of their research, it is unlikely that situations such as those surrounding the Jesse Gelsinger case will be avoided by such recommendations. Some institutional cultures will simply have a different interpretation of when the presumption can be put aside. We suggest, nevertheless, that these recommendations provide an important baseline for evaluating the risk created by financial interests in research and that they should be integrated in more stringent regulatory documents. The recommendations could be refined and strengthened. The premise should be that researchers or institutions with financial interests in the outcome of the research ought not to be involved in the research. Further, review bodies, such as REBs and COI Committees, should issue a formal justification in individual cases where they think it is necessary to make an exception. By qualifying financial interests as a significant risk factor, additional mechanisms seem required when such exceptions are made. They could consist, for example, in requirements that researchers divest themselves of their financial ties: in ordering the research to be conducted and/or monitored outside the institutions; in closer monitoring of the consent process; and in requiring a rigorous external review of the data. Again, it should be emphasized that the introduction of the term "rebuttable" should not create a "business as usual" climate in which the formulation of exceptions becomes a mere bureaucratic hassle.

Governance of Biomedical Research with Human Participants: Proposals for Legal and Structural Reform

Our analysis suggests that risk assessments of gene transfer and stem cell research proceed in the face of considerable uncertainty. We suggest that there is much to be learned about the magnitude and probability of the physical harms this research poses to human participants. Given the national scope of gene transfer and stem cell research, the task of collecting and analyzing risk-related data is beyond the capacity of local REBs. Furthermore, risk assessments are influenced by the value frameworks of the different parties to a risk debate. Assessments that are formulated by those who endorse the research may reflect a value framework that is weighted in favour of taking risks. Patients who seek novel therapy through science can share a strong enthusiasm for research with the industry sponsors and medical investigators who endorse it. Yet if risk estimation can influence perceptions of risk acceptability, then there is at least an apparent COI in allowing those who endorse the research to be the sole arbiters of its estimated risks. We want the law to ensure that the value frameworks of cautious participants who might assume the risks are given equal weight in the process of research review. In short, we envisage a review process that responds to those who might be risk cautious in the face of significant potential benefits.

With these remarks in mind, we want to offer some general recommendations for law reform. These recommendations are not exhaustive. The Canadian funding agencies have embraced a uniform approach that makes the *Tri-Council Policy Statement* applicable to all forms of research with humans in the biomedical and social sciences. We realize that our more elaborate legislative structure may be neither feasible nor necessary for some forms of research. The forms of research to which it ought to apply should also be subject to further debate. We believe that it ought to apply to biomedical research that raises the three risks discussed earlier in this essay.

1 *We recommend federal legislation to govern the oversight of biomedical research in Canada.* Bernard Starkman has summarized a number of reasons for regulating research through legislation instead of guidelines. Legislation is debated openly, its provisions are publicized, and the legislative process provides accountability. Notwithstanding the limitations of our parliamentary democracies, legislators are subject to the electoral process, and parliamentary debates on legislative proposals are subject to public scrutiny. Legislation promotes uniformity, enforceability, and could contain clarifications about the conditions under which vulnerable persons can legally be participants in research. In short, "legislation has all the advantages that have been claimed for guidelines, and none of the disadvantages."[168]

We acknowledge that the protection of human participants in biomedical research may not be seen as a single matter over which either Parliament or the provinces can assert exclusive legislative jurisdiction. Indeed, some might question whether the federal government has any jurisdiction in this area. We do not want to pursue that debate in this essay. The pros and cons of a federal or provincial legislative scheme should also be subject to further debate.[169] Comprehensive legislation to regulate the management of risks to research participants, to the reliability of research, and to the public's trust in the research enterprise would likely require significant cooperation between both levels of government. While we cannot resolve the jurisdiction debate in this essay, we suggest that federal jurisdiction under the criminal law power can recognize significant scope for provincial action.[170] This is reflected in the model outlined in sections 68 and 69 of *An Act Respecting Assisted Human Reproduction and Related Research,* which allows provinces to pass laws equivalent to key sections of the federal legislation.[171]

2 *We recommend the creation of an independent national agency for research review.* This agency could receive a limited regulatory mandate and remain accountable to the federal Parliament. It should be independent from the current government agencies that regulate drugs and fund research. It should have an unequivocal mandate to focus on the protection of human research participants, and it should not be committed to industry development or health-care funding. It could coordinate, accredit, and monitor the activities of local REBs. To these ends, it would formulate research policies, review and publicize significant decisions made by itself and local REBs, and serve as a source to which local REBs could turn for advice and guidance.[172] The oversight of all biomedical

research would be a daunting task for this proposed agency. We suggest an incremental approach by which the agency limits its initial operations to the oversight of gene transfer and stem cell research. The agency could then gradually expand the range of its oversight activities to other types of biomedical research.

3   *We recommend that this national agency have a branch that would gather and analyze data relevant to risk assessments of new biomedical interventions and that it could coordinate activity in this area with Health Canada.* CenterWatch has noted the practical difficulties faced by REBs in coping with the task of monitoring adverse events in hundreds, if not thousands, of clinical trials at individual institutions each year. While some data monitoring is "study specific," there is no mandatory, audited monitoring of adverse events by an outside, independent source.[173] Critics of the current US regulatory system have argued that there is a need for a combination of standardized reporting and auditing by an independent body as opposed to "subjective reporting" by researchers involved in the trials who "decide when something is worth reporting."[174] The task of monitoring international multi-centre trials only adds to this challenge.

With respect to gene transfer and stem cell interventions, the agency we propose would be similar to the Gene Transfer Safety Assessment Board proposed recently by the NIH in response to the Gelsinger case. It would ensure that "the safety, toxicity, and efficacy data accumulated from trials be regularly reviewed ... identify areas of potential promise or concern and ... promote awareness of these findings among the various sectors of the [scientific community and the] public."[175] We envision the creation of a national database to organize the safety data from gene transfer and stem cell research. Like the Gene Therapy Advisory Committee proposed in the United Kingdom, this branch would coordinate the long-term monitoring of research participants.[176] The agency would also ensure that all active medical research studies are registered and that study results are available even if they are not published. This reporting obligation to, and data gathering by, a central agency would aim to prevent the selective use of clinical trial data in the review process.

4   *We recommend that this national agency have a branch that would assist local REBs in the selection and training of participant representatives from relevant consumer health groups.* This training should contain a module on risk analysis.

5   *We recommend that this national agency have a branch that would investigate complaints or concerns about local REBs or clinical trials.* This branch could be similar to the US Office for Human Research Protection.

6   *We recommend that local REBs become part of, and accountable to, this national agency.* On our account, the current Canadian system of REBs is affected by significant COIs, given the close affiliation of most REBs with

research institutions and the fundamental COIs embedded in private, commercial REBs.

7 *We recommend that this national agency develop uniform conflict of interest guidelines and oversight mechanisms for application at the institutional level.*

8 *We recommend that this national agency also function as a public forum for debating the impact of new biomedical research on social values.* It could, for example, take the initiative to debate particular moral concerns raised by the use of embryos in stem cell research or other moral issues in research that affect the values of the wider community.

9 *We support the development of COI Committees within institutions.* These committees should keep data on financial and other relations between clinical researchers and other research personnel. They should determine whether there is a risk that financial or other relations could impact on research activities. The development of more detailed national restrictions would facilitate this task.

10 *We recommend a reporting obligation by the COI Committees to the REBs.*

11 *REBs should receive a clearer, but limited, mandate to review the potential impact of COIs on the conduct of investigators.*

12 *We recommend the integration of a presumption in regulatory policies that individual researchers cannot conduct research in which they have a significant financial interest. We also recommend that similar presumptions be issued with respect to institutions in which the research takes place.*

Acknowledgments
The authors thank William Leiss, James Till, and R. Steven Turner and an anonymous reviewer from the *University of Toronto Law Journal* for comments on an earlier draft. This essay received an award from the Law Commission of Canada. Research for this chapter was also funded by the Ontario Genomics Institute (Genome Canada). In the final stages of preparing this text, Trudo Lemmens benefited from the stimulating environment of the Institute for Advanced Studies in Princeton. Both authors are equally responsible for the conceptual development of the chapter. Duff Waring took the lead in drafting the section on regulatory science and integrating reviewers' comments, while Trudo Lemmens took the lead in drafting the section about risks. Both contributed substantially to each part of the discussion. On 2 June 2003, Duff Waring presented an earlier draft of the text at the joint annual meeting of the Canadian Association of Law Teachers and the Canadian Law and Society Association during the Congress of the Social Sciences and Humanities in Halifax, Nova Scotia.

Notes
1 Kathleen Cranley Glass and Trudo Lemmens, "Research Involving Humans" in Jocelyn Downie, Timothy Caufield, and Colleen Flood, eds., *Canadian Health Law and Policy*, 2nd ed. (Markham, ON: Butterworths, 2002) 459 at 459.

2 *The Canada We Want: Speech from the Throne to Open the Thirty-Seventh Parliament of Canada*, <www.sft-ddt.gc.ca/hnav/hnav07_e.htm.>.

3 We will use the Canadian terminology. In the United States, the common term for such review boards is "institutional review boards." Other countries and some international guidelines prefer the term "research ethics committees."

4 Medical Research Council of Canada, Natural Sciences and Engineering Research Council of Canada, and Social Sciences and Humanities Research Council, *Tri-Council Policy*

Statement: Ethical Conduct for Research Involving Humans (Ottawa: Public Works and Government Services Canada, 1998) at 1.5, 1.7 [hereinafter *Tri-Council Policy Statement*]. For a discussion of research risk and US federal regulations, see Charles Weijer, "Thinking Clearly about Research Risk: Implications of the Work of Benjamin Freedman" (1999) 21(6) Institutional Review Boards: Review of Human Subject Research 1.

5   Compare Paul M. McNeill, *The Ethics and Politics of Human Experimentation* (Cambridge: Cambridge University Press, 1993) at 184-236; Rebecca Dresser, *When Science Offers Salvation: Patient Advocacy and Research Ethics* (New York: Oxford University Press, 2002) at 111-28, 153-72.

6   Conrad Brunk, Lawrence Haworth, and Brenda Lee, *Value Assumptions in Risk Assessment: A Case Study of the Alachlor Controversy* (Waterloo, ON: Wilfrid Laurier Press, 1991). See also Conrad G. Brunk, "Risk Assessment" in Christopher Berry Gray, ed., *The Philosophy of Law: An Encyclopedia*, volume 2 (New York and London: Garland Publishing, 1999) 756; and Roger E. Kasperson, "The Social Amplification of Risk" in Sheldon Krimsky and Dominic Golding, eds., *Social Theories of Risk* (Westport, CT: Praeger Publishers, 1992) 153 at 155.

7   Evelyn Fox Keller, *The Century of the Gene* (Cambridge, MA: Harvard University Press, 2000) at 45-72, 103-32.

8   Kathleen Cranley Glass, Charles Weijer, Denis Cournoyer, Trudo Lemmens, Roberta M. Palmer, Stanley H. Shapiro, and Benjamin Freedman, "Structuring the Review of Human Genetics Protocols Part III: Gene Therapy Studies" (1999) 21(2) Institutional Review Boards: Review of Human Subject Research 1 at 6.

9   *Tri-Council Policy Statement*, supra note 4 at 1.1-1.3; *International Conference on Harmonization of Technical Requirements for Registration of Pharmaceuticals for Human Use – Good Clinical Practice: Consolidated Guideline*, 1 May 1996, <http://www.fda.gov/cder/guidance/iche6.htm >; World Health Organization [hereinafter WHO], *Operational Guidelines for Ethics Committees That Review Biomedical Research* (Geneva: WHO, 2000); Council for International Organizations of Medical Sciences [hereinafter CIOMS], *International Ethical Guidelines for Biomedical Research Involving Human Subjects* (Geneva: CIOMS, 2000); *Food and Drug Regulations*, C.R.C., c. 870 as amended by *Food and Drug Regulations: Amendment* (Schedule no. 1024) Clinical Trial Framework, S.O.R./2001-2003, s. C.05.010(d); World Medical Association, *Declaration of Helsinki: Ethical Principles for Medical Research Involving Human Subjects*, <http://www.wma.net/e/policy/b3.htm> (adopted at the 18th World Medical Assembly [hereinafter WMA] in Helsinki, Finland, in June 1964. Amended at the 52nd WMA General Assembly, Edinburgh, Scotland, October 2000; Note of Clarification on Paragraph 29 added by the WMA General Assembly, Washington, 2002).

10   For a comprehensive discussion of various review issues, see Ezekiel J. Emanuel, David Wendler, and Christine Grady, "What Makes Clinical Research Ethical?" (2000) 283(20) Journal of the American Medical Association 2701.

11   *Tri-Council Policy Statement*, supra note 4.

12   Glass and Lemmens, *supra* note 1 at 460.

13   *Tri-Council Policy Statement*, supra note 4 at 1.5.

14   *Ibid.* at 1.5.

15   Ingar Palmlund, "Social Drama and Risk Evaluation" in Krimsky and Golding, eds., *supra* note 6, 197 at 207.

16   Alison C. Cullen and Mitchell J. Small, "Uncertain Risk: The Role and Limits of Quantitative Assessment" in Timothy McDaniels and Mitchell J. Small, eds., *Risk Analysis and Society: An Interdisciplinary Characterization of the Field* (Cambridge: Cambridge University Press, 2004) 163 at 174-75.

17   *Ibid.* at 164.

18   Mary R. English, "Environmental Risk and Justice" in McDaniels and Small, eds., *supra* note 16, 119 at 121.

19   Paul Slovik, "Perception of Risk: Reflections on the Psychometric Paradigm" in Krimsky and Golding, eds., *supra* note 6, 117 at 118.

20   Vicki M. Bier, Scott Ferson, Yacoy Y. Haimes, James H. Lambert, and Mitchell J. Small, "Risks of Extreme and Rare Events: Lessons from a Selection of Approaches" in McDaniels and Small, eds., *supra* note 16, 74 at 90-91.

21   Brunk *et al.*, *Value Assumptions*, *supra* note 6 at 4.

22 *Ibid.* at 4. See also Kasperson, *supra* note 6 at 155: There can be "a most striking disjunc-ture" between the technical and the socio-perceptual analysis of hazards.
23 English, *supra* note 18 at 121; R. Steven Turner, "Of Milk and Mandarins: RBST, Mandated Science and the Canadian Regulatory Style" (2001) 36 J. Can. Stud. 107 at 126-27.
24 Bier *et al.*, *supra* note 20 at 100.
25 Brunk *et al.*, *Value Assumptions, supra* note 6 at 3 and 33-37; Brunk, "Risk Assessment," *supra* note 6 at 757-58.
26 Brunk *et al.*, *Value Assumptions, supra* note 6 at 2-3.
27 William R. Freudenburg, "Heuristics, Biases, and the Not-So-General Publics: Expertise and Error in the Assessment of Risks" in Krimsky and Golding, eds., *supra* note 6, 229 at 236; Harry Otway, "Public Wisdom, Expert Fallibility: Toward a Contextual Theory of Risk" in Krimsky and Golding, eds., *supra* note 6, 215 at 220-22. Otway claims that the final esti-mates of risk from "technical systems" to the public are "notoriously unreliable." After affirming the importance of the "qualitative dimensions of risk" in the acceptance of new technologies, he urges the public to be cautious about "any suggestion that we know what the 'true' (or objective) risks are because of the size of the effort made to make and refine the estimates." See also Brunk *et al.*, *Value Assumptions, supra* note 6 at 5; and Brunk, "Risk Assessment," *supra* note 6 at 757.
28 Kenneth R. Foster, Paolo Vecchia, and Michael H. Repacholi, "Science and the Precaution-ary Principle" (2000) 288 Science 979 at 979.
29 *Ibid.* at 979.
30 Deborah Borfitz, "Quantifying Risk in Clinical Trials" (2001) 8(10) CenterWatch 1 at 1.
31 *Ibid.* at 1.
32 *Ibid.* at 4.
33 *Ibid.* at 1.
34 *Ibid.* at 5.
35 *Ibid.* at 4.
36 *Ibid.* at 5.
37 Justine E. Bekelman, Yan Li, and Carey P. Gross, "Scope and Impact of Financial Con-flicts of Interest in Biomedical Research: A Systematic Review" (2003) 289(4) Journal of the American Medical Association 454 at 463; Joel Lexchin, Lisa Bero, Benjamin Djulbeg-ovic, and Octavio Clark, "Pharmaceutical Sponsorship and Research Outcome and Qual-ity: A Systemic Review" (2003) 326 British Medical Journal 1167 at 6, full version is available online at <http://bmj.com/cgi/reprint/326/7400/1167.pdf> (date accessed: 4 July 2003).
38 *Ibid.* at 5.
39 Law Reform Commission of Canada, *Working Paper 61: Biomedical Experimentation Involving Human Subjects* (Ottawa: Public Works and Government Services Canada, 1989) at 33.
40 Brunk *et al.*, *Value Assumptions, supra* note 6 at 3.
41 Kenneth R. Chien, "Lost in Translation" (2004) 428 Nature 607.
42 Glass *et al.*, *supra* note 8 at 6.
43 National Institutes of Health Advisory Committee on Oversight of Clinical Gene Transfer Research, Enhancing the Protection of Human Subjects in Gene Transfer Research at the National Institutes of Health (12 July 2000) at Appendix D, <http://www.nih.gov./about/director/07122000.htm>.
44 Kasperson, *supra* note 6 at 163.
45 *Ibid.* at 163.
46 Brunk *et al.*, *Value Assumptions, supra* note 6 at 4.
47 Kristen Shrader-Frechette, *Risk and Rationality: Philosophical Foundations for Populist Reforms* (Berkeley: University of California Press, 1991) at 57. See also Jeremy D. Frailberg and Michael J. Trebilcock, "Risk Regulation: Technocratic and Democratic Tools for Regulatory Reform" (1998) 43 McGill Law Journal 835 at 855.
48 Compare Brunk *et al.*, *Value Assumptions, supra* note 6 at 28-29. Compare Glass *et al.*, *supra* note 8 at 6.
49 Brunk *et al.*, *Value Assumptions, supra* note 6 at 26. Compare Brian Wynne, "Risk and Social Learning: Reification to Engagement" in Krimsky and Golding, eds., *supra* note 6 at 275 at 281-83.

50   Douglas MacLean, "Social Values and the Distribution of Risk" in Douglas MacLean, ed., *Values at Risk* (Totowa, NJ: Rowman and Allanheld Publishers, 1986) 75 at 78.
51   Adil E. Shamoo and David B. Resnik, *Responsible Conduct of Research* (New York: Oxford University Press, 2003) at 281.
52   MacLean, *supra* note 50 at 78.
53   Brunk *et al., Value Assumptions, supra* note 6 at 144.
54   *Ibid.* at 26. For an excellent discussion of the sources of uncertainty in risk assessment, see Frailberg and Trebilcock, *supra* note 47 at 850-57.
55   The following statement appears in the consent form of a Protocol for Treatment of Progressive or Recurrent Pediatric Malignant Supratentorial Brain Tumor with Herpes Simplex Thymidine Kinase Gene Vector Producer Cells Followed by Intravenous Ganciclovir, which was conducted in the Children's Hospital in Washington, DC, in 1995: "We emphasize that we do not know if this therapy will be effective. It is entirely possible that this experimental treatment will have no effect on your/your child's tumor. It is possible that the therapy will make you/your child worse ... This investigational procedure is relatively new and it is possible that despite extensive efforts, other unforeseen problems may occur including the possibility of unknown and possible disabling effects or death." From the Baylor College of Medicine and Affiliates consent form for a Phase 1 Trial of Adenoviral Mediated Suicide Gene Therapy with HSV-tk and Intravenous Ganciclovir in Locally Advanced and Refractory Superficial Bladder Cancer, circa 2001: "It is not known what the long-term consequences are going to be from injecting this virus into tumors such as mine." From the University of Arizona consent form for a Phase 1 Dose Escalation Study of Intraperitoneal E1A-Lipid Complex with Combination Chemotherapy in Women with Epithelial Ovarian Cancer, circa 1999: "Only a limited number of women with ovarian cancer have received E1A-Lipid Complex and it has never been given in combination with chemotherapy. Unpredicted, serious side effects, including life-threatening ones, could occur."
56   Akshay Anand and Sunil K. Arora, "Risk Assessment in Gene Therapy" in G. Subramanian, ed., *Manufacturing of Gene Therapeutics: Methods, Processing, Regulation, and Validation* (New York: Kluwer Academic/Plenum Publishers, 2001) 331 at 336.
57   Keller, *supra* note 7 at 70-72.
58   *Ibid.* at 68-69. Others note this complexity but believe that there will be a Food and Drug Association–approved gene therapy in the clinics by 2005, with open "floodgates" for other treatments between 2005 and 2010. See W. French Anderson, "Editorial: The Current Status of Clinical Gene Therapy" (2002) 13 Human Gene Therapy 1261 at 1261-62.
59· Alison Abbott, "Genetic Medicine Gets Real" (2001) 411 Nature 410 at 410-12. Compare Philip Kitcher, *Science, Truth, and Democracy* (New York: Oxford University Press, 2001) at 5 (Enhanced understanding of genetics and basic biology "*may* bring, several decades or a century hence, significant breakthroughs in the treatment or prevention of diseases that cause suffering and premature death for millions. It would be unwise either to rule out that possibility or to stake the (research) farm on it").
60   Abbott, *supra* note 59 at 410-12.
61   These data are available online at <http://www.wiley.co.uk/genmed/clinical>.
62   Freudenburg, *supra* note 27 at 239.
63   Kenneth R. Foster, David E. Bernstein, and Peter W. Huber, "A Scientific Perspective" in Kenneth R. Foster, David E. Bernstein, and Peter W. Huber, eds., *Phantom Risk: Scientific Inference and the Law* (Cambridge, MA: Massachusetts Institute of Technology Press, 1993) 1 at 1. See also Anna Coote and Jane Franklin, "Negotiating Risks to Public Health: Models for Participation" in Peter Bennett and Kenneth Calman, eds., *Risk Communication and Public Health* (Oxford: Oxford University Press, 1999) 183 at 184 (Health risks that can be credibly assessed, predicted, and known include "the risk of sexually transmitted diseases, teenage pregnancy, coronary heart disease, [and] lung cancer").
64   William E. Bishop, David P. Clarke, and Curtis C. Travis, "The Genomic Revolution: What Does It Mean for Risk Assessment?" (2001) 21(6) Risk Analysis 983 at 987.
65   Brunk *et al., Value Assumptions, supra* note 6 at 141-44.

66 *Ibid.* at 6-7.
67 Declan Butler, "Call for Risk/Benefit Study of Gene Therapy" (1994) 372 Nature 716.
68 Eliot Marshall, "Less Hype, More Biology Needed for Gene Therapy" (1995) 270 Science 1751.
69 Ulrich Dettweiler and Simon Perikles, "Points to Consider for Ethics Committees in Human Gene Therapy Trials" (2001) 15 Bioethics 491 at 498.
70 Julian Savulescu, "Harm, Ethics Committees and the Gene Therapy Death" (2001) 27 Journal of Medical Ethics 148 at 148.
71 E. Marshall, "Gene Therapy on Trial" (2000) 288 Science 951.
72 Michael Siegrist and George Cvetkovich, "Perception of Hazards: The Role of Social Trust and Knowledge" (2000) 20(5) Risk Analysis 713; Michael Siegrist, "The Influence of Trust and Perceptions of Risks and Benefits on the Acceptance of Gene Technology" (2000) 20(2) Risk Analysis 195.
73 We acknowledge that shared assumptions about the "sacred" or "intrinsic" value of human life are open to different interpretations. A mentally competent adult and a fertilized ovum can both be seen as intrinsically valuable human life forms that ought to be respected appropriately. Yet persons differ over the appropriate level of respect that each should receive. Ronald Dworkin argues that what we share in understanding human life to be *prima facie* inviolable is more fundamental than our quarrels over the best interpretation of intrinsic value. See Ronald Dworkin, *Life's Dominion: An Argument about Abortion, Euthanasia, and Individual Freedom* (New York: Vintage Books, 1993) at 70-71, 76.
74 Dettweiler and Perikles, *supra* note 69 at 498; Borfitz, *supra* note 30 at 7.
75 See "US Gene Therapy: Is There Oversight for Patient Safety? Testimony, Senate Subcommittee on Public Health" (2 February 2000), <http://www.hhs.gov/asl/testify/t000202c.html>.
76 E. Schiff, "In the Service of Science," *The Magazine* (26 March 2000), <http://www.cbc.ca/national/magazine/gene>.
77 Raja Mishra, "Gene Therapy Trials Are Restored by FDA Despite Cancer Cases," *Boston Globe* (3 March 2003) at A3.
78 Glass *et al.*, *supra* note 8 at 6.
79 Dettweiler and Perikles, *supra* note 69 at 492-95, 499.
80 Glass *et al.*, *supra* note 8 at 6.
81 Norman C. Nevin and Jayne Spink, "Gene Therapy Advisory Committee: Long-Term Monitoring of Patients Participating in Gene Therapy" (2000) 11 Human Gene Therapy 1253.
82 *US Food and Drug Administration Gene Therapy Tracking System: Final Document* (27 June 2002) at 26-28, <http://www.fda.gov/cber/genetherapy/gttrack.htm>.
83 Canadian Institutes of Health Research, the Stem Cell Oversight Committee, <http://www.cihr-irsc.gc.ca/e/about/19312.shtml>.
84 *An Act Respecting Assisted Human Reproduction and Related Research*, 3rd Sess., 37th Parl., 2004 (assented to on 29 March 2004). The act will come into force on a day or days to be fixed by order of the Governor in Council [hereinafter *Assisted Human Reproduction Act*].
85 *Ibid.* at clauses 21-39 and clause 5(1)a respectively.
86 Bishop *et al.*, *supra* note 64 at 987.
87 Sigrid Grauman, "Some Conceptual Questions about Somatic Gene Therapy and Their Relevance for an Ethical Evaluation" in Anders Nordgren, ed., *Gene Therapy and Ethics* (New York: Uppsala, 1999) 67 at 74-75.
88 Nicholas Rescher, *Risk: A Philosophical Introduction to the Theory of Risk Evaluation and Management* (Washington, DC: University Press of America, 1983) at 7.
89 These points were made to us by Dr. Jonathan Kimmelman, post-doctoral fellow with the Biomedical Ethics Unit of McGill University.
90 Lars M. Bjorklund *et al.*, "Embryonic Stem Cells Develop into Functional Dopaminergic Neurons after Transplantation in a Parkinson Rat Model" (2002) 99(4) Proceedings of the National Academy of Science 2344 at 2345-47.
91 Ron McKay, "Stem Cells: Hype and Hope" (2000) 406 Nature 361 at 361-62.
92 *Ibid.* at 362-63.

93 *Ibid.* at 363.
94 Holger Hoffman-Riem and Brian Wynne, "In Risk Assessment, One Has to Admit Ignorance" (2002) 416 Nature 123 at 123.
95 *Ibid.* at 123.
96 *Ibid.*
97 D.D. Federman, K.E. Hanna, and L.L. Rodriguez, eds., Committee on Assessing the System for Protecting Human Research Participants, Institute of Medicine, *Responsible Research: A Systems Approach to Protecting Research Participants* (Washington, DC: National Academies Press, 2001) at 82 [hereinafter *Responsible Research*].
98 See, among many others, Roy G. Spece, Davis S. Shimm, and Allen E. Buchanan, eds., *Conflicts of Interest in Clinical Practice and Research* (New York: Oxford University Press, 1996); Lexchin *et al.*, *supra* note 37; Bekelman *et al.*, *supra* note 37; Mary Little, "Research, Ethics and Conflicts of Interest" (1999) 25(3) Journal of Medical Ethics 259; Karine Morin *et al.*, "Managing Conflicts of Interest in the Conduct of Clinical Trials" (2002) 287 Journal of the American Medical Association 78; Robert P. Kelch, "Maintaining the Public Trust in Clinical Research" (2002) 346(4) New England Journal of Medicine 285; Joseph B. Martin and Denis L. Kasper, "In Whose Best Interest? Breaching the Academic-Industrial Wall" (2000) 343(22) New England Journal of Medicine 1646; Marcia Angell, "Is Academic Medicine for Sale?" (2000) 342(20) New England Journal of Medicine 1516; Steven Lewis *et al.*, "Dancing with the Porcupine: Rules for Governing the University-Industry Relationship" (2001) 165(6) Canadian Medical Association Journal 783; Thomas Bodenheimer, "Uneasy Alliance – Clinical Investigators and the Pharmaceutical Industry" (2000) 342(20) New England Journal of Medicine 1539; Richard A. Rettig, "The Industrialization of Clinical Research" (2000) 19(2) Health Affairs 129; Jesse A. Goldner, "Dealing with Conflicts of Interest in Biomedical Research: IRB Oversight as the Next Best Solution to the Abolitionist Approach" (2000) 28(4) Journal of Law, Medicine, and Ethics 379; Trudo Lemmens and Peter Singer, "Bioethics for Clinicians: 17. Conflict of Interest in Research, Education and Patient Care" (1998) 159(8) Canadian Medical Association Journal 960; Stuart E. Lind, "Financial Issues and Incentives Related to Clinical Research and Innovative Therapies" in Harold Y. Vanderpool, ed., *The Ethics of Research Involving Human Subjects: Facing the Twenty-First Century* (Frederick, MD: University Publishing Group, 1996) at 185; and Claire T. Maatz, "Comment: University Physician-Researcher Conflicts of Interest: The Inadequacy of Current Controls and Proposed Reform" (1992) 7(1) High Technology Law Journal 137.
99 Louis L. Jaffe, "Law as a System of Control" (1969) 98(2) Daedalus 406 at 416-17; and National Commission for the Protection of Human Subjects of Biomedical and Behavioral Research, *Report and Recommendations: Institutional Review Boards* (Washington, DC: US Government Printing Office, 1978) at 1.
100 For a general overview of historical instances of abuse, see President's Advisory Committee on Human Radiation Experiments, *The Human Radiation Experiments: Final Report of the President's Advisory Committee* (New York: Oxford University Press, 1996); a shorter discussion can be found in Glass and Lemmens, *supra* note 1 at 464-66. For more detailed information, including reprints of original articles and governmental documents on historical cases, see Jay Katz, *Experimentation on Human Beings: The Authority of the Investigator, Subject, Professions, and State in the Human Experimentation Process* (New York: Russell Sage Foundation, 1972).
101 Department of Health and Human Services, Office of Human Research Protection, *Financial Relationships in Clinical Research: Issues of Institutions, Clinical Investigators, and IRBs to Consider When Dealing with Issues of Financial Interests in Human Subject Protection, Draft Interim Guidance* (22 January 2002), <http://ohrp.osophs.dhhs.gov/nhrpac/mtg12-00/finguid.htm> [hereinafter *Financial Relationships*].
102 Task Force on Financial Conflicts of Interest, *Protecting Subjects, Preserving Trust, Promoting Progress: Policy and Guidelines for the Oversight of Individual Financial Interests in Human Subjects Research* (Washington, DC: Association of American Medical Colleges, 2001), <http://www.aamc.org/members/coitf/firstreport.pdf>; and Task Force on Financial Conflicts of Interest, *Protecting Subjects, Preserving Trust, Promoting Progress II: Principles and Guidelines for the Oversight of an Institution's Financial Interests in Human Subjects Research* (Washington,

DC: Association of American Medical Colleges, 2001), <http://www.aamc.org/members/coitf/2002coireport.pdf>.

103 Denis F. Thompson, "Understanding Financial Conflicts of Interest" (1993) 329(8) New England Journal of Medicine 573.

104 See Rettig, *supra* note 98; Adil E. Shamoo, "Adverse Events Reporting: The Tip of an Iceberg" (2001) 8 Accountability in Research 197 at 208

105 T. Lemmens, "Les conflits d'intérêts dans le temple de la science médicale: diagnostic et options thérapeutiques" in Y. Gendreau, ed., *Dessiner la société par le droit/Mapping Society through Law* (Montréal: Les Éditions Thémis, 2004. See also Jocelyn Downie, "Contemporary Health Research: A Cautionary Tale" (2003) Health Law Journal (special edition) 1 at 14-15.

106 "TTOs Endorse Network's Commercialization Plan" (2003) 11 Celllines 1.

107 For a discussion of payment of subjects, see Christine Grady, "Money for Research Participation: Does It Jeopardize Informed Consent?" (2001) 1(2) American Journal of Bioethics 40, with commentaries; and Trudo Lemmens and Carl Elliott, "Guinea Pigs on the Payroll: The Ethics of Paying Research Subjects" (1999) 7 Accountability in Research 3.

108 Trudo Lemmens and Paul Miller, "The Human Subjects Trade: Ethical and Legal Issues Surrounding Recruitment Incentives" (2003) 31(3) Journal of Law, Medicine, and Ethics 390.

109 See the practices discussed in Office of Inspector General, *Recruiting Human Subjects: Pressures in Industry-Sponsored Research* (Washington, DC: Department of Health and Human Services, 2000).

110 For more details, see the discussion in Lemmens and Miller, *supra* note 108.

111 James R. Ferguson, "Biomedical Research and Insider Trading" (1997) 337(9) New England Journal of Medicine 631; and Christopher B. Overgaard, Richard A. van den Broek, Jay H. Kim, and Alan S. Detsky, "Biotechnology Stock Prices before Public Announcements: Evidence of Insider Trading?" (2000) 48(2) Journal of Investigative Medicine at 118.

112 For a good discussion of the case, see Goldner, *supra* note 98 at 379-404.

113 Shamoo and Resnik, *supra* note 51 at 139-42; and *Responsible Research, supra* note 97 at 83.

114 For a general overview, see Morin *et al.*, *supra* note 98; Bekelman et al., *supra* note 37; Lexchin *et al.*, *supra* note 37; Glass and Lemmens, *supra* note 1, in particular at 466-76; and Lemmens and Singer, *supra* note 98.

115 See, for example, Henry T. Stelfox, Grace Chua, and Keith O'Rourke *et al.*, "Conflict of Interest in the Debate over Calcium-Channel Antagonists" (1998) 338(2) New England Journal of Medicine 101.

116 See David Healy, "Is Academic Psychiatry for Sale?" (2003) 182 British Journal of Psychiatry 388; David Healy and Dinah Cattell, "Interface between Authorship, Industry and Science in the Domain of Therapeutics" (2003) 183 British Journal of Psychiatry 22; and Bodenheimer, *supra* note 98 at 1541-42.

117 Jon Thompson, Patricia Baird, and Jocelyn Downie, *The Olivieri Report: The Complete Text of the Report of the Independent Inquiry Commissioned by the Canadian Association of University Teachers* (Toronto: James Lorimer, 2001).

118 Eric G. Campbell, Karen Louis, and David Blumenthal, "Looking a Gift Horse in the Mouth: Corporate Gifts Supporting Life Sciences Research" (1998) 279 Journal of the American Medical Association 995.

119 MacLean, *supra* note 50 at 91.

120 *Ibid.* at 88-89.

121 Frailberg and Trebilcock, *supra* note 47 at 881.

122 See James H. Jones, *Bad Blood* (New York: Free Press, 1981); and President's Advisory Committee on Human Radiation Experiments, *supra* note 100.

123 Shamoo and Resnick, *supra* note 51 at 140.

124 *Ibid.* at 139.

125 Siegrist and Cvetkovich, *supra* note 72. See also Coote and Franklin, *supra* note 63 at 185-86; Paul Slovic, "Perceived Risk, Trust and Democracy" in Paul Slovic, ed., *The Perception of Risk* (London: Earthscan Publications, 2000) 316; Paul Slovik, "Trust, Emotion, Sex, Politics, and Science: Surveying the Risk-Assessment Battlefield" (1999) 19 Risk Analysis 689.

For a contrasting view, see Lennart Sjoberg, "Limits of Knowledge and the Limited Importance of Trust" (2001) 21 Risk Analysis 189.

126   Andrew J. Webster, "Risk and Innovative Health Technologies: Calculation, Interpretation and Regulation" (2002) 4 Health, Risk and Society 221 at 224.

127   *Ibid.* at 224.

128   Webster, *supra* note 126 at 225. See also Brian Salter and Mavis Jones, "Regulating Human Genetics: The Changing Politics of Biotechnology Governance in the European Union" (2002) 4 Health, Risk and Society 325 at 335.

129   MacLean, *supra* note 50 at 92.

130   *Ibid.* at 92.

131   Slovik, *supra* note 125 at 689.

132   See, for instance, Coote and Franklin, *supra* note 63; Peter Glasner and David Dunkerly, "The New Genetics, Public Involvement, and Citizens' Juries: A Welsh Case Study" (1999) 1 Health, Risk and Society 313; Timothy L. McDaniels, Robin S. Gregory, and Daryl Fields, "Democratizing Risk Management: Successful Public Involvement in Local Water Management Decisions" (1999) 19 Risk Analysis 497.

133   Robert M. Veatch, "Human Experimentation Committees: Professional or Representative?" (1975) 5 Hastings Center Report 31; McNeill, *supra* note 5 at 185-87.

134   Brunk *et al., Value Assumptions, supra* note 6 at 143.

135   *Ibid.* at 133.

136   McNeill, *supra* note 5 at 185.

137   *Ibid.* at 206.

138   *Ibid.* at 207.

139   *Ibid.* at 200; Coote and Franklin, *supra* note 63 at 185.

140   McNeill, *supra* note 5 at 202.

141   *Ibid.*

142   *Ibid.* at 205. See also Dresser, *supra* note 5 at 159-65. Dresser proposes three "principles" to guide what she terms "research patient advocates." First, advocates should be accurate and realistic when assessing research, i.e., science may not offer anything approaching salvation. Second, they should appreciate any diversity in the views of their constituents and third, they should "not concentrate solely on research advocacy if significant numbers of constituents lack access to standard treatments of proven benefit."

143   Brunk *et al., Value Assumptions, supra* note 6 at 141.

144   See Schiff, *supra* note 76; Larry Thompson, "Human Gene Therapy: Harsh Lessons, High Hopes," *FDA Consumer Magazine* (September-October 2000), <http://www.fdac/features/2000/500gene.html>.

145   Julian Savulescu, "Two Deaths and Two Lessons: Is It Time to Review the Structure of Research Ethics Committees?" (2002) 28 Journal of Medical Ethics 1 at 1-2; Julian Savulescu and M. Spriggs, "The Hexamethonium Asthma Study and the Death of a Normal Volunteer in Research" (2002) 28 Journal of Medical Ethics 3 at 3-4.

146   Dresser, *supra* note 5 at 153.

147   *Ibid.* at 154.

148   *Ibid.* at 170.

149   Bernard L. Bloom and Shirley J. Asher, "Patient Rights and Patient Advocacy: A Historical and Conceptual Appreciation" in Bernard L. Bloom and Shirley Asher, eds., *Psychiatric Patient Rights and Patient Advocacy: Issues and Evidence* (New York: Human Sciences Press, 1982) 19 at 26, 29.

150   Paul McNeill, "International Trends in Research Regulation: Science as Negotiation" in David N. Weisstub, ed., *Research on Human Subjects: Ethics, Law, and Social Policy* (Oxford: Pergamon Press, 1998) 243 at 250.

151   *Ibid.* at 250.

152   Dresser, *supra* note 5 at 68.

153   *Ibid.* at 69.

154   Alliance for Human Research Protection, "About AHRP," <http://www.ahrp.org/about/about.html>.

155   *Ibid.*

156 Citizens for Responsible Care and Research, "Mission Statement," <http://www.circare.org>.
157 See, for instance *Freedom of Information and Protection of Privacy Act*, R.S.A. 2000, c. F-25.
158 Trudo Lemmens and Benjamin Freedman, "Ethics Review for Sale? Conflict of Interest and Commercial Research Review Boards" (2000) 78 Milbank Quarterly 547.
159 For a good discussion of their role and limitations, see Goldner, *supra* note 98.
160 Kathleen Cranley Glass and Trudo Lemmens, "Conflict of Interest and Commercialization of Biomedical Research: What Is the Role of Research Ethics Review?" in Timothy Caulfield and B. Williams-Jones, eds., *The Commercialization of Genetic Research: Ethical, Legal and Policy Issues* (New York: Kluwer, 1999) at 79.
161 *Food and Drug Regulations, supra* note 9; Regulatory Impact Analysis Statement, <http://www.hc-sc.gc.ca/hpfb-dgpsa/inspectorate/food_drug_reg_amend_1024_gcp_entire_html>.
162 See the two reports by the Task Force on Financial Conflicts of Interest, *supra* note 102; *Financial Relationships, supra* note 101; and *Responsible Research, supra* note 97 at 82-84.
163 McNeill, *supra* note 5 at 194.
164 For further discussion of conflicts of interests and REBs, see Trudo Lemmens and Alison Thompson, "Non-Institutional Research Review Boards in North America: A Critical Appraisal and Comparison with IRBs" (2001) 23(2) Institutional Review Boards: Review of Human Subject Research 1; and Mildred K. Cho and Paul Billings, "Conflict of Interest and Institutional Review Boards" (1997) 45(4) Journal of Investigative Medicine at 154.
165 See the discussion of various models of REB review in Marie Hirtle, Trudo Lemmens, and Dominique Sprumont, "A Comparative Analysis of Research Ethics Review Mechanisms and the ICH Good Clinical Practice Guideline" (2000) 7 European Journal of Health and Law 265.
166 Sheldon Krimsky, *Science in the Private Interest* (Lanham, MD: Rowman-Littlefield, 2003); Sheldon Krimsky, "Reforming Research Ethics in an Age of Multi-Vested Science," presentation at New Directions in Biomedical Research: Regulation, Conflict of Interest, and Liability (Annual Health Law Day, Faculty of Law, University of Toronto, 22 November 2002).
167 See both reports by the Task Force on Financial Conflicts of Interest, *supra* note 102.
168 Bernard Starkman, "Models for Regulating Research: The Council of Europe and International Trends" in David N. Weisstub, ed., *Research on Human Subjects: Ethics, Law, and Social Policy* (Oxford: Pergamon Press, 1998) 264 at 274.
169 For an interesting analysis supporting federal jurisdiction over the regulation of human subjects research, see Jennifer Llewellyn, Jocelyn Downie, and Robert Holmes, "Protecting Research Subjects: A Jurisdictional Analysis" (2003) Health Law Journal, special edition 207 at 216-36.
170 *RJR-MacDonald Inc.* v. *Canada (Attorney General)*, [1995] 3 S.C.R. 199; *R.* v. *Hydro-Quebec*, [1997] 3 S.C.R. 213; and Martha Jackman, "Constitutional Jurisdiction over Health in Canada" (2000) 8 Health Law Journal 95.
171 *Assisted Human Reproduction Act, supra* note 84. Note, however, that the intention in the former Bill C-13 to afford exemptions for provinces that pass equivalent laws has been condemned by Patrick Healy as unconstitutional. He argued that provinces have no power to enact laws equivalent to the severe criminal penalties in Bill C-13, for example, ten years' imprisonment and/or up to half a million dollars in fines. See Patrick Healy, "Statutory Prohibitions and the Regulation of New Reproductive Technologies under Federal Law in Canada" (1995) 40 McGill L.J. 905. His analysis refers to Bill C-13, *An Act Respecting Human Reproductive Technologies and Commercial Transactions Relating to Human Reproduction*, 2nd Sess., 35th Parl., 1996.
172 Jesse A. Goldner, "An Overview of Legal Controls on Human Experimentation and the Regulatory Implications of Taking Professor Katz Seriously" (1993-94) 38(2) Saint Louis U. L.J. 63 at 104. The proposal for such an agency has been made by others. See also Jay Katz, "The Regulation of Human Experimentation in the United States – A Personal Odyssey" (1987) 9 IRB: Rev. Human Subj. Research 1; Carol Levine and Arthur L. Caplan, "Beyond Localism: A Proposal for a National Research Review Board" (1986) 8 Institutional Review Boards: Review of Human Subject Research 7. For a Canadian perspective that argues for a system of provincial oversight, see Simon N. Verdun-Jones and David N. Weisstub, "The Regulation of Biomedical Experimentation in Canada: Developing an Effective Apparatus

for the Implementation of Ethical Principles in a Scientific Milieu" in David N. Weisstub, ed., *Research on Human Subjects: Ethics, Law and Social Policy* (Oxford: Pergamon Press, 1998) 318.
173 Borfitz, *supra* note 30 at 6, quoting Dr. Dan Schuster, associate dean of clinical research at Washington University, St. Louis, Missouri.
174 *Ibid.* at 7, quoting Arthur Caplan, bioethicist at the University of Pennsylvania.
175 National Institutes of Health Recombinant DNA Advisory Committee, "Assessment of Adenoviral Vector Safety and Toxicity" (2002) 13 Human Gene Therapy 3 at 9.
176 Nevin and Spink, *supra* note 81 at 1253.

Bibliography

Abbott, Alison. "Genetic Medicine Gets Real" (2001) 411 Nature 410.

Anand, Akshay, and Sunil K. Arora. "Risk Assessment in Gene Therapy." In G. Subramanian, ed., *Manufacturing of Gene Therapeutics: Methods, Processing, Regulation, and Validation* (New York: Kluwer Academic/Plenum Publishers, 2001) 331.

Alliance for Human Research Protection. <http://www.researchprotection.org>.

An Act Respecting Assisted Human Reproduction and Related Research, 3rd Sess., 37th Parl., 2004 (assented to on 29 March 2004).

Anderson, W. French. "Editorial: The Current Status of Clinical Gene Therapy" (2002) 13 Human Gene Therapy 1261.

Angell, Marcia. "Is Academic Medicine for Sale?" (2000) 342(20) New England Journal of Medicine 1516.

Association of American Medical Colleges Task Force on Financial Conflicts of Interest. *Protecting Subjects, Preserving Trust, Promoting Progress: Policy and Guidelines for the Oversight of Individual Financial Interests in Human Subjects Research* (Washington, DC: Association of American Medical Colleges, 2001), <http://www.aamc.org/members/coitf/firstreport.pdf>.

–. *Protecting Subjects, Preserving Trust, Promoting Progress II: Principles and Guidelines for the Oversight of an Institution's Financial Interests in Human Subjects Research* (Washington, DC: Association of American Medical Colleges, 2001), <http://www.aamc.org/members/coitf/2002coireport.pdf>.

Bekelman, Justine E., Yan Li, and Cary P. Gross. "Scope and Impact of Financial Conflicts of Interest in Biomedical Research: A Systematic Review" (2003) 289(4) Journal of the American Medical Association 454.

Bier, Vicki M., Scott Ferson, Yacoy Y. Haimes, James H. Lambert, and Mitchell J. Small. "Risks of Extreme and Rare Events: Lessons from A Selection of Approaches." In Timothy McDaniels and Mitchell J. Small, eds., *Risk Analysis and Society: An Interdisciplinary Characterization of the Field* (Cambridge: Cambridge University Press, 2004) 74.

Bishop, William E., David P. Clarke, and Curtis C. Travis. "The Genomic Revolution: What Does It Mean for Risk Assessment?" (2001) 21(6) Risk Analysis 983.

Bjorklund, Lars M., *et al.* "Embryonic Stem Cells Develop into Functional Dopaminergic Neurons after Transplantation in a Parkinson Rat Model" (2002) 99(4) Proceedings of the National Academy of Science 2344.

Bloom, Bernard L., and Shirley J. Asher. "Patient Rights and Patient Advocacy: A Historical and Conceptual Appreciation." In Bernard L. Bloom and Shirley J. Asher, eds., *Psychiatric Patient Rights and Patient Advocacy: Issues and Evidence* (New York: Human Sciences Press, 1982) 19.

Bodenheimer, Thomas. "Uneasy Alliance: Clinical Investigators and the Pharmaceutical Industry" (2000) 342(20) New England Journal of Medicine 1539.

Borfitz, Deborah. "Quantifying Risk in Clinical Trials" (2001) 8(10) CenterWatch 1.

Brunk, Conrad. "Risk Assessment." In Christopher Berry Gray, ed., *The Philosophy of Law: An Encyclopedia*. Vol. 2 (New York and London: Garland Publishing Inc., 1999) 756.

–, Lawrence Haworth, and Brenda Lee. *Value Assumptions in Risk Assessment: A Case Study of the Alachlor Controversy* (Waterloo, ON: Wilfrid Laurier Press, 1991).

Butler, Declan. "Call for Risk/Benefit Study of Gene Therapy" (1994) 372 Nature 716.

Campbell, Eric G., Karen Louis, and David Blumenthal. "Looking a Gift Horse in the Mouth" (1998) 279 Journal of the American Medical Association 995.

Canada. "The Canada We Want: Speech from the Throne to Open the Thirty-Seventh Parliament of Canada," Government of Canada <www.sft-ddt.gc.ca/hnav/hnav07_e. htm>.

Canadian Institutes of Health Research. The Stem Cell Oversight Committee, <http://www. cihr-irsc.gc.ca/e/about/19312.shtml>.

Chien, Kenneth R. "Lost in Translation" (2004) 428 Nature 607.

Cho, Mildred K., and Paul Billings. "Conflict of Interest and Institutional Review Boards" (1997) 45(4) Journal of Investigative Medicine 154.

Committee on Assessing the System for Protecting Human Research Participants, Institute of Medicine, D.D. Federman, K.E. Hanna, and L.L. Rodriguez, eds. *Responsible Research: A Systems Approach to Protecting Research Participants* (Washington DC: National Academies Press, 2001).

Coote, Anna, and Jane Franklin. "Negotiating Risks to Public Health: Models for Participation." In Peter Bennett and Kenneth Calman, eds., *Risk Communication and Public Health* (Oxford: Oxford University Press, 1999) 183.

Council for International Organizations of Medical Sciences. *International Ethical Guidelines for Biomedical Research Involving Human Subjects* (Geneva: Council for International Organizations of Medical Sciences, 1993).

Cullen, Alison C., and Mitchell J. Small. "Uncertain Risk: The Role and Limits of Quantitative Assessment." In Timothy McDaniels and Mitchell J. Small, eds., *Risk Analysis and Society: An Interdisciplinary Characterization of the Field* (Cambridge: Cambridge University Press, 2004) 163.

Department of Health and Human Services, Office of Human Research Protections. *Financial Relationships in Clinical Research: Issues of Institutions, Clinical Investigators, and IRBs to Consider When Dealing with Issues of Financial Interests in Human Subject Protection,* Draft Interim Guidance, 22 January 2002, <http://ohrp.osophs.dhhs.gov/nhrpac/mtg12-00/ finguid.htm>.

Dettweiler, Ulrich, and Simon Perikles. "Points to Consider for Ethics Committees in Human Gene Therapy Trials" (2001) 15 Bioethics 491-500.

Downie, Jocelyn. "Contemporary Health Research: A Cautionary Tale" Health Law Journal [forthcoming].

Dresser, Rebecca. *When Science Offers Salvation: Patient Advocacy and Research Ethics* (New York: Oxford University Press, 2002).

Dworkin, Ronald. *Life's Dominion: An Argument about Abortion, Euthanasia, and Individual Freedom* (New York: Vintage Books, 1993).

Emanuel, Ezekiel J., David Wendler, and Christine Grady. "What Makes Clinical Research Ethical?" (2000) 283(20) Journal of the American Medical Association 2701.

English, Mary R. "Environmental Risk and Justice." In Timothy McDaniels and Mitchell J. Small, eds., *Risk Analysis and Society: An Interdisciplinary Characterization of the Field* (Cambridge: Cambridge University Press, 2004) 119.

Ferguson, James R. "Biomedical Research and Insider Trading" (1997) 337(9) New England Journal of Medicine 631.

Food and Drug Administration. *US Food and Drug Administration Gene Therapy Tracking System: Final Document* (27 June 2002) at 26-28, Food and Drug Administration <http:// www.fda.gov/cder/genetherapy/gttrack.htm.>.

Food and Drug Regulations, C.R.C., c. 870 as amended by *Food and Drug Regulations: Amendment* (Schedule No. 1024) Clinical Trial Framework, S.O.R./2001-2003, s. C.05.010(d).

Foster, Kenneth R., David E. Bernstein, and Peter W. Huber. "A Scientific Perspective." In Kenneth R. Foster, David E. Bernstein, and Peter W. Huber, eds., *Phantom Risk: Scientific Inference and the Law* (Cambridge, MA: Massachusetts Institute of Technology Press, 1993) 1.

–, Paolo Vecchia, and Michael H. Repacholi. "Science and the Precautionary Principle" (2000) 288 Science 979-84.

Frailberg, Jeremy D., and Michael J Trebilcock. "Risk Regulation: Technocratic and Democratic Tools for Regulatory Reform" (1998) 43 McGill Law Journal 835.

Freedom of Information and Protection of Privacy Act, R.S.A. 2000, c. F-18.

Freudenburg, William R. "Heuristics, Biases, and the Not-So-General Publics: Expertise and Error in the Assessments of Risk." In Sheldon Krimsky and Dominic Golding, eds., *Social Theories of Risk* (Westport, CT: Praeger Publishers, 1992) 229.

Glass, Kathleen C., and Trudo Lemmens. "Research Involving Humans." In Jocelyn Downie, Timothy Caufield, and Colleen Flood, eds., *Canadian Health Law and Policy*. 2nd ed. (Markham, ON: Butterworths Canada, 2002) 459.

–, Charles Weijer, Denis Cournoyer, Trudo Lemmens, Roberta M. Palmer, Stanley H. Shapiro, and Benjamin Freedman. "Structuring the Review of Human Genetics Protocols Part III: Gene Therapy Studies" (1999) 21(2) Institutional Review Boards: Review of Human Subject Research 1.

Goldner, Jesse A. "An Overview of Legal Controls on Human Experimentation and the Regulatory Implications of Taking Professor Katz Seriously" (1993-94) 38(2) Saint Louis University Law Journal 63.

–. "Dealing with Conflicts of Interest in Biomedical Research: IRB Oversight as the Next Best Solution to the Abolitionist Approach" (2000) 28(4) Journal of Law, Medicine, and Ethics 379.

Grady, Christine. "Money for Research Participation: Does It Jeopardize Informed Consent?" (2001) 1(2) American Journal of Bioethics 40.

Grauman, Sigrid. "Some Conceptual Questions about Somatic Gene Therapy and Their Relevance for an Ethical Evaluation." In Anders Nordgren, ed., *Gene Therapy and Ethics* (New York: Uppsala, 1999) 67.

Healy, David. "Is Academic Psychiatry for Sale?" (2003) 182 British Journal of Psychiatry 388.

–, and Dinah Cattell. "Interface between Authorship, Industry and Science in the Domain of Therapeutics" (2003) 183 British Journal of Psychiatry 22.

Healy, Patrick. "Statutory Prohibitions and the Regulation of New Reproductive Technologies under Federal Law in Canada" (1995) 40 McGill L.J. 905.

Hirtle, Marie, Trudo Lemmens, and Dominique Sprumont. "A Comparative Analysis of Research Ethics Review Mechanisms and the ICH Good Clinical Practice Guideline" (2000) 7 European Journal of Health Law 229.

Hoffman-Riem, Holger, and Brian Wynne. "In Risk Assessment, One Has to Admit Ignorance" (2002) 416 Nature 123.

International Conference on Harmonization of Technical Requirements for Registration of Pharmaceuticals for Human Use – Good Clinical Practice: Consolidated Guideline, 1 May 1996, US Food and Drug Administration <http://www.fda.gov/cder/guidance/iche6.htm>.

Jackman, Martha. "Constitutional Jurisdiction over Health in Canada" (2000) 8 Health Law Journal 95.

Jaffe, Louis L. "Law as a System of Control" (1969) 98(2) Daedalus 406.

Jones, James H. *Bad Blood* (New York: Free Press, 1991).

The Journal of Gene Medicine Clinical Trial Site. "Gene Therapy Clinical Trials Worldwide": Charts and Tables, <http://www.wiley.co.uk/genmed/clinical>.

Kasperson, Roger E. "The Social Amplification of Risk." In Sheldon Krimsky and Dominic Golding, eds., *Social Theories of Risk* (Westport, CT: Praeger Publishers, 1992) 153.

Katz, Jay, ed. *Experimentation on Human Beings: The Authority of the Investigator, Subject, Professions, and State in the Human Experimentation Process* (New York: Russell Sage Foundation, 1972).

–. "The Regulation of Human Experimentation in the United States – A Personal Odyssey" (1987) 9 Institutional Review Boards: Review of Human Subject Research 1.

Kelch, Robert P. "Maintaining the Public Trust in Clinical Research" (2002) 346(4) New England Journal of Medicine 285.

Keller, Evelyn Fox. *The Century of the Gene* (Cambridge, MA: Harvard University Press, 2000).

Kitcher, Philip. *Science, Truth, and Democracy* (New York: Oxford University Press, 2001).

Krimsky, Sheldon. "Reforming Research Ethics in an Age of Multi-Vested Science." Presentation at New Directions in Biomedical Research: Regulation, Conflict of Interest and Liability. Annual Health Law Day, Faculty of Law, University of Toronto, 22 November 2002.

–. *Science in the Private Interest* (Lanham, MD: Rowman-Littlefield, 2003).

Law Reform Commission of Canada. *Working Paper 61: Biomedical Experimentation Involving Human Subjects* (Ottawa: Public Works and Government Services Canada, 1989).

Lemmens, T. "Les conflits d'intérêts dans le temple de la science médicale: diagnostic et options thérapeutiques." In Y. Gendreau, ed., *Dessiner la société par le droit/Mapping Society through Law* (Montréal: Les Éditions Thémis, 2004).

Lemmens, Trudo, and Carl Elliott. "Guinea Pigs on the Payroll: the Ethics of Paying Research Subjects" (1999) 7(1) Accountability in Research 3.

–, and Benjamin Freedman. "Ethics Review for Sale? Conflict of Interest and Commercial Research Review Boards" (2000) 78 Milbank Quarterly 547.

–, and Paul B. Miller. "The Human Subjects Trade: Ethical and Legal Issues Surrounding Recruitment Incentives" (2003) 31(3) Journal of Law, Medicine, and Ethics 390.

–, and Peter S. Singer. "Bioethics for Clinicians: 17. Conflict of Interest in Research, Education and Patient Care?" (1998) 149(10) Canadian Medical Association Journal 1401.

–, and Alison Thompson. "Non-Institutional Research Review Boards in North America: A Critical Appraisal and Comparison with IRBs" (2001) 23(2) Institutional Review Boards: Review of Human Subject Research 1.

Levine, Carol, and Arthur L. Caplan. "Beyond Localism: A Proposal for a National Research Review Board" (1986) 8 Institutional Review Boards: Review of Human Subject Research 7.

Lewis, Steven, *et al.* "Dancing with the Porcupine: Rules for Governing the University-Industry Relationship" (2001) 165(6) Canadian Medical Association Journal 783.

Lexchin, Joel, Lisa Bero, Benjamin Djulbegovic, and Octavio Clark. "Pharmaceutical Sponsorship and Research Outcome and Quality: Systemic Review" (2003) 326 British Medical Journal 1167.

Lind, Stuart E. "Financial Issues and Incentives Related to Clinical Research and Innovative Therapies." In H.Y. Vanderpool, ed., *The Ethics of Research Involving Human Subjects: Facing the Twenty-First Century* (Frederick, MD: University Publishing Group, 1996) 185.

Little, Mary. "Research, Ethics and Conflicts of Interest" (1999) 25(3) Journal of Medical Ethics 259.

Llewellyn, Jennifer, Jocelyn Downie, and Robert Holmes. "Protecting Research Subjects: A Jurisdictional Analysis" (2003) special ed. Health Law Journal 207.

Maatz, Claire T. "Comment: University Physician-Researcher Conflicts of Interest: The Inadequacy of Current Controls and Proposed Reform" (1992) 7(1) High Technology Law Journal 137.

McDaniels, Timothy L., Robin S. Gregory, and Daryl Fields. "Democratizing Risk Management: Successful Public Involvement in Local Water Management Decisions" (1999) 19 Risk Analysis 497.

McKay, Ron. "Stem Cells: Hype and Hope" (2000) 406 Nature 361.

MacLean, Douglas. "Social Values and the Distribution of Risk." In Douglas MacLean, ed., *Values at Risk* (New Jersey: Rowman and Allanheld Publishers, 1986) 75.

McNeill, Paul M. *The Ethics and Politics of Human Experimentation* (Cambridge: Cambridge University Press, 1993).

–. "International Trends in Research Regulation: Science as Negotiation." In David N. Weisstub, ed., *Research on Human Subjects: Ethics, Law, and Social Policy* (Oxford: Pergamon Press, 1998) 250.

Marshall, Eliot. "Less Hype, More Biology Needed for Gene Therapy" (1995) 270 Science 1751.

–. "Gene Therapy on Trial" (2000) 288 Science 951.

Martin, Joseph B., and Denis L. Kasper. "In Whose Best Interest? Breaching the Academic-Industrial Wall" (2000) 343(22) New England Journal of Medicine 1646.

Medical Research Council of Canada, Natural Sciences and Engineering Research Council of Canada, Social Sciences and Humanities Research Council of Canada. *Tri-Council Policy Statement: Ethical Conduct for Research Involving Humans* (Ottawa: Public Works and Government Services Canada, 1998).

Mishra, Raja. "Gene Therapy Trials Are Restored by FDA Despite Cancer Cases." *Boston Globe* (3 March 2003) A3.

Morin, Karine, *et al.* "Managing Conflicts of Interest in the Conduct of Clinical Trials" (2002) 287(1) Journal of the American Medical Association 78.

National Commission for the Protection of Human Subjects of Biomedical and Behavioral Research. *Report and Recommendations: Institutional Review Boards* (Washington DC: US Government Printing Office, 1978).

National Institutes of Health Advisory Committee on Oversight of Clinical Gene Transfer Research. Enhancing the Protection of Human Subjects in Gene Transfer Research at the National Institutes of Health (12 July 2000), National Institutes of Health <http://www.nih.gov./about/director/07122000.htm.> at Appendix D.

Nevin, Norman C., and Jayne Spink. "Gene Therapy Advisory Committee: Long-Term Monitoring of Patients Participating in Gene Therapy" (2000) 11 Human Gene Therapy 1253.

Office of Inspector General. *Recruiting Human Subjects: Pressures in Industry-Sponsored Research* (Washington, DC: Department of Health and Human Services, 2000).

Otway, Harry. "Public Wisdom, Expert Fallibility: Toward a Contextual Theory of Risk." In Sheldon Krimsky and Dominic Golding, eds., *Social Theories of Risk* (Westport, CT: Praeger Publishers, 1992) 215.

Overgaard, Christopher B., Richard A. van den Broek, Jay H. Kim, and Alan S. Detsky. "Biotechnology Stock Prices before Public Announcements: Evidence of Insider Trading?" (2000) 48(2) Journal of Investigative Medicine 118.

Palmlund, Ingar. "Social Drama and Risk Evaluation." In Sheldon Krimsky and Dominic Golding, eds., *Social Theories of Risk* (Westport, CT: Praeger Publishers, 1992) 197.

Patterson, Amy. *Gene Therapy: Is There Oversight for Patient Safety?* Testimony, Senate Subcommittee on Public Health, 2 February 2000. <http://www.hhs.gov/asl/testify/t000202c.html>.

President's Advisory Committee on Human Radiation Experiments. *The Human Radiation Experiments: Final Report of the President's Advisory Committee* (New York: Oxford University Press, 1996).

R. v. Hydro-Quebec, [1997] 3 S.C.R. 213.

Regulations Amending the Food and Drug Regulations (1024 – Clinical Trials), P.C. 2001-1042, C. Gaz. 2001.II.1116.

Rescher, Nicholas. *Risk: A Philosophical Introduction to the Theory of Risk Evaluation and Management* (Washington, DC: University Press of America, 1983).

Rettig, Richard A. "The Industrialization of Clinical Research" (2000) 19(2) Health Affairs 129.

RJR-Macdonald [1995] 3 S.C.R. 199.

Salter, Brian, and Mavis Jones. "Regulating Human Genetics: The Changing Politics of Biotechnology Governance in the European Union" (2002) 4 Health, Risk and Society 325.

Savulescu, Julian. "Harm, Ethics Committees and the Gene Therapy Death" (2001) 27 Journal of Medical Ethics 148.

–. "Two Deaths and Two Lessons: Is It Time to Review the Structure of Research Ethics Committees?" (2002) 28 Journal of Medical Ethics 1.

–, and M. Spriggs. "The Hexamethonium Asthma Study and the Death of a Normal Volunteer in Research" (2002) 28 Journal of Medical Ethics 3 at 3-4.

Schiff, E. "In the Service of Science," *The Magazine* (26 March 2000), <http://www.cbc.ca/national/magazine/gene>.

Shamoo, Adil E. "Adverse Events Reporting: The Tip of an Iceberg" (2001) 8 Accountability in Research 197.

–, and David B. Resnik. *Responsible Conduct of Research* (New York: Oxford University Press, 2003).

Siegrist, Michael, and George Cvetkovich. "The Influence of Trust and Perceptions of Risks and Benefits on the Acceptance of Gene Technology" (2000) 20(2) Risk Analysis 195.

–, and George Cvetkovich. "Perception of Hazards: The Role of Social Trust and Knowledge" (2000) 20(5) Risk Analysis 713.

Sjoberg, Lennart. "Limits of Knowledge and the Limited Importance of Trust" (2001) 21(1) Risk Analysis 189.

Slovik, Paul. "Perception of Risk: Reflections on the Psychometric Paradigm." In Sheldon Krimsky and Dominic Golding, eds., *Social Theories of Risk* (Westport, CT: Praeger Publishers, 1992) 117.

–. "Trust, Emotion, Sex, Politics, and Science: Surveying the Risk Assessment Battlefield" (1999) 19(4) Risk Analysis 689.

–. "Perceived Risk, Trust and Democracy." In Paul Slovik, ed., *The Perception of Risk* (London: Earthscan Publications, 2000) 316.

Spece, Roy G., Davis S. Shimm, and Allen E. Buchanan, eds. *Conflicts of Interest in Clinical Practice and Research* (New York: Oxford University Press, 1996).

Starkman, Bernard. "Models for Regulating Research: The Council of Europe and International Trends." In David N. Weisstub, ed., *Research on Human Subjects: Ethics, Law, and Social Policy* (Oxford: Pergamon Press, 1998) 264.

Stelfox Henry T., Grace Chuay, Keith O'Rourke *et al.* "Conflict of Interest in the Debate over Calcium-Channel Antagonists" (1998) 338(2) New England Journal of Medicine 101.

Thompson, Denis F. "Understanding Financial Conflicts of Interest" (1993) 329(8) New England Journal of Medicine 573.

Thompson, Jon, Patricia Baird, and Jocelyn Downie. *The Olivieri Report: The Complete Text of the Report of the Independent Inquiry Commissioned by the Canadian Association of University Teachers* (Toronto: James Lorimer, 2001).

Thompson, Larry. "Human Gene Therapy: Harsh Lessons, High Hopes," *FDA Consumer Magazine* (September-October 2000), Food and Drug Administration, <http://www.fdac/features/2000/500gene.html>.

"TTOs Endorse Network's Commercialization Plan" (2003) 11 Celllines 1.

Turner, R. Steven. "Of Milk and Mandarins: RBST, Mandated Science and the Canadian Regulatory Style" (2001) 36 Journal of Canadian Studies 107.

Veatch, Robert M. "Human Experimentation Committees: Professional or Representative?" (1975) 5 Hastings Center Report 31.

Verdun-Jones, N. Simon, and David N. Weisstub. "The Regulation of Biomedical Experimentation in Canada: Developing an Effective Apparatus for the Implementation of Ethical Principles in a Scientific Milieu." In David N. Weisstub, ed., *Research on Human Subjects: Ethics, Law, and Social Policy* (Oxford: Pergamon Press, 1998) 318.

Webster, Andrew J. "Risk and Innovative Health Technologies: Calculation, Interpretation and Regulation" (2002) 4 Health, Risk and Society 221.

Weijer, Charles. "Thinking Clearly about Research Risk: Implications of the Work of Benjamin Freedman" (1999) 21(6) Institutional Review Boards: Review of Human Subject Research 1.

World Health Organization. *Operational Guidelines for Ethics Committees That Review Biomedical Research* (Geneva: WHO, 2000).

Contributors

Steve E. Hrudey is a member of the Environmental Appeal Board in the province of Alberta and a professor in the Department of Health Sciences in the Faculty of Medicine and Dentistry at the University of Alberta.

William Leiss is a professor in the School of Policy Studies at Queen's University, a scientist at the McLaughlin Centre for Population Health Risk Assessment at the University of Ottawa, and a visiting professor at the Haskayne School of Business at the University of Calgary.

Trudo Lemmens is an associate professor in the Faculty of Law at the University of Toronto.

Ron Levi is an assistant professor in the Centre of Criminology at the University of Toronto.

David MacAlister is an assistant professor in the School of Criminology at Simon Fraser University.

Dawn Moore is an assistant professor in the Law Department at Carleton University.

Danielle Pinard began her career as a clerk for Supreme Court Justice Antonio Lamer and then as visiting professor in the Faculty of Law at McGill University. Since 1987, she has been a professor in the Faculty of Law at the Université de Montréal.

Dayna Nadine Scott is a PhD candidate in Law at Osgoode Hall Law School at York University. She is currently a Fulbright Scholar and a visiting researcher in the Hauser Global Law School Program at New York University School of Law.

Mariana Valverde is Professor of Criminology and Law at the University of Toronto.

Duff R. Waring is an assistant professor of philosophy at York University.

Index

Printed and bound in Canada by Friesens
Set in Stone by Artegraphica Design Co. Ltd.
Copy editor: Stacy Belden
Proofreader and indexer: Deborah Kerr